the cinema of

DAVID LYNCH

american dreams, nightmare visions

edited by

erica sheen & annette davison

WALLFLOWER PRESS LONDON & NEW YORK

First published in Great Britain in 2004 by
Wallflower Press
4th Floor, 26 Shacklewell Lane, London E8 2EZ
www.wallflowerpress.co.uk

A catalogue for this book is available from the British Library

ISBN 1-903364-85-X (paperback)
ISBN 1-903364-86-8 (hardback)

Book design by Rob Bowden Design

Printed in Great Britain by Antony Rowe, Chippenham, Wiltshire

CONTENTS

ACKNOWLEDGEMENTS

The editors would like to acknowledge all participants of the 'Weird on Top: The Films of David Lynch' conference at the University of Sheffield, UK, in February 1999, and thank the Departments of English Literature and Music for secretarial and administrative support. For help at various stages of the project we thank Matthew Bradshaw, Eric Clarke, Julian Crockford, John Croft, Anne Delnevo, Catherine Haworth and Suzanne Spiedel. At Wallflower Press, Yoram Allon and Hannah Patterson have provided much appreciated support.

Grateful acknowledgement too for the use of the following excerpts:
Twin Peaks
By Angelo Badalamenti & David Lynch
© Copyright 1991 Universal/MCA Music Limited
All rights reserved. International Copyright Secured.
Laura
Music by David Raksin.
© Copyright 1944, copyright renewed in 1972 by Twentieth Century Fox.
Reprinted by permission of Warner Bros. Publications/Warner Chappell.
All rights reserved.

Sheli Ayers teaches Writing and Literature at Loyola Marymount University. Recent publications include 'Virile Magic: Baudelaire/Ballard/Bataille' in *Speed* and 'Rhapsody' in *Trepan: a Literary Journal*. She lives in Los Angeles and is currently writing a book on retro fashion.

Jana Evans Braziel is Assistant Professor in English, University of Cincinnati. She has co-edited *Theorizing Diaspora* (Blackwell, 2003) with Anita Mannur, *Bodies Out of Bounds: Fatness and Transgression* (University of California Press, 2001) with Kathleen LeBesco and published articles in *Meridians: feminism, race, transnationalism*; *Callaloo: Journal of African Diaspora Arts and Letters*; *Journal x: a journal in culture and criticism*; *Tessera: Feminist Interventions in Writing and Culture*; and the *Journal of North African Studies*.

Annette Davison is Lecturer in Music, University of Leeds. She has published articles on cinema soundtracks in *Indiana Theory Review*, *Music Analysis* and in Scanlon and Waste (eds) *Crossing Boundaries* (Sheffield Academic Press, 2001). She has just completed her first book – *Hollywood Theory, Non-Hollywood Practice: Cinema Soundtracks in the 1980s* (Ashgate, 2004).

Greg Hainge is Senior Lecturer in French at the University of Adelaide, Australia. He is the author of *Capitalism and Schizophrenia in the Later Novels of Louis-Ferdinand Céline: D'un … l'autre* (Peter Lang, 2001) and has published widely on literature, film, theory and noise. He serves on the editorial board of *Culture Theory and Critique* and recently edited a special issue of this journal on the subject of Fascism and Aesthetics. He is currently preparing edited volumes on noise and Björk.

Sam Ishii-Gonzales is a doctoral candidate in Cinema Studies at New York University, and teaches aesthetics and film history at NYU and the Film/Media Department at Hunter College. He is the co-editor with Richard Allen of two volumes on *Hitchcock: Centenary Essays* (BFI, 1999) and *Past and Future* (Routledge, forthcoming). His dissertation examines the works of Fassbinder, Pasolini and Warhol in relation to Deleuze's semiotics of film.

Anne Jerslev is Associate Professor in the Department of Film and Media at the University of Copenhagen, Denmark. She has published books on David Lynch (also translated into German), cult movies and young people's video communities, and articles in Danish and Scandinavian journals and anthologies. Her latest book is on media and intimacy (Gyldendal, 2004).

Joe Kember is Lecturer in film studies at the University of Teesside. He has published articles on early film history and theory, and is co-author of *Early Cinema: From Factory Gate to Dream Factory* (Wallflower Press, 2004).

Martha P. Nochimson is the author of *The Passion of David Lynch: Wild at Heart in Hollywood* (University of Texas Press, 1997), *No End to Her: Soap Opera and the Female Subject* (University of California Press, 1993) and *Screen Couple Chemistry: The Power of 2* (University of Texas Press, 2002). She is a frequent contributor to *Film Quarterly* and *Cineaste*. She is Director of the Film Studies Program at Mercy College in Dobbs Ferry, NY, and a member of the Advisory Board of the Columbia University Seminar on Cinema and Interdisciplinary Interpretations.

John Richardson is an Academy of Finland Research Fellow at the University of Jyväskylä in Finland. He has previously worked at City University in London and De Montfort University in Leicester. He is the author of *Singing Archaeology: Philip Glass's Akhnaten* (Wesleyan University Press, 1999) and co-editor of *Beatlestudies 1* (University of Jyväskylä Press, 1998). His specialisms include contemporary music theatre, film music studies and popular music studies.

Nicholas D. Rombes is Associate Professor of English at the University of Detroit Mercy, where he teaches courses in film and co-founded the Electronic Critique programme, an interdisciplinary major. He also co-edits the journal *Post Identity*. His work has appeared in *Post-Script*, *Arizona Quarterly*, *Literature/Film Quarterly*, and many other journals. He is currently working on a book on the intersection between surveillance culture and cinema.

Steven Jay Schneider is the author of *Designing Fear: An Aesthetics of Cinematic Horror* (Routledge, 2004); editor of *The Horror Film and Psychoanalysis: Freud's Worst Nightmares* (Cambridge University Press, 2003), *New Hollywood Violence* (Manchester University Press, 2004) and *Fear Without Frontiers: Horror Cinema Across the Globe* (FAB Press, 2003); and co-editor of *Understanding Film Genres* (McGraw-Hill, 2004), *Traditions in World Cinema* (Edinburgh University Press, 2004) and *Horror International* (Wayne State University Presss, 2004). His co-edited collection, *Underground U.S.A.: Filmmaking Beyond the Hollywood Canon* was published by Wallflower Press in 2002.

Erica Sheen is Lecturer in the School of English, University of Sheffield. Recent and forthcoming publications include studies of adaptation, Hollywood and Shakespeare. She teaches and researches in early modern studies, film history and film and literary theory.

American Dreams, Nightmare Visions

Erica Sheen & Annette Davison

ABCNEWS.com runs an online feature called The Wolf Files written by Buck Wolf. Late in summer 2000, Wolf posted an item called 'A Topless Cow in New York' which related a recent incident in the career of David Lynch. Lynch – 'one of the country's darkest directors' – had been asked to provide a statue for New York City's Cow Parade and what he came up with was, apparently, 'gruesome':

> The fibreglass heifer is quite a sight. Its severed head rests on bloody, gorged-out shoulders. Forks and knives have been stabbed into the rump. And scrawled across the side are the words: 'Eat My Fear'. (Wolf 2001)

City Parks Commissioner Henry J. Stern compared the statue to the work of Charles Manson: 'These cows are meant to be PG,' Stern said. 'Would you want a swastika cow, or a KKK cow, or a cow performing an obscene act?'

Needless to say, the statue was not included in the parade. It was stored in a warehouse in Connecticut and finally exhibited in an art gallery in downtown Manhattan. Lynch, whom the article also described as 'a notorious shock artist', commented, 'I'm happy folks got a chance to see what they missed'. When asked what he was 'trying to say', Lynch replied, 'I never interpret my art. I let the audience do that.'

The question, 'what are you trying to say?' is a clichéd address to, perhaps even an accusation of, artistic impenetrability. It implies that any difficulties experienced in understanding an artwork derive from the formal struggle between artist and medium. It is symptomatic of the facile interpretability of Hollywood cinema that the phrase is rarely applied to mainstream film-makers, and that we are rarely invited to see the medium as one that produces formal struggle. David Lynch is an exception on both these counts. He is a director who has sought to position his work within mainstream production, yet whose creative practices constantly defamiliarise his chosen medium.

As the essays in this collection show, Lynch's work can be seen as an anticipation of, even a formative influence on, the independent aesthetic that has become increasingly dominant in Hollywood over the last fifteen years. Beginning his career in fine art and mixed media, Lynch entered mainstream movie-making at a time when it was in a state of economic and technological transformation. After *Eraserhead* (1977) and *The Elephant Man* (1980), he took the opportunity of *Dune* (1984) to gain access to a system of production that has consistently appeared puzzled by or suspicious of his way of seeing. Since then his work has been distinctively situated at the nexus of changing systems of distribution and exhibition: the introduction of video and pay television at the end of the 1970s and across the 1980s; the rise of the multiplex, with its extended market reach; the growth of the regional independent cinemas.

From the arthouse avant-garde of *Eraserhead*, to the blockbuster *Dune*, the television serial *Twin Peaks* (1990), the porn video culture of *Lost Highway* (1997) and the 'Disney' family film *The Straight Story* (1999), Lynch's films give aesthetic form to the synergies of post-classical Hollywood in a way no other contemporary film-maker's work has done. If the intellectual consistency of his vision suggests we might approach him as an auteur, the formal and generic range of his work raises questions about that status. Like classical directors who brought European aesthetic traditions to studio-system working practices, he has a quality more pertinent to our understanding of his work than either narrative or genre: an intensely creative approach to the activity of production. In his partnerships with Alan Splet and Angelo Badalamenti or with the veteran British cinematographer Freddy Francis, Lynch displays an almost utopian sense of Hollywood as an ideal system of production that plays against his parallel perception of it as an oppressive commercial dystopia. As Martha Nochimson's chapter in this collection suggests, *Mulholland Drive* (2001) is a particularly well-developed statement of this position. In an interview about ABC-Disney's failure to option the pilot, Lynch was asked if he had ever thought of moving to Europe, where his work is always better received. His reply was paradoxical:

'Yeah. I've thought about it quite a bit. But I love Los Angeles.'
'What do you love about it?'
'The light ... and the feeling in the air ... the feeling of optimism.'
(Lynch in Lantos 1999: 71)

There is a link between this 'feeling of optimism' and his openness to critical freedom: 'I never interpret my art. I let the audience do that.' The writers of the essays in this collection take up this invitation, but they also seek to focus the implications of his paradoxicality.

Recent scholarship has tended to situate Lynch's complexities within the critical frame of postmodernism. Many of these essays adopt that position; many are openly critical of it. But they all push beyond it towards a fuller account of the cultural contexts and intertexts within which Lynch's work has been situated, and of his intense creative engagement with the specific working practices of his industry. Thus Sheli Ayers, Jana Evans Braziel, Greg Hainge and Anne Jerslev offer new readings of Lynch's films in relation to the work of Jean Baudrillard, Walter Benjamin, Paul Virilio and Slavoj Žižek and – particularly – Gilles Deleuze, and Deleuze and Félix Guattari, whilst Joe Kember looks at Lynch's approach to dialogue and the close-up, Annette Davison and John Richardson discuss his work on sound, and Erica Sheen and Martha Nochimson consider his relation to the industry as a whole. In his almost excessive attention to the complete range of working practices at his disposal, Lynch encourages a reconsideration of the periodicity of cinema: Ayers, Hainge and Sheen show that his work breaches boundaries between old and new media, while Kember suggests continuities with the pragmatics of early cinema – a continuity Lynch himself explored directly in his 52-second contribution to *Lumière et Compagnie* (1995). These continuities illuminate our understanding of the sources of Lynch's own creativity, but they also identify his role in a twenty-first-century cinema that is more in a state of becoming than of having been.

In this respect, one of the most important features of Lynch's work is his continuing engagement with the *noir* aesthetic. Arguably the strand of film-making that has maintained the disruptive potential of European traditions within mainstream production, *noir* has emerged in post-classical Hollywood as the narrative and stylistic template for an independent aesthetic. Jerslev, Richardson and Braziel all offer accounts of the Lynchian *noir*, the latter two in relation to its implications for gender-based responses to his work. Like most writers in this collection, Braziel engages strongly with the work of leading Lynch scholar Martha Nochimson, whose immensely rich reading of female performance in *Mulholland Drive* – 'Lynch's own *Sunset Boulevard*' – suggests the extent to which the *noir* paradigm has provided Lynch with a position of critical response to the failure of creativity in Hollywood cinema.

Braziel's Deleuzean account of 'becoming woman' as a process of 'spilling over' in *Blue Velvet* (1986) and *Wild at Heart* (1990) finds resonance with Schneider's reading of *Eraserhead* as a horror film. According to Schneider, horror results from violations of existing cultural categories – living/dead; human/machine; inside/outside. Hainge, Jerslev and Davison find a related effect in the deconstruction of depth and surface produced by a magnified focus on textures – both auditory and visual. Hainge and Davison link these moments of *jouissance* with a dissolution of the spectator's engagement with the narrative.

Nicholas Rombes situates *Blue Velvet* within the context of 1980s post-modernism, but finds that a reading of the film as ironic critique of American suburban values cannot adequately account for the film's disturbing mood and effects. For him, Lynch's films are simply not 'safe enough' to allow us to side-step the disquieting process of reading them as 'straight' stories. Taking up a position which both complements and contrasts this view, Ayers argues that the postmodern critique offered by *Twin Peaks* was to acquire distinctly non-ironic connotations when the programme reached its second series. Rather than being too uncomfortable to accommodate a retreat into irony or parody, *Twin Peaks* ceased to imply self-conscious critique, because – for its fans – it increasingly felt too much like home. Lynch's juxtaposition of the homely and the strange is a recurring preoccupation in this book: thus Hainge discusses the 'unhomeliness' of *Lost Highway* in relation to the deforming aesthetic of Francis Bacon's paintings, and Ishii-Gonzales offers a particularly full new reading of the relation between *Blue Velvet* and Freud's study of the Wolfman.

Such strange familiarity is ultimately unsettling and the case of Laura Palmer, so lovingly mourned on television only to be resurrected in order to die again in the cinema, aptly demonstrates how Lynch can push his spectators into reviewing their terms and conditions of reception. From this perspective, Laura Palmer is an emblem of his position as a director whose films have pre-eminently achieved success on video and television, and whose work is as a consequence distinctively located in a critical and academic context rather than merely one of entertainment.

What these similar yet divergent readings imply is the difficulty Lynch's viewers have in locating stable interpretative positions, both within individual works and in relation to generic or media conventions. What they all suggest is that the process of watching Lynch's work is just that: a continuing, unfixed, fluctuating experience. These are narratives that perhaps above all never seem or want to finish. Lynch's work tells a story of artistic and professional struggle which neither concludes nor allows for easy conclusions.

CHAPTER ONE

The Essential Evil in/of Eraserhead (or, Lynch to the Contrary)

Steven Jay Schneider

I like things that go into hidden, mysterious places, places I want to explore that are very disturbing. *In that disturbing thing, there is sometimes tremendous poetry and truth.* (Lynch in Jerome 1990: 82 [my emphasis])

For various reasons, and in various ways, commentators on *Eraserhead* – David Lynch's first feature-length production, released in 1977 – have attempted to mitigate the film's cynicism and nightmarish qualities. It is as if they feel (but refuse to admit) that the picture cannot be celebrated as a work of brilliance unless its manifest horror is somehow redeemed. However, such a redemptive impulse, perpetuated by the director himself in published interviews, actually serves to render this already challenging text *less*, rather than more, coherent. In fact, *Eraserhead* offers little if any hope of salvation, liberation or deliverance from evil; even those characters and scenes typically held up as beacons in the midst of the film's literal and metaphorical darkness (for example, The Lady in the Radiator, Henry's 'mercy killing' of his diseased infant, his tryst with the Beautiful Girl Across the Hall) are *themselves* sources of disgust, loathing and fear. In what follows, I will attempt to show how *Eraserhead* relies upon formal and thematic techniques familiar within the horror genre in order to engender its uncanny effects. To the extent that this analysis contradicts statements made by others, including Lynch himself, concerning the film's romantic, cathartic, even comedic dimensions, it will stand as a useful corrective to the naïve version of auteurism which so often accompanies the director's work. By contextualising *Eraserhead*, highlighting its debt to generic horror conventions both traditional and modern, the conception (including the *self-conception*) of Lynch as an eccentric *artiste* working in a cinematic vacuum may be somewhat damaged, though not his status as an innovative, immensely talented film-maker.

The Primacy of the Image in Eraserhead

Eraserhead's unconventional plot, post-industrial wasteland setting and imagery which seems to have been extracted from the subconscious mind of a neurotic nebbish has drawn comparisons to the expressionist *mise-en-scène* of Robert Weine's *The Cabinet of Dr Caligari* (1920), the futuristic urban decay of Fritz Lang's *Metropolis* (1927) and the absurdist/surrealist dreamscape of Luis Buñuel's *Un Chien Andalou* (1929) – and all with some justification, despite Lynch's repeated insistence that these films were not direct influences and that, for example, it was not until much later that he even saw the last one on this list.[1]

Although most critics and commentators begin their discussions of *Eraserhead* by noting that the question 'What is this film *about?*' is misplaced, if not wholly irrelevant, they typically proceed to argue that 'despite its gaps and incoherences, *Eraserhead* is a narrative film with a dialogue, a hero and a linear story' (Chion 1995: 41);[2] and that the best way to analyse *Eraserhead* is to decipher the ways in which its meaning 'falls out' from its storyline. So, for example, Cynthia Freeland writes that *Eraserhead* is 'in part "about" cycles of life and death, meaning and meaningless – where death and meaningless are real contenders in the struggle' (Freeland 2000: 232), those quotation marks around the word 'about' signifying the author's reluctance to make even a qualified statement of this sort. K. George Godwin, meanwhile, in a lengthy *Cinefantastique* article, concludes that *Eraserhead* is primarily concerned with dramatising 'the self-defeating tensions which result from man's inability to reconcile his intellect with other, equally potent aspects of his nature' (Godwin 1984: 54).

The first of the above two arguments is difficult to deny, considering the film's bizarre prologue and corresponding epilogue involving the so-called 'Man in the Planet' (Jack Fisk), the fashioning of Henry Spencer (Jack Nance) as more-or-less sympathetic protagonist, and the admittedly loose cause-and-effect relationship holding between various events in the plot. But the second one (less an argument than a critical tendency or unacknowledged strategy), is extremely problematic. For it fails to appreciate the extent to which Lynch – whose earlier shorts (*Six Figures* (1966), *The Alphabet* (1968), *The Grandmother* (1970), *The Amputee* (1974)) make manifest his desire to create 'film paintings' (Lynch in Chion 1995: 10) – asserts the primacy of the audiovisual image in *Eraserhead*; and this *despite* the film's recognisable narrative elements. As Kenneth Kaleta remarks, 'a detailed summary of [the film's] plot actions neither replicates nor illuminates the film. Images from the subconscious are not merely tied to the plot; in *Eraserhead*, images from the subconscious *are* the plot … *Eraserhead* gains its force from presenting images that somehow affect the viewers' (Kaleta 1993: 16). At the very least, rather than it being the case that the film's meaning 'falls out' from its storyline, it is the film's *storyline* which gets determined, or else disrupted, by its *images*.

By way of defending this claim, I shall turn to three methods by which Lynch renders narrative continuity subservient to visual and auditory material. But first, for those who may be completely unfamiliar with *Eraserhead*'s plot, a reasonably straightforward synopsis of events is necessary. The following, courtesy of Lynch biographer Chris Rodley, is as clear and succinct as any:

> In the depths of The Planet, a Man pulls levers. Images implying conception and birth occur. We surface. On arriving home at his strange, squalid apartment in the midst of a desolate industrial landscape, Henry Spencer is told by a neighbour that his girlfriend Mary has invited him for dinner at her parents' home. Once there, he discovers that he has fathered a premature 'baby', which is still at the hospital. Mary moves in with Henry but soon returns to her parents, unable to sleep through the 'baby's' constant crying. Henry fantasises about a lady who appears on a stage inside his radiator. She sings about Heaven, while stamping on strange worm-like creatures. The 'baby' falls ill and, having been seduced by his neighbour, Henry fantasises about being on the radiator stage. His head is pushed off by the 'baby' growing inside him and is taken to a workshop to be processed into pencil-top erasers. Henry finally kills the 'baby', causing a cosmic catastrophe. The Planet explodes, despite the efforts of The Man at its centre, pulling levers in vain. A blinding white flash. Henry meets The Lady in the Radiator in what might be the afterlife. They embrace tenderly. (Rodley 1997: 246–7)

Clear and succinct indeed! The fact is, no mere summation of *Eraserhead*'s narrative, however 'accurate' it may be, can possibly succeed in conveying the *tone* of this picture, the feelings of unease, uncanniness and out-and-out horror which result from watching it and which only increase in intensity upon repeated viewings. At best, descriptive statements of the sort provided by Rodley *et al.* may serve as points of reference in the discussion to follow, which concerns the three methods employed by Lynch in order to assert the primacy of the audio-visual image in *Eraserhead*.

First and most obvious are the inexplicable, surrealistic set-pieces that Lynch spaces out over the course of the picture. These set-pieces – which resemble nothing so much as the miraculous stop-action shorts of Czechoslovakian film-maker/animator/ puppeteer Jan Švankmajer – include one in which a man-made, oven-roasted miniature chicken begins haemorrhaging blood and involuntarily moving its legs up and down after Henry sticks a fork in it in preparation for carving; and another in which a tiny worm-like creature left for Henry as an anonymous gift begins performing and doing backflips for its bemused owner.[3] In the literature on *Eraserhead*, one of the main areas of interest has been the manufacturing of the baby – is it a puppet, a mechanical prop, an animal foetus perhaps?[4] Lynch's staunch refusal to reveal the answer on the grounds that 'magicians keep their secrets to themselves' (Lynch in Rodley 1997: 78) has only served to stoke people's curiosity. To date, however, insufficient attention has been paid to the film's *other* special-effects feats (such as the two just mentioned), feats which operate so as to disrupt narrative continuity by encouraging viewers to marvel at their life-likeness while simultaneously acknowledging their impossibility. As Buñuel said of his collaboration with Salvador Dali on *Un Chien Andalou*: 'Our only rule was very simple: no idea or image that might lend itself to rational explanation of any kind was to be accepted.'[5]

Second, at numerous points during *Eraserhead*, Henry – and along with him, the audience – is confronted by what appears, at least at first, to be unmotivated behaviour on the part of other characters in the film. Such behaviour is manifested frequently during Henry's brief yet somehow interminable dinner at the family home of his girlfriend, Mary X (Charlotte Stewart). First comes a succession of tics and spasms on Mary's part, which only subsides after her mother holds her face and runs a brush firmly through her hair. During dinner, as the mini-chicken described above begins spewing its bloody contents onto Henry's plate, Mary's mother falls victim to a quasi-epileptic fit of her own. Later, the woman begins kissing her soon-to-be son-in-law's neck in a vaguely incestuous gesture reminiscent of a similarly disturbing scene (involving a father and his adolescent daughter) in David Cronenberg's 1975 cult horror film, *Shivers*. Such episodes of bizarre, irrational behaviour can be found in almost all of Lynch's films, including even the so-called *The Straight Story* (1999), and might reasonably be labelled one of his directorial signatures.[6] But it should be kept in mind that the 'associational' component here – because the activity in question gets placed within a pre-existing narrative context, viewers are encouraged to look for some connection – has always been a favoured strategy of experimental and avant-garde film-makers, and betrays Lynch's debt to these established traditions.[7] Lynch exhibits his mastery of this strategy during the scene in which Mary prepares to leave Henry's apartment due to lack of sleep and an inability to keep the baby quiet ('You're on vacation now; you can take care of him for a little while!' she sobs). Before exiting through the front door, Mary walks back to the bed still occupied by Henry, crouches down and starts violently shaking the frame. The disquieting effect this seemingly unmotivated behaviour has on both Henry and the audience evaporates once it is revealed that she has simply been struggling to pull her suitcase out from under the bed.

Finally, throughout *Eraserhead*, the audience is confronted with excessive, hyperbolic 'gross-out' shots: typically extreme close-ups (many of them inserts) which effectively force viewers to contemplate the opening up, leakage and/or utter decay of various bodies, human as well as non-human. I shall have reason to return to this technique later on, since it stands as one of *Eraserhead*'s prime means of generating horror and disgust; for present purposes, one example should suffice. After Henry's baby gets sick approximately two-thirds of the way through the picture, the viewer is suddenly 'treated' to an extreme close-up of its diseased face, complete with leprous growths, rolled-back eyes and a mouth completely rotted on the inside.[8] Kaleta writes that '*Eraserhead* poses a quantitative imagery question. And it is characteristically a question of excess. Who would have thought that a world could have so many bodily fluids in it' (Kaleta 1993: 22). This is right, as far as it goes. But it is not simply the *quantity* of images, bodily fluids in particular, that raises questions of excess and functions to interrupt the film's narrative flow, but the *proximity* such images have to the audience; that is, the way Lynch shoves them in our face.

The above three methods – surrealistic set-pieces, apparently unmotivated behaviour and hyperbolic gross-out shots – are by no means the only ones Lynch employs in order to render narrative continuity subservient to visual and auditory material. Additionally, I would briefly draw attention to the presence of unexpected and/or unnerving sounds – puppies suckling their mother in the middle of the X family's living room, for example, and the roaring hiss of Henry's radiator – which engender feelings of dread when such a response would not have been otherwise called for. And then there is the quick cutting to shots (not necessarily close-ups) of objects and events neither predictable nor obviously relevant if one considers the context – a sort of cinematographic equivalent to the second method discussed above. With all this in mind, I shall now proceed with an analysis of some of *Eraserhead*'s most disturbing/horrifying scenes and sequences; my goal here will be to identify those formal and thematic techniques relied upon by Lynch in order to produce such negative (upsetting, unpleasant, undesirable) emotional responses in viewers. I intend to demonstrate that many of these techniques find their origins in horror films of a far more generic nature. The conclusions reached in this next section will, among other things, lay the groundwork for my eventual discussion and critique of *Eraserhead*'s supposedly 'redemptive' moments.

Eraserhead's Horror Effects

The following are brief descriptions of five of *Eraserhead*'s most unnerving scenes, in order of their appearance within the film. Although there is a degree of arbitrariness in the selections – there are, without a doubt, *other* unnerving moments, and perhaps not *everyone* will find those listed here especially effective or interesting – most of the scenes in question have been deemed worthy of attention in the critical literature on *Eraserhead*. After describing these scenes, I shall proceed to compare, contrast and analyse them in greater detail, and in the process situate them within various already-existent horror traditions:

(a) Early in the film, and after an innocent-enough walk home, Henry enters his apartment building and presses the elevator button. What follows after the doors open is an extremely disconcerting period of waiting (approximately 13 seconds) for them to close again, and then an equally disconcerting ride up to Henry's floor. It is not so much that anything 'happens' during this sequence – though the lights in the elevator flicker, and briefly go out a couple of times – but our sense of foreboding is primed nevertheless, and carries over to subsequent scenes.

(b) While alone at the table with Mary's father Bill (Allen Joseph) during his dinner at the Xs', Henry sits uncomfortably for what seems like an eternity while Bill just stares at him, his body completely still, his face frozen in the mask of a goofy smile. At the same time, in an effectively eerie juxtaposition of contrasting moods, Mary can be seen crying in the background.

(c) Henry and the audience suddenly discover (in the scene discussed briefly above) that the baby – already malformed and not entirely human – is sick, and not just sick, but suffering terribly.

(d) In the midst of a fantasy sequence that we eventually discover is a dream (or rather, a nightmare), Henry climbs up onto the stage inside his radiator and attempts to make physical contact with the blonde, ovarian-cheeked 'Lady in the Radiator' (Laurel Near) who occasionally performs a song-and-dance routine there for him. His attempt at touching her fails, however, and The Lady disappears in a flash of blinding white light. Henry backs up slowly as a small tree on a dolly rolls to centre stage. Then, just before the tree begins oozing blood down its sides, our hero's head literally pops off, only to be replaced by that of his mutant child's.

(e) Just prior to the film's epilogue, Henry takes a pair of scissors and cautiously yet determinedly cuts open the bandages in which his paraplegic infant has been mummified for what we can only assume has been its entire life. What gets revealed to Henry and the audience is far more disgusting than anyone could have guessed, far more than anyone could have imagined. After an extreme close-up of the baby's now exposed internal organs, out from every orifice mushrooms a foamy waste material that threatens to remain in a state of perpetual and ever-increasing discharge. (Kaleta's remark, quoted above, concerning the 'quantitative imagery' of *Eraserhead* is most appropriate here.)

One obvious difference between the first two scenes on this list is that the former involves just Henry and an inanimate object (the elevator), while the latter centres on a bizarre interaction taking place between two people, neither of whom we would be inclined to call 'normal', but one of whom – Henry – serves as our surrogate for much of the picture. Nevertheless, it could plausibly be argued that these scenes engender their disturbing effects primarily the same way: not through special effects, manipulative camerawork or hyperbolic gross-out shots, but through images which instil in viewers a palpable feeling of uncanniness.[9] Before I defend it, this claim requires both qualification and clarification: the Lynchian uncanny is not – at least not primarily – explicable in Freudian/psychoanalytic terms (that is, via a return to consciousness of some previously repressed ideational content, or else via a reconfirmation in depicted reality of some previously 'surmounted' belief or beliefs), so much as in the terms proffered by Noël Carroll, a contemporary philosopher of film who attributes feelings of horror and uncanniness to apparent transgressions or violations of existing cultural (in some cases, conceptual) categories. Examples of such categories, according to Carroll, are the mutually exclusive dyads 'me/not me, inside/outside ... living/dead' and human/machine (Carroll 1990: 32).[10]

In both (a) and (b), Henry waits and waits ... and waits ... for something to happen (the elevator door to close; Bill X to stop grinning), without actively seeking to change his situation. In part, this is a symptom of his passivity, a character defect which is at least partially responsible for the problems he faces at home, and one which is dramatically overcome – with tragic consequences – when he finally decides to undress/murder his own child. But it is also no real surprise, since Henry has every reason (every *right*) to expect the 'somethings' in question to change of their own accord, and in a timely manner. It is precisely because Lynch intentionally primes, only to violate, Henry's – as well as our own – expectations concerning what is and is not 'appropriate' (standard operating procedure for a familiar piece of machinery; normal human social behaviour) that most viewers experience a feeling of uncanniness upon watching these scenes. At the imagistic level, both (a) and (b) also exhibit a *second* level of uncanniness: for there is a sense in which, arguably, the elevator displays a primitive consciousness of sorts, intentionally and perhaps spitefully 'teasing' Henry; and Bill X, by sitting utterly motionless for so long, in addition manages to violate the cultural/conceptual schema distinguishing animate from inanimate bodies. (Apparently this is a trait that runs in the X family, as Mary's grandmother displays some extreme corpse-like symptoms of her own.)

Without for a moment wishing to deny the effectiveness and creativity of the scenes in question, it should be pointed out that, at the level of *types* rather than *tokens*, the uncanny images just described do not originate with *Eraserhead*. On the contrary, the transgressive trope of non-living objects exhibiting some degree of proto-consciousness is a central feature of most – if not all – haunted-house movies (consider, for example, *The Haunting* (Robert Wise, 1964), *The Legend of Hell House* (John Hough, 1973) and *The Changeling* (Peter Medak, 1980)). Michel Chion writes that the shots of Henry waiting for the elevator and confronting evil in the form of electrical failures once inside it, 'betray the successfully assimilated influence of Kubrick, Fellini ... and, of course, Tati' (Chion 1995: 31). With respect to Kubrick, it is true that his *own* unforgettable elevator sequence, in *The Shining*, appeared three years *after* Lynch's.[11] Similarly, confusion over the ontological status of a particular individual – *Is s/he awake or asleep, conscious or unconscious, alive or dead?* – can be found in such a diverse collection of horror film narratives as *Mystery of the Wax Museum* (Michael Curtiz, 1933), *I Walked With a Zombie* (Jacques Tourneur, 1943), *House of Wax* (André De Toth, 1953), *A Bucket of Blood* (Roger Corman, 1959) and the post-*Eraserhead* pictures *The Texas Chainsaw Massacre 2* (Tobe Hooper, 1986), *The Serpent and the Rainbow* (Wes Craven, 1988) and *Se7en* (David Fincher, 1995). In the last example, a motionless, emaciated male figure is discovered tied to his bed in a dilapidated apartment by Detectives Somerset (Morgan Freeman) and Mills (Brad Pitt). Considering the wretched state of the body, and the largely 'realistic' world in which *Se7en* takes place, there seems no way this person could be alive. Curiosity and comfort lead the partners to bend over and examine the man, who suddenly jolts into consciousness with a vitality that fills most audience members with equal parts terror and disgust. Here we are approaching that most prolific of horror sub-genres, the zombie film, where the non-existent boundary separating animate from inanimate matter is frequently expressed by the term 'undead'. In Bill X's case, and especially that of Grandma X, however, a more fitting expression would be 'unliving'.

The point to take from this discussion is that Lynch's genius, as evidenced throughout *Eraserhead* in such simple yet compelling scenes as (a) and (b) above, should not automatically be taken as an indication of utter novelty and nonconformity with respect to established codes of cinematic discourse, even *generic* codes, despite the director's own denials of influence (which may or may not be true, the question of Lynch's conscious or direct influences making next to no difference to the soundness of the claim). Rather, one of the most important (yet to date, least popular) tasks of the Lynch scholar should be the systematic investigation and illumination of those *continuities* between his film work and the various texts and conventions – both classic and modern, local and foreign – to which this work is indebted.[12] For it is only by *contextualising* a film such as *Eraserhead* that we may fully appreciate the extent to which Lynch displays not just originality and creativity, but an awareness of existing traditions, and an expertise in the technical production of uncanny effects.[13]

In order to further support these assertions, I propose to look more closely at another pair of scenes from the list above: (c) and (e). Because both scenes centre on Henry's freakish, physically- (not to mention psychologically-) indeterminate infant, it is no surprise that the predominant emotional response generated in each of them is disgust. Nor is the stylistic means by which Lynch seeks to achieve this response surprising, namely through the use of what I have been referring to as 'hyperbolic gross-out shots' (of the baby's face in the first instance; of its body in the second). A staple of modern horror fare, the technique of quick cutting to extreme close-ups of disturbing content became the defining feature of low-budget 'splatter' films, as pioneered by underground auteur Herschell Gordon Lewis (*Blood Feast*, 1963; *Color Me Blood Red*, 1965) and popularised in such immediate *Eraserhead* predecessors as Wes Craven's *Last House on the Left* (1972) – in which an innocent young girl is stabbed to death and disembowelled by her sadistic tormentors – and Tobe Hooper's *Texas Chain Saw Massacre* (1974).[14] But considering that, in Lynch's film, the focus is primarily on the 'guts' component of the splatter sub-genre's 'blood-and-guts' formula, it would be remiss not to mention *Eraserhead*'s similarity in this respect to a pair of modern Italian horror classics: *Black Sunday* (Mario Bava, 1960) and *Suspiria* (Dario Argento, 1977).

In *Black Sunday*, there is an unprecedented and thus truly shocking moment near the end of the film in which the viewer is presented with a close-up of the reincarnated vampire-witch Aja's (Barbara Steele) rotting innards, which had previously been kept hidden by a mere article of clothing – just as the makeshift bandages encasing the Spencer baby's limbless body are the only things keeping its viscera 'under wraps'. Where are the layers of epidermis to protect this otherwise helpless being, to ensure that its insides *remain* inside? Although, as Freeland notes, nowhere in the published interviews does Lynch make actual direct reference to *Repulsion* (Roman Polanski, 1965), J. Hoberman and Jonathan Rosenbaum must be onto something when they describe the baby as 'an illegitimate monster – a mewling, eye-rolling first cousin to the skinned-rabbit centrepiece of Roman Polanski's [film]' (Hoberman and Rosenbaum 1983: 214). Whatever sympathy some viewers may feel for this creature – and let me emphasise the word *may* here, not wishing to assume any uniformity of audience response on this point – the 'monster' appellation is fitting. By fashioning Henry's baby skinless, boneless and poised to spill its guts out all over the place, Lynch forces Daddy and audience alike to contemplate a living, breathing (temporarily, at least) transgression of the deeply-entrenched cultural opposition, inside vs. outside.

Carroll writes that '[monsters] are un-natural relative to a culture's conceptual scheme of nature. They do not fit the scheme; they violate it. Thus, monsters are not only physically threatening; they are cognitively threatening. ... [T]hey tend to render those who encounter them insane, mad, deranged, and so on' (Carroll 1990: 34). This last is certainly a point to which Henry could testify, despite the utter lack of danger represented by his newborn; after all, with no arms or legs, how on earth – besides its incessant, exasperating crying – could it possibly harm him? In fact, the interactions between Henry and the baby, culminating in Henry's extra-uterine abortion of the baby (there *is* something distinctly surgical about the scene in question, what with the baby wrapped in bandages and Henry methodically snipping his way through them), leads me to propose a slight modification of the standard Carrollian view: monsters may be physically *or* cognitively threatening to those who encounter them – either type of threat is sufficient, neither by itself is necessary. For the sake of comparison, it is worth quoting here the mad, overanxious narrator of Edgar Allen Poe's 1843 short story, *The Tell-Tale Heart*:

> The disease had sharpened my senses – not destroyed – not dulled them. Above all was the sense of hearing acute. I heard all things in heaven and in the earth. I heard many things in hell. ... It is impossible to say how first the idea entered my brain: but once conceived, it haunted me day and night. ... I loved the old man. He had never wronged me. He had never given me insult. ... I think it was his eye! yes, it was this! One of his eyes resembled that of a vulture – a pale, blue eye, with a film over it. Whenever it fell upon me, my blood ran cold; and so by degrees – very gradually – I made up my mind to take the life of the old man, and thus rid myself of the eye forever (Poe 1980: 186).

Although his own monomania – *What lies underneath those bandages?* – only reveals itself towards the end of *Eraserhead's* narrative, Henry's striking resemblance to the Poe narrator should be obvious: both men possess excessively keen senses and what can only be considered hyperactive imaginations; neither has anything to fear, physically-speaking, from his eventual victim; both are spurred to violence by characteristics and qualities that challenge their traditional way of looking at, and so understanding, the worlds in which they live; and both wind up paying (more or less intentionally) a heavy price for the murders they commit.

With respect to (c), the sudden close-up of the baby in the throes of its mysterious, ulcerous illness finds an analogue in *Suspiria*, Argento's masterpiece of supernatural horror, released in the same year as *Eraserhead*. In this film, the discovery of infestation in the ceiling of a famous dance academy leads to a quick zoom-in to a nest of maggots, followed immediately by a close-up of a young girl's face covered with the vile insects – the resultant image is surprisingly similar to what we see of Henry's infant. Also crucial here is the sudden introduction of a high-pitched, monotonic, non-diegetic sound, an effect which serves as an aural correlate to the unsettling visuals. Lynch employs precisely the same technique in (c) – as well as in the scene when Henry discovers a multitude of stringy, sperm-like creatures (foetuses?) under the covers of his bed[15] – resulting in nearly exactly the same bi-sensory shock effect.

Finally, we come to (d), a scene that stands alone in this brief survey not least because of its fantastic/surrealistic atmosphere and images. As is so often the case with highly effective horror scenes, even *knowing* what to expect here fails to provide a shield against its disturbing impact.[16] In order to examine the reasons for (the 'causes of') this impact, I shall divide (d) into the following three segments: Henry's brief encounter with The Lady in the Radiator; his behaviour as the tree rolls out onto the radiator stage; and the loss and subsequent replacement of his head. What emerges from this division is that each sequence possesses its *own* horror effects, effects which nevertheless work together to add to the overall power of the scene, and which, after they are identified, serve to render the scene as a whole somewhat less mysterious (though certainly no less frightening).

In the first of the above segments, Henry approaches The Lady in the Radiator, whose chipmunk cheeks, adorable smile and saccharine voice still betray something distinctly ominous (I shall return to this point below). With a look of desperation mixed with apprehension on his face, he reaches out to touch her, but at the moment of contact the screen goes blindingly white and the omnipresent 'white noise' of mechanistic energy suddenly rises to a near-deafening crescendo (once again we are provided the auditory correlate to a striking visual display). Henry pulls back in surprise and, perhaps wanting to verify the strange cause-and-effect process he has seemingly initiated, tries touching her again – with the same result. Except that this time, after turning away momentarily, what he (and we) see in place of The Lady is the hideous visage of The Man in the Planet. This unexpected switch functions as a very effective scare tactic, as an associative link is established between apparent opposites (good and evil, appealing and repulsive, etc.) and what was originally thought to be safe is now revealed as a threat.[17] Lynch would repeat himself 15 years later in the underrated *Twin Peaks: Fire Walk with Me* (1992) when the face of Laura Palmer's (Sheryl Lee) demonic attacker is momentarily replaced by that of her own father. But this tactic has a long history and can be found in numerous vampire, shape-shifter and *doppelgänger* films, as well as in such otherwise non-generic horror fare as *Don't Look Now* (Nicholas Roeg, 1973) and, more recently, *Jacob's Ladder* (Adrian Lyne, 1990).[18]

In the second sequence from (d), Henry, even more unnerved after the shock of what just happened, slowly backs away from the centre of the stage, finally standing

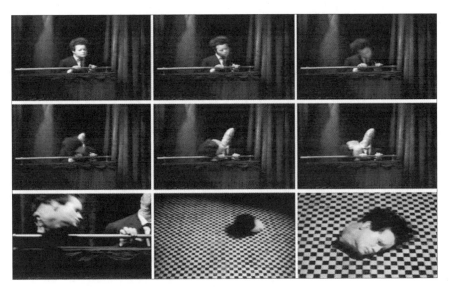

Henry loses his head in *Eraserhead*

behind a railing as the tree makes its special guest appearance. Crucial to notice here (but next to invisible if one is not looking for it) is the compulsive manner in which Henry twists his hands around the rail, reminiscent of the fits experienced by Mary and her mother at the X family home, like a needle stuck in the groove of a phonograph record. Whether consciously registered by the viewer or not, Henry's repetitive, masturbatory hand motion only increases the overall feeling of dread and fearsome anticipation.

And we are not disappointed. For in the scene's final segment, Henry's head suddenly pops off, or, to be more precise, is forced off its moorings by an erect phallus erupting from somewhere inside his body. This shocking sight is accompanied by a loud noise reminiscent of a cartoon spring being released from a broken jack-in-the-box. His hands continue their circular movements around the railing, even though Henry is, at least for the time being, dead; think of a chicken with its head cut off, still running frantically around the pen until its body finally gets the message. Henry's decapitation is so horrific in part because of the way it happens. We have no time to prepare ourselves as the executioner readies his sword, the killer wields his knife, etc.; rather, it happens pretty much all on its own, via some kind of internal mechanism, and if Henry can lose his head so easily, what does that say about the rest of him ... and us? I have made it this far without resorting to hackneyed Freudianisms, but the castration anxiety manifested in this sequence is just too transparent – and too effective – not to mention. The slow, steady rise of the baby's (penis) head in place of Henry's own signals Oedipal wish-fulfilment and in fact serves to over-determine psychoanalytic interpretation: are we witnessing Henry's nightmare, the baby's fantasy, both at once? Ultimately, the horror of this sequence is the horror of *attack from within*, whether psychically, socially ('As the internalisation of social labels, this interior "baby" is an impediment to the fulfillment Henry seeks' (Nochimson 1997: 160)), or at a more primitive, bodily level. In this respect, it bears comparison with such *Eraserhead* contemporaries as *Shivers* (aka *They Came From Within*) (David Cronenberg, 1975), *The Manitou* (William Girdler, 1978), *The Beast Within* (Philippe Mora, 1982) and, of course, *Alien* (Ridley Scott, 1979), with its infamous male birthing scene of an extra-terrestrial infant, a close cousin to Henry's own.

The Essential Evil in/of Eraserhead

The two-part thesis of this essay has been, first, that rather than treating *Eraserhead* as an isolated masterpiece, one whose 'genuine strangeness [of] cinematography ... is not easy to define and cannot be reduced to the use of particular techniques' (Chion 1995: 42), the film's pervasive uncanniness is most fruitfully explained, though never explained away, when situated within the context of the horror genre and its established traditions; and second, that if such a reading of *Eraserhead* is at odds with Lynch's own denials of influence, so much the worse for the director (but not at all for the film itself). In support of these claims, I have analysed a number of *Eraserhead*'s most disturbing scenes, seeking to reveal and partially expose their dependence on and interaction with particular currents in horror film-making past and present.

As alluded to above, even the film's purported oases of contentment have a dark and ominous feel to them. Consider The Lady in the Radiator – whom Nochimson claims 'represents a feminine energy that prohibits castration' (Nochimson 1997: 164) and of whom Lynch disingenuously states that 'inside is where the happiness in her comes from. Her outside appearance is not the thing' (Lynch in Rodley 1997: 67) – what with her seductive song promoting suicide ('In heaven, everything is fine...'), her ritualised acts of violence (stomping to death the falling foetuses as part of a formal dance routine) and her funhouse-mirror Marilyn Monroe looks (those chubby cheeks are less cute than regressive, even grotesque). Similarly, Henry's night of passion with the Beautiful Girl Across the Hall possesses its share of distressing elements: for he must forcibly prevent the woman from focusing on the hysterical baby, who is indeed stuck witnessing a variant of the primal scene; and the couple's potentially 'romantic' dissolution into a pool of milky water closes with a disconcerting image of the woman's hair floating on the surface (what happened to *Henry's* famous coiffure? and is there any doubt that the woman's hair has become unattached from her scalp?). Although Freeland views Henry's infanticide as 'a matter less of revenge than of consuming curiosity or even mercy' (Freeland 2000: 230), we have already seen (with reference to Poe) that it is Henry's very obsession with 'ridding himself' of that which he is responsible for but cannot comprehend that renders his act of murder less merciful than (mono)maniacal.

There can be no denying the fact that *Eraserhead* is a complex and challenging film. The extent to which Lynch here renders plot and narrative subservient to what we have called 'the primacy of the audio-visual image' has been amply demonstrated. But it is an overstatement to claim that 'the uncanny in *Eraserhead* is what literally exceeds the limits of representation' (Freeland 2000: 234), or that 'all structures of representation ... in *Eraserhead* ... always feign totality in their absurd incompleteness' (Nochimson 1997: 158). The brilliance of this film lies in the director's extraordinary command of proven horror techniques: in *Eraserhead*, it is precisely what *can* be represented (despite its impossibility) that generates such powerful feelings of uncanniness, anxiety and disgust.[19]

Notes

1 'I never saw, I still haven't seen a lot of Buñuel', Lynch told a *Rolling Stone* interviewer in 1990. 'I saw *An Andalusian Dog* a lot later. I don't even know that much about surrealism – I guess it's just my take on what's floating by' (Lynch in Breskin 1990: 62; cf. Chion 1995: 25). It is true that Lynch screened Billy Wilder's creepy *film noir*, *Sunset Boulevard* (1950), for his actors and crew before starting shooting on *Eraserhead*, but he has since downplayed even the influence of this film: 'there wasn't anything in particular about it that related to *Eraserhead*. It was just a black-and-white experience of a certain mood' (Lynch in Rodley 1997: 71). Moments later, however, Lynch qualifies this remark: 'Obviously, there's gotta be something similar because I love it so much. But I don't know what it is' (ibid.).

2 Cf. Freeland: 'the plot [of *Eraserhead*] is straightforward in its own odd way' (2000: 226). Martha Nochimson offers an interesting contrast to this position when she states that 'the end of *Eraserhead* represents the two incommensurable regimes of energy and structure together, never to be harmonised but sometimes in a blinding flash to be balanced. *We have narrative closure, but only as a result of having broken free from narrative structure*' (Nochimson 1997: 162 [my emphasis].

3 See, in particular, Švankmajer's *The Last Trick* (1964), *Jabberwocky* (1971) and *Dimensions of Dialogue* (1982). For an introduction to the work of Jan Švankmajer, see Uhde 2003.

4 See, for example, Godwin 1984: 48, Freeland 2000: 229, and Hoberman and Rosenbaum, who argue that 'the taboo aspect of this question [whether the baby can be defined as a living creature] is, in fact, central to the film's impact' (Hoberman and Rosenbaum 1983: 242).

5 Interview with Buñuel, *Un Chien Andalou*. Interama Video Classics, 1990.

6 Tico Romao, in e-mail correspondence with the author (1 December 2001), makes the point that it is productive to situate Alvin Straight's (Richard Farnsworth) characterisation in *The Straight Story* with respect to the ways in which Lynch routinely departs from mainstream character depiction: 'While ... Straight does not provoke the category confusion of, say, the "baby" in *Eraserhead*, nor does he manifest the psycho-sexual pathologies that are exhibited in certain characters of *Blue Velvet* and *Twin Peaks*, he nonetheless uses a lawnmower as his principal mode of transport and eats raw wieners along the way!'

7 See the essays in Mendik and Schneider 2002.

8 The baby's desperate gasps for breath are also amplified for the duration of this shot.

9 The word 'uncanny' comes from the German 'unheimlich' (literally 'unhomely'), a fact which has special relevance here considering the domestic locales in which the scenes in question take place.

10 The classic statement of Freud's position on the uncanny can be found in Freud (1919/58). For more on the relevance of this account to horror film theorising, see Schneider (1997). For Carroll's non-psychoanalytic alternative, see Carroll 1990: 31–5. For discussion and critique of the Carrollian view, see Schneider 2000.

11 See also Dick Maas's Dutch horror film, *De Lift* (1983), remade in Hollywood in 2001 under the title *Down*. Freeland writes that '*The Shining* and *Eraserhead* share a number of features. Each is the story of a father threatened by an uncanny or monstrous child. Because he attempts to destroy this child, the father himself must die. Conditions surrounding this family melodrama make father and child seem as much victims as they are monsters. [...] The evil that dominates the worldview of these films is not just a product of literary elements; its evocation fundamentally involves the filmic medium as a whole' (Freeland 2000: 215–16).

12 Note that I have not restricted myself in this sentence to mention of *filmic* texts and conventions, thus leaving open the possibility (and possible utility) of cross-media analyses.

13 Had this way of conceiving of Lynch and his work gained credence earlier, it may not have come as such a surprise – even shock – to find the director so successful at making the seeming transition to 'mainstream' Hollywood narrative in *The Straight Story*, questions concerning the status of *Mulholland Drive* notwithstanding.

14 Though retrospectively taken to task by Chion, Hoberman and Rosenbaum, *et al.*, perhaps the contemporary review of *Eraserhead* which appeared in *Variety* (23 March 1977) was not *entirely* off-target when it stated that 'Lynch seems bent on emulating Herschell Gordon Lewis, the king of low-budget gore'.

15 As reported by Godwin, 'these "foetuses" were actually human umbilical cords, which Catherine Coulson obtained from a hospital' (Godwin 1984: 64).

16 The very interesting question that arises here is whether knowing what to expect in such scenes actually *increases* their disturbing impact (and if so, why?).

17 Contrast this analysis with that of Nochimson, who writes that 'In a series of images after Henry reaches for the lady, we see the man in the planet as an internal pressure on Henry to lose the vision of the lady, leaving empty space where she had been' (Nochimson 1997: 159). Perhaps a threatening space, but by no means is it empty.

18 For an extended discussion of the *doppelgänger* trope in modern horror cinema, see Schneider 2001.

19 Sincere thanks to Annette Davison, Peter Krämer, Tico Romao and Erica Sheen for helpful comments and suggestions on earlier versions of this essay.

CHAPTER TWO

David Lynch and the Mug Shot: Facework in The Elephant Man and The Straight Story

Joe Kember

[Close-up of braunschweiger and wieners at the checkout of Joyce's Store. Brenda the shop girl speaks to Rose Straight]

Brenda:	Having a party?
Rose Straight:	O Jeez ... I love ... a party!
Brenda:	O! Me too!
Rose:	So ... where's it ... at?
Brenda:	Where's what at?
Rose:	... Your ... party?
Brenda:	I'm not having a party. I thought *you* were having a party.
Rose:	... I *am*?
Brenda:	Well, yah! Look at all that braunschweiger...

In this brief scene from *The Straight Story* (1999) Rose Straight (Sissy Spacek) discusses her unusually large purchase of braunschweiger and wieners with the grocery store checkout girl, Brenda (Jennifer Edwards-Hughes). Rose attempts to conform to the conversational rationale in the store, but struggles against her speech impediment within the formality of their polite dialogue. Speaking at cross-purposes, they misunderstand one another, and the conversation descends into a series of double takes and non sequiturs. The two women, smiling good-naturedly, pursue a gestural conversation with little more success. The facial expression of each is captured by a series of reaction shots, and the scene draws to an abrupt close when they mug back and forth their mutual dislike for braunshweiger. Their agreement returns the scene to its opening shot of the offending cold cuts and contributes to a pervasive sense of inertia and inconsequence for which the narrative offers no explanation. The film simply pauses for a moment around the opacity of their faces and the clumsiness of their communication. The smooth economy of looks and speech typically associated with shot/reverse-shot congeals into a faltering and thoroughly comic redundancy.

The scene is remarkable for its abeyance of the conventional intersubjective routines that the two-shot has customarily sought to reproduce. In place of free-flowing dialogue, Spacek enacts speech which is strangely free from nuance, and which emerges breathlessly, word by word, as if overcoming physical hindrance. Like her speech, her face accomplishes an extraordinary staccato rhythm, freezing momentarily before passing, with seemingly mechanical effort, into new configurations. Rose's disability seems to affect only her capacity to communicate and makes the work inherent to such social interactions as small talk painfully obvious. Writing about such social interactions for ordinary individuals, Anthony Giddens notes that 'much of this labour passes unnoticed, so deeply engrained is it in practical consciousness in terms of bodily control and facial expression' (Giddens 1991: 61). By contrast, the labour of Rose's small talking with Brenda is immediately apparent because Rose's bodily, facial and vocal control proves inadequate to the social interaction at hand. Spectators accustomed to the transparent dissemination of character psychology during dialogue scenes (and in day-to-day life) are forced to address a face and a voice whose connections with character are uncertain, or, at least, unfamiliar. Disability, a frequently repeated motif of David Lynch's films, thus becomes the structuring principle around which this scene revolves. The lingering close-ups of Rose's face capture the hesitation between the intersubjective promise of her eyes and the physical obstruction posed by the face's disobedient mobile features – especially the mouth. Assumptions concerning characterisation and 'deep' motivation are countered by the irresolvable play of the face's surface structures. Expressive and incoherent by turns, Rose typifies the ambivalence of the mug shot in Lynch's cinema, promising an implicit empathetic access to her character and motivations, but always threatening to expose the chaotic and uncontrolled relationships such understanding seeks to repress.

Lynch's cinema has consistently exploited this ambivalence of the face. Through-out most of his films, however, the problem of the human face is not somatic, as in the case of Rose, but derives from its inability to express inhuman or perverse desires. Conflicts of identity/dispersal, interior/surface, control/powerlessness are instigated by events as simple as the discovery of an ear (*Blue Velvet*, 1986) or as unprecedented as the agonising conversion of one face into another (*Lost Highway*, 1997). In *Wild at Heart* (1990), Marietta Fortune (Diane Ladd) plasters her face with red lipstick and gazes at a mirror in which her reflected image seems flattened and dehumanised. Only the eyes stand out from this wall of red, and these compromise the obliteration of personality Marietta has attempted.[1] The scene carries a potent insinuation of schizoid disembodiment fully realised in *Lost Highway*, where a parallel scene at Andy's party similarly instils a pervasive sense of menace. In this latter scene, the extreme close-up shot/reverse-shot sequence between Fred Madison (Bill Pullman) and the Mystery Man (Robert Blake) destabilises the communication between these characters to such an extent that the alignment of space, sound, time and identity conventionally assured by this continuity technique is itself subjected to scrutiny. In these films the human face no longer guarantees access to character or personality. Instead, the face becomes notable more for the uncanny underworld it masks than for the communication it promises.

These scenes also exemplify Lynch's inclusion within a certain modern tradition of American film-making in which faces are often disguises, and shield a variety of unspeakable desires and perversities. Consider, for example, Lecter's face-wearing episode in *The Silence of the Lambs* (1991), or the persistent appearance in the 1980s and 1990s of plastic surgery and shape-shifting among evil or non-human characters, as in *Terminator 2: Judgment Day* (1991), *Face/Off* (1997) or *Die Another Day* (2002). Each of these mainstream Hollywood productions routinely delivers a narrative payoff in which the faces of protagonists are revealed as manipulated and corrupt. 'Perversion is no longer subversive', writes Slavoj Žižek of Lynch's contribution to this tradition; 'the shocking excesses are part of the system, which feeds on them in order to reproduce itself'. (Žižek 2000b). More generally, according to Jacques Aumont's study of international trends of facial representation in film, the face has often been fragmented and de-socialised in this 'marginal but certainly significant' tradition of modern film-making:

> Its own beauty, its meaning, even its expression are emptied. Stripped of sense, stripped of value, this face just barely enters into any exchange, and forbids contemplation. … It insinuates itself, erratic, incomplete, in the shape of obstinate effects all sharing a common resemblance to a ruin, to an abandonment, an undoing. A certain inclination of the cinema, let us say, of the 1970s and 1980s, has de-faced the face. (Aumont 1992: 149–50, my translation)

The face in modern cinema is sometimes no more than the sum of its ruined individual features, an object defying communication and empathy. It is as if the lights and colours comprising the film image possess 'an autonomous life of their own, more living than that of faces', which deny the face's gestaltic signification of selfhood (1992: 154, my translation). Aumont defines this face-ruin primarily in opposition to the 'ordinary face of cinema' associated with the classical American cinema of the 1930s (1992: 43–69, my translation). This ordinary face served within classical film as a central figure and premise for representation itself, prefiguring the swift exchange of glances, speech and of empathy between characters as it did more broadly between characters, cameras, film-makers and audiences. Lynch's cinema, I believe, consistently mediates between these two alternatives, and it does so in two closely related ways. In the most Lynchian films, such as *Wild at Heart* or *Lost Highway*, we learn that the human face is a peculiarly expressive mask whose apparently ordinary countenance is compromised and ultimately ruined by the emergence of passions it can neither suppress nor express. However, in *The Elephant Man* (1980) and *The Straight Story*, the mask-faces worn by John Merrick and Rose are not disguises, but disabilities to be borne and overcome. Furthermore, the faces of other characters within these films are also defined by their efforts to communicate. Beginning as ruins, the triumphant emergence of these extraordinary faces as ordinary marks their entrance into a world of competent, meaningful and often highly sentimental communication. That is to say, they aspire to the transparency of classical modes of representation.

Lynch has acknowledged that *The Elephant Man* and *The Straight Story* are unique among his films in their attempt 'to create a pure emotion with images and sound' and to communicate straightforwardly the touching and morally instructive story of the 'lone man' (Henry 1999: 17, my translation). Both dwell upon the faces of their central characters in a series of protracted and intimate mug shots, especially in the course of face-to-face conversations. Both, moreover, are biopics which appear to celebrate the transcendence of bodily limitations and the pursuit of mundane normalcy: Merrick (John Hurt) wishes to sleep lying down like everybody else; Alvin Straight (Richard Farnsworth) wants to visit his brother in spite of old age, infirmity and the distance between them. However, Lynch's apparent reversion to a conventional Hollywood sentimentalism, rewarded in both films with Oscar nominations, has discomfited some critics.[2] Furthermore, the transcendence of physical disability and grandiose achievement of ordinariness in these films has provoked substantial criticism from a disabled perspective. Paul Anthony Darke has challenged Lynch's consistent use of physical abnormality and disability as a curio or motif, and has condemned *The Elephant Man* in particular for its normalisation of the extraordinary body (Darke 1994). Ostensibly, this film benevolently uncovers the everyday personhood behind Merrick's monstrous body. Darke objects to what he sees as Lynch's acquiescence with a prescriptive bourgeois blueprint for this everydayness. The supposed benevolence of the film's perspective dissolves because it malignly suppresses the radical challenge of an everyday existence that is unable to conform.[3] The representation of Joseph Merrick – the incorrectly named John Merrick of the film[4] – insidiously 'turn[s] full circle and return[s] abnormality to the metaphysical and moral arena of sin' (1994: 328).

The same objection might also be levelled, with some qualification, at the representation of Rose Straight. Spacek's performance as Rose appears to dramatise an internal struggle with disability, and hence reinforces the aspirational drive for 'normal' selfhood that Darke found insupportable in *The Elephant Man*. However, the restless ambivalence of her face, tautly poised moment to moment between ordinariness and ruin, also suggests a kind of answer to Darke, or at least a moderation of his objection. In one emotionally charged scene, Rose sadly watches a child retrieve his ball in her front yard. Although we have not yet learned that Rose has lost her own children to a prejudiced child welfare system, Spacek

'The triumphant emergence of these extraordinary faces as ordinary': John Merrick (John Hurt) in *The Elephant Man*

evokes a keen sense of sadness or pensiveness. In this silent scene her speech impediment is irrelevant: her face is both seen and seeing, a permeable membrane with a recognisably human profile granting spectators access to her emotions and personality. Her face alone proves capable of eliciting emotions in spectators, a phenomenon Carl Plantinga, following recent cognitive research into the face, has called 'emotional contagion' (Plantinga 1999: 243). 'The art of the actor', Plantinga has written of classical narrative film, is to make available 'a direct, sensory, representation of human emotion, more accessible and more sensual than any other medium' (Plantinga 1993: 20).[5] In this scene, Spacek offers emotions consistent with this classical vision of ordinary selfhood. But, when Rose speaks with others, as in the scene with Brenda, the peculiar thematics of her face ensure that this self becomes intermittently difficult to negotiate. Its various components – the mouth, the eyes, the eyebrows – seem to act independently, as if emphasising the miracle of these components' evocation of character in the first place. 'The orderliness of day-to-day life is a miraculous occurrence', confirms Giddens, 'yet the slightest glance of one person towards another, inflexion of the voice, changing facial expression or gestures of the body may threaten it' (Giddens 1991: 52). In the case of Rose, the face-ruin automatically re-emerges during conversation, continually reminding us of an extraordinary and sometimes unsettling pattern of selfhood which, as in the case of Merrick, cannot conform.

In Rose's case, the aspiration to ordinariness, to which Darke objects, also inevitably delivers the radical challenge to ordinary selfhood he wishes to celebrate. Her face works laboriously and fitfully during conversation and encourages close scrutiny, but this scrutiny results not in better understanding of her character, but in the fragmentation of the face's components. The spectator's secure sense of connection with this character, a reassurance traditionally associated with the mug shot, is thus supplemented by existential anxieties associated with the face-ruin. But this ruined face is never the empty undoing of meaning described by Aumont.

Crucially, in *The Elephant Man* and *The Straight Story* the fragmentation of the face is merely an external register of a deeper and resolutely Lynchian fragmentation of character and personhood. The troubled play of surface structures in even the most static, passive faces of the protagonists of these films implies the deeper operation of chaotic internal structures. Protagonists such as Merrick and Rose have a unique significance in Lynch's work, since they sometimes enable spectators to read these internal structures directly from the face without having to see through the facial disguises worn by such characters as Marietta Fortune or the Mystery Man. Rudolf Arnheim has also described these deep structures associated with the perception of human physiognomy as a complex 'configuration of forces' with universal significance:

> Such a configuration interests us because it is significant not only for the object in whose image it appears, but for the physical and mental world in general. Motifs like rising and falling, dominance and submission, weakness and strength, harmony and discord, struggle and conformance, underlie all existence. We find them within our mind and in our relations to other people, in the human community and in the events of nature (Arnheim 1956: 368).

This series of abstract forces structure our relationships with other people as they do the world in general. We may recognise in Rose, for example, the motifs of harmony and discord, struggle and conformance, and in doing so we also recognise that she embodies an individual example of these universal forces acting throughout everyday existence. Her face renders such primordial motifs legible and thus sustains an immanent critique of subject-centred models of selfhood.

The face of John Merrick poses a different set of somatic and social problems with a distinct impact on sentimental narrative entailments. Unlike Rose, Merrick's face is physically distorted to such an extent that facial emotional contagion is near impossible, and empathy for this character is achieved by other means with the utmost difficulty. Merrick's face is a ruin in a literal sense, a face unmade by the encroaching distortion of his features since childhood. Rose's communicative difficulties ultimately result in awkwardness, especially during set-piece conversations, but for Merrick, having overcome the horrified response of his audiences, the problems arise because his face is almost incapable of emoting. Merrick's immobile features make of his countenance an object which his extraordinary body does little to humanise.

Without the intersubjective attraction of the emoting, mobile face, Merrick's face becomes an attraction in *The Elephant Man* in two related senses. Firstly, it becomes an objectified exhibit for the cinema audience as it is in the film's freak show and medical lecture scenes. Indeed, this principle of objectification, which Lynch arguably exploits as much as his predecessors, was clearly understood by the real Joseph Merrick and his exhibitor (real name, Tom Norman), who sold thousands of pamphlets outlining the 'Life of the Elephant Man' to fascinated customers (Norman n.d.).[6] Norman would stand outside or within the freak show, introducing his exhibit by describing its bestial and nonhuman face, but, as in all subsequent representations of Merrick, he also exaggerated the humanity within. Secondly, in Sergei Eisenstein's sense of a 'cinema of attractions', Merrick's face is a fascination of the eye, inviting strategies of shock, defamiliarisation and distanciation amongst the film's spectators (Eisenstein 1988: 39–58). Significantly, both senses of the term 'attraction' are most closely associated with the earliest aesthetics of the cinema. Unlike recent cinematic facial vocabularies, the early cinema consistently lingered on the grotesque and unsettling effect of the facial close-up, making representation of the face a showcase for the capacities of the new medium, as well as a stark expression of a distinctly modern sense of alienation (see, for example, Gunning 1997 and Kember 2001). Lynch has openly experimented with this early aesthetic of defamiliarisation in his 52-second contribution to Sarah Mohn's *Lumière et Compagnie* (1995), entitled 'Premonitions Following an Evil Deed', in which he uses an original Lumière camera to capture a series of unsettling images of the human face and body. In this short film, as in *The Elephant Man*, the dynamic of the attraction precludes the possibility of easy facial transparency and emotional contagion, and sometimes threatens to submerge the seeing and speaking personality 'behind' the face in the sheer volume of unfocused and appropriative gazes that slide across it.

The reproduction of the freak show dynamic in Lynch's film has troubled several commentators, who have regularly emphasised the delayed appearance of Merrick's face in the film (Kaleta 1993: 49–50; Alexander 1993: 69; Chion 1995: 57; Nochimson 1997: 138–40). Wishing to see the phenomenon for himself, Frederick Treves (Anthony Hopkins), like the cinema audience, is thwarted by the enforced closure of the freak show. Treves returns some time later to try again at the filthy and damp quarters of the film's showman figure, Bytes (Freddie Jones). Bytes delivers a well-practiced spiel to Treves but, gazing outward to the left and right of the screen, he ominously addresses it to absent 'ladies and gentlemen'. The tale he tells invites curiosity and cynicism in equal measure and thus tends to include spectators of the film within the dynamic of the freak show attraction. Despite the ambiguous promise of his address (and the appearance in the screenplay of a facial close-up at this stage) we spectators are frustrated once again by a distant and heavily shadowed partial profile of the coveted and feared face-object. Instead, a protracted close-up of Treves' frozen and astonished face, a tear rolling from his eye, serves to sentimentalise and prolong the suspense. Throughout the film, a succession of shocked and horrified faces are emotionally focused in this manner by Merrick's distorted features. But on this occasion the audience is also implicated in Treves' enterprise. The intensity of the lingering mug shot of Treves is likely to elicit a powerful form of emotional contagion in spectators, bordering on an uncomfortable identification with his acquisitive desire to see 'it'.[7]

Throughout these episodes Merrick himself remains silent, unresponsive and all but invisible, his face hidden beneath his cap and hood or behind curtains and medical screens. These boundaries are defended by a series of judicious cuts: 'I think I'll examine you now', threatens Treves in his office, advancing toward the camera with a predatory gesture barely arbitrated by a fade to black. Shortly afterwards, a medium close-up mug shot of Merrick occurs when Nora (Lesley Dunlop) brings him a bowl of soup. Nora's terrified reaction is this time focused by the appearance of Merrick's unresponsive face, but the shots of him are brief and flatten his face against the surface of the wall behind him, again tending to frustrate rather than indulge us. Eventually, the camera's predatory tendencies are satisfied unexpectedly, the loud tolling of a bell causing Merrick to start up in bed and reveal his face in extreme close-up. The long-desired mug shot is violently invasive, brutally realising for us the desire to examine the face closely. It is achieved by means of an inversion of the discovery scene experienced earlier by Treves: if Merrick has been the occasion of shock in other characters, it is Merrick himself who experiences the shock here. Furthermore, his startled reaction is caused by the bell, a mechanism which creaks punctually into operation as if heralding the film's inevitable and systematic violation of his space and face. This is the first acknowledgement not only of the internal intelligence able to hear and to respond coherently to the bell (until now we, like Treves, are reassured that Merrick is a 'complete imbecile'), but also of a potent insinuation that the invasive scrutiny levelled by the camera at the surface of his body is the occasion of his shock. His face reflects back to us a revulsion at the monstrous appetites of camera and spectators – and at their inevitable satisfaction.

Such self-reflexive moments are repeated on several further occasions in the course of the film. The audience's self-reflexive sense of discomfort with its own viewing practices thus achieves what Merrick's face cannot: a degree of empathy and emotional participation. More sophisticated evocations of his personality are accomplished throughout by manipulation of the point-of-view shot, by the 'corporeal implication' of his wheezing and pained 'pre-vocal' voice, and by the more diffuse emotional evocations of extra-diegetic music (Chion 1982: 56, my translation).[8] Soon after the intrusion of the bell, Merrick is depicted gazing intently at the portrait of his mother. The point-of-view shot establishes his capacity for an interpersonal relationship whose content, however, cannot be specified from his face. His fascination with this facial portrait, and indeed with the numerous 'beautiful' and 'noble' photographic portraits that populate the film once again brings to light the ungenerous qualities of our own gaze. As Merrick gazes at the image of an ordinary face, ordinary cinema audiences are offered an inverted and generous parallel for their own abusive strategies of face-reading. Indeed, throughout this scene, the camera dwells unmercifully on Merrick's face, enabling us to gratify fully our acquisitive gaze (Holladay and Watt 1989).

Significantly, the scene is cross-cut by the approach of the night porter (Michael Elphick), the most abusive of all sites of vision incarnated by the film. His invasion of Merrick's room reproduces our own, and the shots associated with his point of view also dwell on the face. Meanwhile, harsh lighting from Merrick's left and front demonstrates a cartographer's concern with the tumescent mass of its right side. The porter's point of view, like our own, is associated with a levelling and decentring of *mise-en-scène*. Spectators are denied a specific facial feature upon which the wandering eye can settle. This technique was predetermined at an early stage of production by the adoption of CinemaScope format, and by the decision made, as Mel Brooks put it, 'to hold back some of the more horrible aspects of the deformity' by shooting in black-and-white (Woods 1997: 45). Unusually for a widescreen production, the camera in this scene is static and offers Merrick's face in close-up, allowing the eye to slide across textures and details of this face as it does, more generally, across the screen. The night porter pokes crudely at a single point in the expanse of skin, as if to focus the spectator upon a single point. But the decentring of *mise-en-scène* ensures that our sensual and visceral negotiation of the face is condemned to a restless wandering, threatening at points to lose even the single familiar landmark of Merrick's eyes. The mobile eye seeks in vain at this stage for more than a fleeting correlative to the personality and intellect that we have simultaneously learnt Merrick possesses. Like the motif of billowing smoke or steam which appears in several of Lynch's films, this face reduces the cinema screen momentarily to a moving, textured surface, whose fascination for audiences is not mimetic, but kinetic.

The opening scenes of *The Elephant Man* thoroughly expose our difficulties in experiencing empathy for an inexpressive face. However, from the first close-up, and with progressively greater frequency and confidence, strategies of expression associated with the point-of-view shot, with Merrick's strangely musical and refined voice, and with the gradual emergence of his eyes, begin to penetrate the permeable membrane of the face, assuring intersubjective passage above and beyond the dynamics of the attraction. The transformation from 'imbecile' to individual is completed when Merrick confesses to Treves and Carr Gomm (John Gielgud) that he can read: a qualification necessary not only for intersubjective competence, but also for bourgeois social acceptance. In fact, the film is dedicated to representing Merrick's problems in achieving such acceptance, a point made most bluntly when Madge Kendal's (Anne Bancroft) reading of *Romeo and Juliet* spurs her, disconsonantly and absurdly, to call him 'Romeo' (Nochimson 1997: 138–9). Merrick's own desire for inclusion within this romantic bodily ideal is starkly expressed by the strongly subjective montage sequence at Drury Lane Theatre, an episode which ultimately inspires Merrick to sleep lying down, and thus brings his ideal into lethal conflict with the unique requirements of his body.

Accusations of cloying sentimentality and, more importantly, of the film's legitimation of a bourgeois intolerance of difference thus rest on Merrick's gradual inclusion within personal and social conventions. As Darke argues, *The Elephant Man* confronts the monstrous surface with the bourgeois human normalcy within, seeking to reinstate the face's transparency. Indeed, representations of Merrick's progression into this narrowly defined vision of normalcy was deliberately enabled by the painstaking design of Hurt's make-up. Unlike the original body suit Lynch had designed for Hurt, which permitted no movement and therefore no expressiveness at all, this make-up permitted very restricted mobility and allowed for the gradual development of Merrick's personality. However, in spite of this narrative investment in Merrick's personal growth into everyday bourgeois culture, Lynch's camera frequently exposes another more radical and progressive version of everydayness. In certain key scenes, *The Elephant Man* reflects back to us deep structures that are no less chaotic than the surface of Merrick's face.

The montage sequences which open and close the film and the meticulous dream sequence at its centre are the film's clearest representations of threatening and universal deep structures corresponding with such vision. In the dream sequence the camera tracks across Merrick's sleeping figure, offering a rare extreme close-up of the varied textures of his head as it passes, before sliding significantly onwards through the eyehole of his mask. The camera traces a slimy progression inwards, along pipes and through dank corridors: passages, as Michel Chion describes them, between alternative worlds and forms of vision (Chion 1995: 181). Images of the workhouse, of childhood, of a beating and a previously unseen view from the inside of his old cell at Bytes' quarters suggest an impressionistic record of Merrick's experiences. At one point in the dream, Merrick's face is transformed into that of an elephant, then his own face returns, but accompanied by the eerie bellowing sound associated with elephant imagery throughout. Merrick, of course, is not an animal, but this difficult juxtaposition of faces acknowledges the multiple and often conflicting deep structures underlying the face of the Elephant Man, wherein bestial and monstrous components inevitably play a part. The dreamscape offers a welter of chaotic symptoms associated as much with our vision as with Merrick's interiority. As Martha Nochimson argues, such sequences in the film comprise an 'empathic mode of seeing, which precedes "normal" modes of objectification' (Nochimson 1997: 138–9). They bring to light, as Arnheim has it, a series of universal structures 'distinguishing between animate and inanimate things, human and nonhuman creatures, the mental and the physical' and more (Arnheim 1956: 369).

John Merrick enacts a traumatic pursuit of bourgeois acceptance. This pursuit is also enacted by spectators whose customary adherence to transparent modes of character engagement progressively seems to overcome the attractionist fascination with the extraordinary and monstrous body. However, everydayness in *The Elephant Man* is also characterised by the reappearance of this monstrosity within certain traumatic deep structures. Passing inwards and between textures and structures unglimpsed by transparent determinations of identity and character, our negotiation of the Elephant Man ironically renders his face as the only legible transcription of a radical interiority. The eye's slippage across Merrick's face is an echo of the heterogeneous deep structures captured by the dream sequence. In this respect, Merrick's face is less an isolated site of resistance to everyday modes of expression and perception than an incarnation of the multiplicity and insurgency that comprise everydayness in the first place. Indeed, while watching the face we are encouraged, according to the unattractive qualities of our own gaze, to enact its monstrosity, inhumanity, bestiality, feebleness and discordance.

This self-reflexive spectatorship, however, is also mitigated within the film by the appearance within Merrick's face of a kind of glamour or 'star quality'. John Hurt's performance has widely been recognised as a foremost attraction of the film, and this actorly value sometimes appears to overwrite the existential anxieties evoked by Merrick's ruined face. Hurt 'emotes to the heavens behind a suit of tumescent, crepuscular make-up', one admirer claims, advertising an exemplary human personality underneath the mask (Woods 1997: 45) Although we are unable to see his face, Hurt acquires a face value whose status we might compare favourably with other Hollywood stars. Indeed, the inexpressive face worn by certain stars has conventionally encouraged spectators, unwilling to accept a simple absence of meaning, to look deeper for an 'authentic' expression. Arguably, Nicolas Cage as the Elvis-esque Sailor Ripley in *Wild at Heart* both encourages and ironises this search for authenticity. Lynch has also exploited his own face value. Reviewers, interviewers and critics dwell on the peculiarities of his face and especially on the unusualness of his haircut, an idiosyncrasy that he shares with several characters in his films. Bizarre biographical details circulate in ever-deepening layers of authenticity, as if justifying the peculiarities of this face.[9] Technics and American Express have recently used photographic portraits of Lynch in their advertising campaigns, exploiting both his recognisability to a select demographic and the long-established values of individuality and innovation with which he is associated: 'An American Original' proclaims an American Express campaign.

The search for authenticity, however, is at odds with the often uncomfortable fragmentation of face and character in *The Elephant Man*. It returns us to a quality of glamour belonging to the cinema industry, a quality that remains extrinsic to the face whose content it manipulates and commodifies (Aumont 1992: 64). It becomes difficult to read the complexities of Merrick's face across the unifying idea of Hurt's performance. By contrast, in *The Straight Story* the search for authenticity has tended to reinforce strategies of performance and face representation. In the protracted round of interviews preceding and following the release of this movie in the USA and worldwide, David Lynch has consistently emphasised the saliency of the film's central character, Alvin Straight, and the crucial impact of Richard Farnsworth in this lead role: 'My film hangs on his performance,' Lynch has claimed with some justification (Lynch in Dwyer 1999). Farnsworth is present in all but a few of the film's scenes and the camera lingers on his face, offering a portrait that is at once characterised by its claim to documentary veridicality and to an intense signification of interiority. The glamour associated with the role appears to emerge from an intrinsic quality. Speaking about Farnsworth, Lynch notes, 'I had seen his work and I had seen his face and those eyes. There's something about him that people just like and he's got a natural innocence, strength. You see his soul as he works, and so when his name came up, because you consider many people, but up comes a name … and that was Richard, born to play this role' (Lynch in Ross 1999).

The association of Farnsworth with the role inevitably finds focus in the representation of the face, recalling Roland Barthes' remarks on Audrey Hepburn (Barthes 1972: 63–4), or Lawrence Shaffer on Montgomery Clift: 'the actor's face is inseparable from the character's that it "embodies" an identity so close that "represents" is too weak a description of it' (Shaffer 1977–8: 3). This near identity has always informed the work of cinema's character actors, in particular, and may be read as a conventional commodification of film's representative capacities in general. But explicitly surfacing in Lynch's remarks, and indeed in the overwhelming media

Richard Farnsworth in *The Straight Story*: 'my film hangs on his performance'

adulation for Farnsworth's performance, has been an unexpected appeal to historical biography which has scored through the iconic status of the filmic image, making of it an index for a secondary identity of character, even of soul: 'He is so much like Alvin', emphasises Lynch, adding that both Straight and Farnsworth began their careers in the rodeo, wore cowboy hats, and underwent considerable discomfort *en route*, cowboy-style, without complaint (Lynch in Dwyer 1999). Shortly following the film's release, it emerged that during filming Farnsworth had been suffering from a painful illness which he knew to be terminal. This revelation has inevitably reoriented the epitaphic quality of the film, evidenced, most obviously, by the memorial to Alvin Straight that heads the closing credits. Acting as a tribute to Farnsworth too, the film bespeaks an unusual affiliation between two types of authenticity: that associated with the glamour of a powerfully charismatic actor and that associated with an entire generation and the mid-western way of life. Furthermore, the genuine affection and sentimentality for which the film has been criticised and praised in turn suggests a certain legibility of character familiar in classical film-making.

The conventional opening shots of the movie progress fluidly inwards from the small mid-western town of Laurens to the exterior of a house. We hear the noise of somebody falling inside the house but, in a strategy that initially resembles the frustrations created by *The Elephant Man*, the camera does not invade this space until Bud (Joseph A. Carpenter) and Dorothy (Jane Galloway Heitz) have done so. Once again, the intrusion is not altogether welcome, but on this occasion it is associated with a benevolent form of vision and the conventional, well-humoured economy of looks and dialogue which Aumont has described in relation to the ordinary face in classical cinema. The easy circulation of empathy between protagonists deflects our curiosity about Alvin and sets in motion the equally mobile gazes of the camera and audience. Their discovery of him on the floor initiates a complex interchange of objectifying relations such that each face becomes fleetingly the object of another's: Bud complains; Dorothy panics; Rose misunderstands; Alvin settles the matter by simply requesting help. Alvin is already, transparently, both bearer and object of the gaze and the voice. This structure offers the face as the central figure and foundation for communication, its permeable surface offering an ostension of character and soul that extends into intersubjective space.

In fact, there are other moments when a variant of the attractionist aesthetic dominates *The Straight Story*. When Alvin rides past Laurens' community of old men or the bewildered inhabitants of a farmhouse, or when he encounters the incredulous gaze of the young runaway, Crystal (Anastasia Webb), the spectacle of his crawling progress across the American landscape is also offered up to us for consumption. Patterns of self-reflexivity are repeated, too, when Alvin is passed by a group of cyclists moving at high speed in a scene inflected by the unsettling mechanical hum of wheels on the road. Rather like the scenes in which he encounters heavy traffic, or is dwarfed by juggernauts and full-sized tractors, Alvin's surprise is an inverted reflection of the incredulity which greets his journey. Accustomed to the rhythm and pace dictated by his John Deere lawnmower (Lynch had completed Alvin's journey twice, sometimes at mower-pace), audiences too are momentarily forced to address the bizarre spectacle of such everyday activities as cycling and driving, and the direction of the objectifying gaze is turned sharply around.

Thus, in *The Straight Story* self-reflexive strategies serve primarily the same ends as do the series of cross-generational dialogues depicted. In each case the circulation of empathy, described by Lynch as a dialogue between teachers and students, and also as a 'dialogue between audiences and picture', enables meaningful intersubjective contact between generations on-screen and in the theatre, a familiar sentimental strategy valorising ideals of mutual comprehension (Sragow 1999). Throughout the film this reciprocity is accomplished above all by storytelling. Repeatedly, storytelling bridges the gap between generations, and between screen and audience, making teller and listener subject to the same trustworthy intersubjective conventions. This dynamic is clearly illustrated by the dialogue between Alvin and Verlyn Heller (Wiley Harker). As the two old men sit face-forwards at a bar, the camera passes from a two-shot emphasising the space between them to a series of extreme facial close-ups in which this space becomes intimately punctuated by intangible structures of memory and release. Each shares an emotive story concerning wartime experiences, the camera engaging each face in close-up for prolonged periods as they speak. The emotional upheaval occasioned by each story is conveyed by a gestaltic effect of physiognomy unbroken by alternative forms of 'dream-vision' or flashback. 'All of my buddies' faces are still young,' admits Alvin, and the surface of his own aged face negotiates strongly visual deep structures communicated by the voice and by the interposition of non-diegetic noises of warfare. This seamless communication of traumatic memories exemplifies the transparency of the face in scenes throughout the film.

There is, therefore, a consistent dependence upon conventional intersubjective routines in *The Straight Story* typified by the theme of separation/reunion which drives the film. Reportedly, this sense of intimacy was deliberately fostered by

Lynch's selection of octogenarian Freddie Francis as his director of photography. Francis maintained a close rapport with Farnsworth and other elderly actors on set and behind the camera. However, as the example of Rose has already demonstrated, the face also preserves a certain ambivalence in *The Straight Story*. The hesitation between empathetic understanding and the chaotic irresolution that plays back and forth across the surface of Rose's face is also evident in the regular appearance of prolonged mug shots of Alvin. Emotional contagion is elicited by Alvin's dialogue with Verlyn, but at certain points the face's physical occupation of space, its unique configuration of faltering lines, lead the spectator's eye to stray from the charismatic intersubjective promise of Alvin's eyes. The effect is emphasised on those occasions that his face remains unfocused by obvious external influences. On one occasion, reflecting presumably upon the bad news he has received from the doctor concerning his failing health, Alvin contrarily lights a cigar, and the illegibility of his face elicits an uncompromising scrutiny of its component elements. In a shot lasting almost 40 seconds, Alvin gazes restlessly from left to right, his brows knit, his eyes and mouth working unconsciously. The camera pans slightly to accommodate his movement; shallow focus renders the background indeterminate, and the camera proffers an intricate and silent portrait incommensurable with the circulation of empathy. The face becomes identical to itself, negotiating movement across its surface identical to the slippage of the spectator's eye across the screen. Within these moments, in particular, the resonance of Farnsworth's face becomes inextricably and harmoniously affiliated with his role; as in *The Elephant Man*, the face momentarily bodies forth the very means and medium of its textual production above and beyond any evocation of character.

On other occasions the sliding of the eye across signifying surfaces is fostered by a strongly two-dimensional understanding of *mise-en-scène*. In a crucial scene, Alvin and Rose sit with their backs to a wall watching a lightning storm, the light casting watery shadows from the window onto Alvin's face and across the room. The flattening effect of this evenly textured distribution of light is emphasised by the slow, rhythmic tracking of the camera between the two as they speak, as if it were unable to accommodate both faces at the same time. The shot achieves fragmentation of their faces and dissolution of the intrinsic verticality and depth of the face within the lateral logic of the scene. Unlike *The Elephant Man*, however, this fragmentation and decentring of *mise-en-scène* does not seem to put Alvin and Rose at the mercy of a hostile environment. Rather, the lightning storm elicits an openness and appreciation of nature that authorises their inclusion within a thoroughly benign (and apparently anti-Lynchian) environment. Later in the scene, when Alvin responds in extreme close-up and at length to the unexpected news of Lyle's illness, this environment even seems to share in the highly contagious expression of distress Alvin wears. The convenient strike of a lightning bolt at this instant reinforces his anxiety. This knowingly 'hammy' device also tends to reinforce a sense of benevolence associated with the camera (as in the rapid zoom on Alvin's face when a car unexpectedly collides with a deer) that fondly re-enacts the Hammer shot vocabulary for which Francis is best known.

Representation in *The Straight Story* persists in this acquiescence with and subordination to the environment. Aerial shots travel across harvest scenes, and subjective shots reproduce Straight's progress across the country. 'The important thing for me', Lynch has claimed, 'is the vast expanse of the landscape, this impression of floating inside nature' (Lynch in Henry 1999: 18, my translation). In Gus Van Sant's *My Own Private Idaho* (1991), a similar mid-western agricultural landscape with its single road stretching endlessly into the distance is envisioned by Mike (River Phoenix) as a 'fucked-up face'. Straight's perspective is more reminiscent of the 'anthropomorphous world-vision' celebrated by early film theorist Béla Balázs, who argued that, 'we rejoice in the landscape which looks back at us with friendly and intelligent recognition, as if calling us by name' (Balázs 1972: 92). The physiognomy of Alvin's landscape is characteristically American. The monotonous mid-western landscape permeates the film with a mythic sense of everydayness associated at points with kindly community spirit, with the crossing of the Mississippi River, and above all, perhaps, with the figure of the cowboy. If Alvin presages a return of straightness to modern American cinema, this is in part because his face resonates with a universal natural physiognomy, promising transparent harmony between the individual and the world.

The Straight Story resurrects harmonious deep structures of wisdom and human community. This is reflected by the predominance of the mid-western landscape, in place of the traumatic dreamscapes of *The Elephant Man*, as the ultimate expression of everyday perception enacted by the movie. Žižek has described Straight as an 'ethical hero', distinct from an earlier series of 'Lynchean perverts', embodying a subversive alternative to the modern tradition of film-making in which the face-ruin is prevalent (Žižek 2000b). However, another kind of subversiveness has always been predicated by facial representation in Lynch. Specifically, it resides in the systemic hesitation between the face's promise of empathy and its status as a face-object. The transparency of facial representation, cherished by classical cinema, is intermittently supplanted by an opacity that acknowledges the face's surface structures. Whether Lynch's protagonists in *The Elephant Man* and *The Straight Story* float through landscapes or through internal dreamscapes, whether their faces emote or do not, the surfaces of these faces allow us to experience more than mere empathy. We also begin to see the operation of the deep structures that bring these everyday configurations into being in the first place. Thus, in *The Straight Story*, beyond the reinforcement of classical principles of characterisation, the eye's slippage across the surface of Alvin's/Farnsworth's face also evokes our sense of the embracing actions of primordial and benign universal designs. When, at the end of both films, the camera mysteriously captures the sensation of floating between stars, it conveys not only the moment of transcendence implied by Merrick's death and Alvin's reunion, but also a kind of pure physical immanence. This is a passage which, unencumbered by physical reference points, promises to make tangible the motifs that underlie all existence, seemingly offering us an experience of movement that precedes all everyday structures.

Notes

1   For more on this, see Jana Evans Braziel's chapter in this collection.
2   See, for example, Jackson 1999.
3   On the distinction between radical and bourgeois forms of everydayness, see Roberts 1999 on a contemporary philosophy of praxis.
4   Lynch's primary source for the film is Sir Frederick Treves' account of the Elephant Man. This is the likely source of the name John, as opposed to Joseph, and indeed for most of the other factual inaccuracies in the film (Treves 1923: 1–37).
5   Cognitive theories of emotional character engagement in film have attracted a good deal of attention in film studies in recent years. See, for example, Smith 1995, Carroll 1996, Neill 1996 and Tan 1996: 153–93.
6   A selection from this manuscript version produced by the family is more widely available as Norman 1985.
7   Graham and Oehlschlaeger note that the single-eyed light that appears at the beginning and end of the lecture room scene is actually called a 'camera' in the screenplay, implicating not only the audience, but also the film-makers and the camera itself in this troubling series of gazes (Graham and Oehlschlaeger 1992: 143).
8   On the emotional impact of Samuel Barber's 'Adagio for Strings' on the final scene, see Smith 1999.
9   On this reading of star systems and authenticity, see Dyer 1991.

CHAPTER THREE

Going into Strange Worlds: David Lynch, Dune and New Hollywood[1]

Erica Sheen

Special effect is the hallmark of postmodern cinema. Taking his cue from Jean Baudrillard, Fredric Jameson and Paul Virilio, Sean Cubitt describes it as a process of loss that exemplifies the death of reality and its replacement by the hyperreal, a 'crisis of signification' by which representation becomes detached from external referents and confronts us instead with the spectacle of the image: 'we confront in the special effect … not representation but its obverse: the sublime' (Cubitt 1998: 127).

From this perspective, *Dune* (1984), a special-effects blockbuster based on Frank Herbert's cult science fiction novel, should be David Lynch's most obvious candidate for a postmodern reading. But, as Martha Nochimson has said, it is also 'the only Lynch film about which there is a valid general agreement that it doesn't work' (Nochimson 1997: 123), and the consequence of this is that almost nothing of interest has been written about it.[2] Clearly, there is something of a contradiction here. No self-respecting crisis of signification should be in a position to make prescriptive statements about whether texts work or not, or to sustain prolific systems of educational or critical production based on the institutional valorisation of such statements. In this chapter, I seek to examine the implications of this contradiction, and suggest that it calls into question the academic tendency to do readings of Lynch's films at the expense of a consideration of the industrial and institutional context within he worked. I will therefore discuss the production history of *Dune* as a paradigm of Lynch's often difficult and always critical relations with the film industry, reassess the film's position in his career and reconsider the question of its status as a success or failure.

Dune was released in 1984, at a time when cinema was preoccupied with science fiction and science fiction horror, and academic discourse saw this preoccupation as symptomatic precisely of a postmodern crisis of signification. In 1987, Vivian Sobchack began the new fourth chapter in the second edition of her study *Screening Space: The American Science Fiction Film* with an assertion that:

> Any understanding of the aesthetics of the contemporary SF film depends on our understanding the ways in which the experience of time and space have changed for us and the cinema in this last and most popularly electronic decade of American culture. As a major capitalist industry and institution, American cinema has increasingly incorporated the new electronic technology into its very modes of production, distribution and exhibition. And, as a symbolic medium whose function is representation, the American cinema has also increasingly articulated the new 'sense' and 'sensibility' generated by this technology and its spatial and temporal transformation of contemporary experience. As might be expected, this articulation is nowhere more evident or given more emphasis than in the SF film – for SF has always taken as its distinctive generic task the cognitive mapping and poetic figuration of social relations as they are constituted and changed by new technological modes of 'being-in-the-world'. (Sobchack 1987: 223–5)

In what follows Sobchack situates *Dune* firmly in a postmodern context, but she too identifies it as a failure. In comparison with Ridley Scott's *Blade Runner* (1982) – 'elegantly poised at the precise point where the high-modern and the postmodern meet to diverge' (1987: 272) – *Dune* is 'a schizophrenic text, and symptomatic of the breakdown of high-modernism in the context of postmodern culture's weakened temporal logic' (1987: 279):

> While *Blade Runner* successfully balances itself narratively and visually between high-modern and the postmodern, the high modernist narrative of *Dune* plunges fatally into the absolute space of the postmodern and breaks down into a heap of fragments. (Sobchack 1987: 278)

Reading behind Sobchack's highly evaluative metaphors, it is hard to see any difference between these two analyses. By her own account, *Dune* is an exemplary instance of the postmodern aesthetic, so why, when *both* films flopped at the box office, is one a failure and the other a success? In order to answer this question we have to pursue the logic of late capitalism into an area of analysis typically elided by academic postmodernism, that of the film's production history. As we have seen, Sobchack begins by acknowledging that American cinema has 'incorporated the new

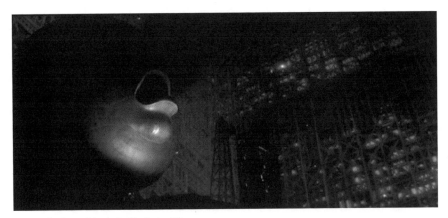

Awe in the face of the technological sublime

electronic technology into its very mode of production, distribution and exhibition', but her account is seriously unnuanced – '*a* major capitalist industry and institution'; '*the* new electronic technology'; '*a* symbolic medium' [my emphases] – and she directs it towards a description of the 'function' of cinema as 'representation', rather than its work as production.[3] Postmodern film and media theory is founded broadly on precisely this substitution, and one of the points of this chapter is to address *Dune* as a case-study of why it is inadequate.

As a starting point we might observe that the changes Sobchack records above all have a bearing on our understanding of the historical nature of reception, not least because they are the basis on which film has been assimilated into the academic canon since the early 1980s. As Douglas Gomery and Tino Balio have shown, terms of access to film changed drastically across the 1980s.[4] Videotapes began to be released in 1977, two years before *Alien*; video renting began in the early 1980s. In 1980 only 2 per cent of American homes had VCRs; by 1990, that figure had risen to 66 per cent. By 1986, video rentals and sales surpassed box-office takings: according to Balio, 'theatrical box office reached a new high of $5 billion in 1989, but video sales and rentals surpassed that figure by a factor of two' (Balio 1999: 58). Video stores flourished: Gomery records an instance of a company that increased from seven outlets in 1982 (the year *Blade Runner* was released) to fifty in 1985 (the year after *Dune*) and one hundred in 1986, the year Sobchack was presumably writing her new chapter. These figures demonstrate a complex symbiosis between, and radical transformation of, the mechanisms and institutions of film and video production and reception. As Balio puts it:

> Home video naturally stimulated demand for product. Domestic feature film production jumped from around 350 pictures a year in 1983 to nearly 600 in 1988. (Balio 1999: 58–9)

He points out that this influx came not from the majors but from independents and 'mini-majors', amongst them Dino De Laurentiis Entertainment, the company that made *Dune*. Taking into account the fact that the same period saw the rise of pay television, with channels like HBO dedicated to the production and exhibition of film, the terms on which the mini-majors entered the market were increasingly made possible by these new media:

> These companies entered the business knowing that even a modest picture could recoup most of its costs from the pre-sale of distribution rights to pay-cable and home video. (1999: 59)

The period has been seen as one characterised by a new form of vertical integration, a conglomerate vertical integration that 'positioned the film industry at the gateway of an emerging field of new technologies and markets' (Neale and Smith 1999: xvi). This development was accompanied by a corresponding 'horizontal' dynamic: the desire to strengthen distribution by cross-marketing a commodity in multiple media.

These then are the terms on which film became available in the 1980s as an object of study; yet they are elided by the theoretical discourses emerging from the academy during the same period, precisely because those discourses naturalised the textual frames of reference that characterise the academy's own cross-marketing of its commodities. In this respect, an account of the film industry as 'a symbolic medium whose function is representation' (Sobchack 1987: 224) mimics conglomerate vertical integration and naturalises its synergies as the historical condition for production. From such a perspective, the supersession of the real by the hyperreal is necessarily attended by the supersession of the media by the hypermedia: thus Wolfgang Coy's assertion that 'all written, optical and electric media, with the use of micro-electrics and computer techniques, finally will merge into one universal digital medium' (Coy in Spielman 1998: 143). Accounts like this are utopian, in Žižek's sense of the word: they suppress the material facts of the working practices that characterise this period of historical transformation. They are 'universality without its symptom' (Žižek 1989: 35).

We have, then, to start any account of *Dune* with an understanding that it articulates a highly specific set of industrial determinants, and that the way it does so is likely to be in a contradictory relation to the terms on which it might be 'read' academically as a text. From this perspective Lynch's own description of *Dune* as a 'fiasco' (Lynch in Rodley 1997: 116) is a better starting point than the concept of failure, because it makes us see the film as an expression of a mode of production, not reception. If Hollywood's 'orientation to crisis' underpins the aesthetics of the classical paradigm (Woolacott in Maltby 1981: 52) then 'fiasco' – defined by the Oxford English Dictionary as 'a failure or breakdown esp. in dramatic or musical performance' – might appropriately express the potentially catastrophic relation between the proliferating modes of production that characterise this period of industrial history, their drive towards a system of finance based on interests external to the industry itself, and the stylistic and narrative forms they generate. In *Mulholland Drive* (2001), the relation between Adam and the mysterious powerbroker Mr Roque, and its subsequent effect on the shape of the narrative of which they are a part, supplies a clear demonstration of this idea.[5] An account of *Dune*'s production history, and of its relation to Lynch's subsequent career, reveals not so much a 'failure' as a film-maker who realised fully the *fiscal* potential of a changing system of production. The story that follows is familiar. My aim here is to make a number of less familiar proposals about how we should understand it.

Frank Herbert's cult science fiction novel *Dune* was published in 1965. Attempts to film it began about ten years later and have continued to the present: John Harrison's miniseries, *Frank Herbert's Dune*, aired in the US on the SCI-FI channel in December 2000.[6] An awareness that what is under consideration here is a 25-year period of continuing production is fundamental to this analysis. One of its significant features is the extent to which the people involved in it keep turning up at different points in the story – like the malevolent neighbourhood ensembles that recur in Lynch's films from *Blue Velvet* (1986) on, now clearly identified in *Mulholland Drive* as an image of Hollywood itself. In the mid-1970s, Chilean director Alejandro Jodorowski tried to put together a French-financed production package with a screenplay by Dan O'Bannon. When this collapsed, O'Bannon moved on to Ridley Scott's *Alien*; after *Alien* and *Blade Runner*, Scott was asked by Dino De Laurentiis to direct *Dune*; when Scott pulled out, Lynch was brought in. Cinematographer Vittorio Storaro was approached by Jodorowski in the 1970s, and finally worked on Harrison's miniseries. He referred to his involvement in a *Dune* project as 'some kind of destiny', and described it not only as a continuation in some sense of his early involvement with Jodorowski, but also as a reaction to Lynch: 'you watch someone else doing that project, somehow it never exactly matches what you have in mind'.[7] Actor William Hurt, who plays Duke Leto in the miniseries, had a similar experience:

> When [Lynch's production] first came out I wanted to be part of it … I put in a call but didn't get called back. I was really upset for a short time, but when I saw the movie I was relieved, because I didn't think it was true to the book.[8]

What is distinctive in all this is a sense of a *Dune* project as a complex dynamic of becoming flowing from one actualisation to another, but not realised by any of them. Characteristic of this project was the frequently expressed sense that the novel was unadaptable, thus ensuring that a film of it remained, in Deleuze and Guattari's terms, a potential rather than a possibility.[9] Lynch seems himself to have been attracted to the production for precisely that reason:

> I probably shouldn't have done that picture, but I saw tons and tons of possibilities for things I loved, and this was the structure to do them in, there was so much room to create a world.[10]

From *Dune* on he begins to emerge as a director who is consistently attracted to projects that have a potential beyond the context of production within which he is working, and who consistently describes that potential as a 'world'.

After Ridley Scott pulled out, De Laurentiis, impressed by the eight Oscar nominations recently received by *The Elephant Man* (1980), offered the film to Lynch. Lynch turned down *Return of the Jedi* (1983) in its favour; as he saw it, 'I wouldn't have been able to influence *Return of the Jedi* because that's totally George's picture' (Lynch in Woods 1997: 57). It is indicative that his acceptance of *Dune* followed his refusal of a film in which he thought that he might not have freedom to do what he wanted. As he later put it, '*Dune* was like a kind of studio film' and we should be clear about what, in the early 1980s, that actually meant (Lynch in Rodley 1997: 120). As we have seen, Dino De Laurentiis Entertainment was a mini-major. According to Balio, the mini-majors emulated the structure of the large studios, and, in an industry characterised by diversification into television and video, this was one of the reasons for their failure (Balio 1999: 64). If the classical style was inflected by changes in the economic structure of post-classical Hollywood, so too was the 'classical' relation between director and producer. Lynch's work on *Dune* began to demonstrate one of the most symptomatic features of this change: a destabilisation of the fundamental conception of a film's length, or perhaps one should say of the institutional relation between length and running time. Like Michael Cimino only a year or so earlier, he planned and shot five hours of film, but the fate of United Artists was still raw in the industrial memory, and distributor Universal insisted on a standard theatrical release of 137 minutes.[11] Without the right of final cut, Lynch had no alternative but to provide it. He subsequently recognised that this situation closed down his own vision of what Nochimson describes as 'an entirely Lynchian project in a possible film of *Dune*' (Nochimson 2002: 124):

> There was a kind of poetry to many of the things in it that were abstract ... I shot a lot of stuff like that: the water drops underground, and the ceremonies and things they did and the way they lived ... A world of stuff had to go. (Lynch in Rodley 1997: 116)

Clearly, one of the fascinating things about this period of industrial history is this radical destabilisation of what the industry itself perceived as the relation between creative and institutional frames of reference. Lynch was assiduous in taking responsibility for the film's difficulties ('It's no one's fault but my own'),[12] but his position raises crucial questions about the paradigm of authorship that emerges from this period of industrial history. The classical concept of the auteur is founded on the idea of a functional dissociation between the director's sensibilities and the material limitations of the system within which he or she works, a dissociation that provides him or her with a mode of being-in-the-world that is both dependent on and differentiated from the technical and institutional constraints that are effectively his or her conditions of employment. This idea collapses under the pressure of the complex dilations of New Hollywood production deals. David Lynch is an exemplary instance of a director that many critics, and most film buffs, want to describe as an auteur, but whose working practices articulate the complexities of a system that has superseded the context to which the term can be applied.

Lynch's original contract with De Laurentiis was a two-picture deal, and he had evidently intended to use the footage not included in the first film to make a sequel. He had even begun to write the script. But because of *Dune*'s failure at the box office, these plans came to nothing. After its unsuccessful theatrical run, *Dune* was released on video and soon began to be played in the US on cable television. Then in 1988, MCA TV made a 'special edition' of the film, and this was released in two parts on the Universal Pictures Debut Network. This included most of the original material, but it also included new scenes constructed from out-take and test footage. At this point, Lynch finally broke his association with the production. He had his name as director taken off the credits and replaced by that of the infamous Allen Smithee, and his name as screenwriter replaced by that of 'Judas Booth'. This name is allegedly made up from Judas Iscariot, Christ's betrayer, and John Wilkes Booth, the assassin of President Lincoln[13] – an amalgam that frames the production with something of the film's own epic narrative of betrayal and assassination, and recasts it as a kind of Benjaminian allegory of its own loss of innocence, thereby anticipating the narrative mode of *Twin Peaks*, then only a year or so away, which Sheli Ayers in this volume describes as a 'profane allegorical world [that] yearns toward the redemption it excluded from the frame of representation' (Ayers 2004: 94). In 1992, when *Twin Peaks* was at its height of success, KTVU produced a third version of *Dune* that synthesised the theatrical release with the Allen Smithee version. Remarkably, this used the main credits from the Allen Smithee version and the end credits from the original theatrical release, so that Lynch, rather like the enigmatic split personalities of *Lost Highway* (1997) and *Mulholland Drive*, is both absent and present in his own film. Even before *Mulholland Drive* it would have been tempting to see the so-called 'psychogenic fugue' of *Lost Highway* as an expression of institutional schizophrenia. After it, it would be hard not to. It is precisely at the point when Adam, the director, succumbs to the requirement that he concede all artistic autonomy to his producers that the plot splits into an impossible loop of frustration and defeat. These plots have found a very precise formal equivalent for the fiasco: the breakdown of the relation between potential and possibility.

It is thus also tempting to see *Twin Peaks* as in some sense a 'special edition' of the story of *Dune*. Clearly, there was already within this film a fatal attraction to televisual endless flow. This attraction articulates both technological and institutional changes within the industry, and Lynch's own particular receptivity to them. On one hand, his excessive extra footage was made under the rubric of a film industry dominated by the sequel, with its complexly symbiotic relation to video and television;[14] on the other, Lynch himself was obviously already deeply drawn to the continuing narrative. Tony Krantz, the television agent who packaged *Twin Peaks* for ABC and subsequently became Lynch's production partner in *Mulholland Drive*, has referred to television as a 'Scheherazade-like medium',[15] an appealing expression that alerts us not only to its indefinities, but also to the fiascal exigencies that determine them. Scheherazade is the new bride from the *Thousand and One Nights* who endlessly defers and is finally reprieved from the execution that attends marital consummation by telling her husband stories instead of letting him have sex. The story of her storytelling, and its eventual abruption, might be seen as the *locus classicus* of narrative not as desire but as fiasco ('breakdown esp. in dramatic or musical performance'). Speaking of his more recent fiasco with ABC over *Mulholland Drive*, he observed,

> I was lured back because of a really strong desire to tell a continuing story in which you go deeper and deeper into a world and you get lost in that world. A pilot is open-ended, and, when it's over, you feel all these threads going out into the infinite which, to me, is a beautiful thing. It's like a body with no head. (Lynch in Lantos 1999: 70)

By this stage, it should be clear that we cannot approach the relation in Lynch's career between film and television in terms of the idea of 'merging' media. Obviously, we need a model of analysis that allows us to examine a far more complex dynamic of continuity and discontinuity. Such a model is, I suggest, offered by Jay David Bolter and Richard Grusin's (1999) concept of *remediation*. According to Bolter and Grusin, old and new media borrow each others' resources in order to compete in a society in which technological innovation is the basis of competition and a source of prestige. The relation is one of 'oscillation' rather than supersession, and it is structural to the history of media: it manifests itself as much in the relationship between painting and photography as in that of film and television. David Lynch's work is strongly marked by such an oscillation, whether between sculpture and film, as in his early installation *Six Men Getting Sick* (1967), or between film and television (*Dune* to *Twin Peaks*), or television and film (*Twin Peaks* to *Twin Peaks: Fire Walk with Me* (1992); *Mulholland Drive* to *Mulholland Drive*). Sheli Ayers draws our attention to *Twin Peaks*' address to a 'target audience that prides itself on its own ability to distinguish "good", that is, cinematic entertainment from the dross of network television' (Ayers 2004: 95) but comes to the conclusion that 'one of the most striking innovations of the series is that it took television seriously as a site of consumption' (2004: 105). I think we can go further than this and suggest that, despite the high level of constraint associated with a system regulated by the Federal Communications Commission, it is actually to network television that Lynch has consistently been drawn, like a moth to one of his own eternally returning flames. In a period in which cable television became an alternative source of funding for film production, Lynch's continuing involvement with ABC is both distinctive and paradoxical. When in 1992 ABC axed his sitcom *On the Air* after three episodes, he vowed he would never work for television again. *Mulholland Drive*, however, went through exactly the same process, with exactly the same network: early enthusiasm; funding for a pilot; final rejection – and a vow from Lynch that he will never work for television again.[16] As he commented to Chris Rodley, 'TV is just for selling products. It's just a little rig for that' (Lynch in Rodley 1997: 175). But it is hard for him to conceal a compulsion for its distinctive aesthetic. Asserting a preference for the medium of film over television, he observed that,

The power of most movies is the bigness of the image and the sound and the romance. On TV the sound suffers and the impact suffers. With just a flick of the eye or turn of the head you see the TV stand, you see the rug, you see some little piece of paper with writing on it, or a strange toaster or something. You're out of the picture in a second. (ibid.)

Lynch is ostensibly referring here to a Benjaminian distracted spectator (Benjamin 1977), but it is unmistakably his own very attentive director's eye that 'flicks' onto the world around the television set and brings its Lynchian objects – a little piece of paper with writing on it; a strange toaster – into the frame. 'The picture' thus becomes precisely what cinema strives to exclude: the everyday context of televisual reception, and the bizarre secret lives that inhabit it. Given that the aesthetics of television is founded on an equivalence between the domestic interior from which television is viewed and the commodity-fetishistic composition of its image, Lynch's visual imagination reveals itself as more televisual than cinematic: more to do with objects than framing; more to do with glow than lighting. His films repeatedly record the transfiguration of the object by emanation – what Homer Simpson refers to as the 'warm glowing warming glow' of television.[17] 'Glow' is one of Lynch's most distinctive stylistic features, from Paul Muad'dib's spice-changed eyes to Alvin Straight's glowing face as he sits in front of his campfire. It brings to his stories meanings that reveal themselves only when the narrative comes to an end, yet which all but prevent it from doing so. Lynch's glowing objects illuminate a narrative which purports to require answers conventionally accessed by finite resources of plot, but actually serves only to postpone them, and ultimately to resolve the enigma by revealing that its only purpose is to prolong the narrative indefinitely. From this perspective, Lynch's enigmas have an utter clarity of purpose that can be understood by anyone who has experienced, perhaps not the death of reality, but certainly the catastrophic loss of watching the final episode of a television series.

I conclude with a discussion of a document that appears to justify the approach to *Dune* I have tried to develop in this chapter. This document is a transcription of an online panel discussion, hosted by the SCI-FI channel shortly after the airing of Harrison's miniseries, and held simultaneously with a broadcast of the original version of *Dune*. Advertised as a 'moderated chat mirroring the broadcast of David Lynch's *Dune*, now airing on SCI-FI', it ran for three hours, covering the time of the film itself and then that of an 'open chat' following it.[18] This is an instantiation of the process of remediation at its most complex, and of the modes of spectatorship and criticism that derive from it. At its most simple, it is merely a running commentary on the film *Dune* taking place while it is being broadcast – for anyone who has ever tried to watch a film in the company of someone who will not stop talking about it, a classic act of distraction. But in the context of a remediated spectatorship, the concept of 'distraction' itself needs reformulating: at one point in the proceedings, one of the participant's eyes is caught by the Atreides' pug, and he interjects, 'is anyone else distracted by that damn dog?' thereby calling the participants' attention *to* the television screen, and *away* from the VDU.

At the most immediate level of reception, the panel discussion quite simply marked out the narrative sequence of the film:

rickaustin: Lynch really captured the navigator in this scene … This is
                a beautiful sequence, with the eno music and rolling sands.

At the same time, it also acknowledged its format as a broadcast, as well as the way the spectator's film-based memories and anticipations are mapped *against* the format of the medium to which it has been transferred:

Edelman: Forget the dog alert – spittle alert! Another sign of Lynch's
                love of the grotesque … Ah well – the spittle comes – after
                – the commercial.
rickaustin: I don't think we get to see the spittle in this version! … do we??
Edelman: Yes, we do.

It also maintains a well-informed critical debate based on a comparison between the film versions and the novel:

Edelman: Since we are discussing the differences between the Dunes,
                perhaps we should mention we already heard the word
                melange tonight, which was not in the miniseries version…
rickaustin: The gom jabbar is a critical scene handles well in both
                versions.

Beyond this, there is an ongoing registration of the contrasting responses of the wider audience, brought into the discussion by the moderator:

Moderator: Many of the people in our audience seem to share the
                opinion that the miniseries handled DUNE the story far
                better, but Lynch really captured the feel of the world.

But we began with special effects, and here the commentary is particularly revealing. As we have seen, Sean Cubitt describes special effect as a 'crisis of signification' by which representation becomes detached from external referents and confronts us instead with the spectacle of the image. How did this particular group of spectators, elegantly poised between past and present, film and television, experience this fatal plunge into the absolute space of the postmodern?

Well, there was very little sense of awe in the face of the technological sublime. For Rick Austin, the first navigator scene was 'the coolest effect in the movie'. John Gardner observed that 'if the rest of the movie had lived up to that moment, it'd been a masterpiece' and that 'the shield effect really holds up for a digital effect from '84'. Edelman did not agree, but remembered that he had liked it at the time: 'The level of early '80s effects can be seen far too plainly here. But in my memory it was state-of-the-art.' Their observations demonstrate a nuanced sense of industrial and technological history, a critical awareness of the way special effect situates a film at the nexus between the two, and perhaps above all no facile sense of what in such a context might constitute success or failure:

Gardner:	Of course, the Special Effects in the miniseries were not up to things like the Worm-riding sequences, or making the deserts at all convincing, but you've got to cut them some slack for that, I think…
Moderator:	The audience likes how the miniseries handled the first appearance of the Worms. Personally this is one thing I like better in the Lynch film, just for the visual impact…
rickaustin:	The TV version had the benefit of an advance in technology, but they are really great in the first sighting.
Edelman:	The sparks that accompany the worms were interesting – perhaps Lynch thought that the only way to make them visual enough. But I don't believe Herbert had that.
rickaustin:	The Lynch ones were done by Carlo Rambaldi, and were completely mechanical.
Edelman:	Who also did ET
rickaustin:	so they didn't move right and sometimes the scale of the surroundings felt wrong…
Moderator:	there does seem to be a feeling that the worm riding sequences in the miniseries weren't very good…
Gardner:	No it wasn't … But I'm willing to cut the miniseries some slack. Not as big a budget…
rickaustin:	I agree about the worm riding, but it wasn't great in the Lynch version either. Both suffer from 'guy standing in front of blue-screen' problems.

Clearly, there is something fundamentally remediative about special effects, something fundamentally opposed to, or disruptive of, the very idea of a textual reading. Far from fixing our attention to the specific moment of its realisation, the special effect distracts us. With a flick of the eye, it takes us 'out of the picture', makes us look around for what we should not be seeing, the television stand or a strange toaster; it oscillates in pursuit of an expressive potential it seems to desire but refuses to realise. One of the participants availed himself of a literary version of the same idea – Harold Bloom's account of the Oedipal confrontation between an originary text and its remake – to evaluate the relation between the two film versions and the 'unadaptable' novel on which they were based:

Some film versions are swerves, in the Harold Bloom sense – certainly the Lynch was. There was no swerve in the TV version; just a moderately seemly commodification.

The idea of a 'seemly commodification' – and by implication the idea that Lynch's *Dune* is in some way neither seemly nor a commodification – is a useful one with which to conclude. Like Lynch himself, what these spectators respond to in this film is the process of becoming it exemplifies, indeed, the process of becoming it appears to leave still open to the future.[19] At the end of a conversation notable for its critical deployment of counterfactual thinking – an activity rarely acknowledged in academic paradigms of spectatorship but fundamental to the way film-makers and their audiences live together inside the thinking machine of cinema – the Moderator asked the panel 'how Lynch might have handled *Dune* different [sic] if he was doing a limited series for television … as he later did with *Twin Peaks*?' Setting aside the fact that Lynch's original, unused footage was eventually used to make a television film, Edelman considered instead the possibility of a Lynch *Dune* conceived and produced within the medium of television; a Lynch *Dune* that would allow Lynch himself to go deeper and deeper into the world he saw in this story, even perhaps to get lost in it; a Lynch *Dune* that might perhaps begin life as a television pilot and end up in the cinema:

> It would have been interesting if he'd had more time. If he'd taken the events of the final hour and paced them as he did at the beginning, you'd have had three more hours right there.

Rick Austin put the whole thing more succinctly: 'It would have been lots weirder if he did it for TV.'

Notes

1   'That's what's so important about film to me. I just like going into strange worlds' (Lynch in Chion 1995: 180).

2   Chion presents by far the most sympathetic and interesting account of the film. In light of the discussion that follows, it is relevant to note that he points out that the film was a major box-office success in France (Chion 1995).

3   For a critique of functionalism see Giddens 1981.

4   The account that follows draws on Gomery 1992 and 1999, and Balio 1999.

5   See Martha Nochimson' chapter in this volume for a detailed elaboration of this idea.

6   Harrison's miniseries is called *Frank Herbert's Dune* because the Dino De Laurentiis Corporation still holds the rights to the title *Dune,* a fact that paradoxically situates Lynch's film as the 'original'. However, in online discussions about his film before its release, Harrison refused to describe his miniseries as a 'remake': 'Suffice it to say we are not remaking the Lynch version. In any case it would be truly presumptious and hubristic of me to try to better the work of a film-maker I truly admire. This miniseries will not reflect the vision or style of his film in any way.' (Available at www.scifi.com/dune (18 November 2000).)

7   Available at www.scifi.com/dune (18 November 2000).

8   Available at www.scifi.com/dune (18 November 2000).

9   For an account of Deleuze and Guattari's distinction between potential and possibility see Massumi 1992: 35-41.

10 Lynch, quoted in *The City of Absurdity* website. Available at www. geocities.com/ Hollywood/2093/dune/index.html (25 April 2001).

11 In 1981, Michael Cimino shot a five-hour cut of *Heaven's Gate*, which he subsequently cut to 3 hours 40 minutes. Following its failure at the box office, United Artists cut the film by a further 70 minutes, and re-released it, but the film sent them into bankruptcy. They were acquired by MGM and ceased to exist as a separate company.

12 Lynch, quoted in *The City of Absurdity* website. Available at www. geocities.com/ Hollywood/2093/dune/duneabout.html (25 April 2001).

13 For this suggestion see the *Dune: The Arrakis File* website, http://members. aol.com/hiphats/arrakis1.html (15 August 2000).

14 See Sheen 1994 for an account of this complex symbiosis in the *Back to the Future* films (1985/1989/1990).

15 Krantz, quoted in *The City of Absurdity* website. Available at www. geocities.com/ Hollywood/2093/intnewyorker02.html (25 April 2001).

16 For a full account of the televisual pre-history of *Mulholland Drive* see Buckland 2003.

17 In 'Treehouse of Horror V', *The Simpsons*, Sixth Season, 2F03, Gracie Films, Twentieth Century Fox.

18 Panel members were identified as: 'Rick Austin, Vice President of On-Air for SCIFI, and former co-producer of the MTV Music Awards; Scott Edelman, four times Hugo Award Nominee and editor of SCI-FI's Science Fiction Weekly; noted science-fiction critic John Clute, the author of both *The Encyclopedia of Science Fiction*, the *Multimedia Encyclopedia of Science Fiction* and the *Encyclopedia of Fantasy*…' The transcription of the event was lodged on the SCIFI Dune website. Available at www.scifi.com/dune (27 March 2001).

19 At the time of writing, SCI-FI are about to air a sequel to *Frank Herbert's Dune* called *Frank Herbert's Children of Dune*. On its website, there is hyperlink to a source for what it describes as a 'rare' video: *Dune: Extended Version*. Available at www.scifi.com/dune (28 April 2003).

CHAPTER FOUR

Mysteries of Love:
Lynch's Blue Velvet/Freud's Wolf-Man

Sam Ishii-Gonzales

Within the extensive critical literature which David Lynch's film *Blue Velvet* (1986) has amassed in the past 15 years you will find almost without fail mention of two central psychoanalytic tropes: the Oedipus complex and the primal scene. This is the case whether the essay in question is primarily psychoanalytic in its methodology or not. Yet whereas the Oedipus complex often serves in these writings as the focal point for a series of observations into the nature of Lynch's work, the primal scene is either evoked in passing or subsumed into the imperatives of the former, as though it were nothing more than a preparatory stage in the realisation of the subject's (and text's) Oedipal destination. It is the claim of this essay that a more detailed analysis of the primal scene both as it appears in psychoanalytic thought, as an example of what Freud calls 'primal fantasy', and in Lynch's film identifies a resistance to the inevitability of this normative structure, and its function in advancing the claims of conscience, morality and heterosexual object-choice against the perversions of desire.

This examination of primal scenes and fantasies will allow us to reconsider several of Freud's writings, in particular *From the History of an Infantile Neurosis*, better known as the case history of the Wolf-Man.[1] My discussion of *Blue Velvet* will illuminate some strange and fascinating qualities of the film, one of which is a remarkable character trait shared by the film's notorious Frank Booth (Dennis

Hopper) and Freud's Wolf-Man patient. This involves what Freud describes as 'ceremonial breathing', namely the ritualised taking-in and exhalation of breath. This peculiar act is emblematic, in the case history, of the patient's inability or unwillingness to control or settle the contrary subject positions made available to him within the socio-cultural realm of language and paternal law instituted by (or through) the Oedipal trajectory. In *Blue Velvet* this obsessive behaviour is beautifully and uncannily embodied in Frank Booth's intoxicant machine which he keeps ready at his side, ready for any and all contingencies: desire, murder, memory. As we shall see, it is just one of several points in Lynch's film where the linearity of narrative is met with a counter-movement which is fantasmatic in nature.[2]

Scenes from Childhood

> He still remains fixated, as though by a spell, to the scene which had such a decisive effect on his sexual life. (Freud 1918: 101)

Let me begin by answering the question, 'What is the primal scene?' Laplanche and Pontalis describe it thus: 'A scene of sexual intercourse between the parents which the child observes, or infers on the basis of certain indications, and phantasies. It is generally interpreted by the child as an act of violence on the part of the father' (Laplanche and Pontalis 1973: 335). As they explain, although there is mention of a primal scene (*Urszenen*) as early as 1897, Freud's original use of the term refers more generally to forms of 'traumatic infantile experiences' (ibid.). It is in the case history of the Wolf-Man that the primal scene is given its more strict definition as the witnessing (in reality or fantasy) of parental intercourse by the small child. Indeed, Freud's central claim in this work is that the periodic outbreak of severe neurotic symptoms in his 23-year-old patient's life are the result of the continuing influence and the repercussive effects of the primal scene on the analysand's unconscious: between the ages of three to eight, an anxiety-hysteria related to an animal phobia followed by a period of obsessive religious piety; from the age of 17 until the beginning of analysis, intestinal problems psychosomatic in nature.

According to Freud, it is not the actual observation of the primal scene at the age of one-and-a-half which causes the analysand's psychological disturbance; instead, this is triggered by a reproduction of the scene, in a dream the patient has about wolves, immediately before his fourth birthday. In the dream the small boy awakes in the middle of the night and is presented with this tableau outside his bedroom window: six or seven wolves, perched motionless on the branches of a tree, gaze fixedly at him, their ears rigidly erect. Freud suggests that this dream reactivates the primal scene, and endows it with its newly discovered (or recovered) traumatic meaning for the subject.[3] Using the methods developed in *The Interpretation of Dreams* to analyse the way the dream-work transforms latent thoughts into manifest dreams through condensation, displacement and reversal, he argues that what we discover about the Wolf-Man's dream is this: the stillness and the attentive gaze are an attribute, not of the wolves, but of the dreamer himself; in a similar vein, what the still and attentive little boy witnesses is not a scene of repose, but of violent, agitated movement. Thus, the small child is perplexed and frightened both by what he witnesses – some type of ferocious activity – and by his own passive fascination with what he sees: Why do *I* remain immobile and attentive? Why are *my* ears pricked?

This recurring nightmare involving wolves allows the child to experience in a manifest form the contents of the primal scene, and this second witnessing allows this little boy (who, by the age of four, has already experienced in words or gestures both seduction and the threat of castration) to comprehend (retroactively) or give meaning to two details.[4] First, the spectacle that he has witnessed is an act of pleasure, an expression of love between his parents: 'He assumed to begin with, he said, that the event of which he was a witness was an act of violence, but the expression of enjoyment which he saw on his mother's face did not fit in with this; he was obliged to recognise that the experience was one of gratification' (Freud 1918: 45). Second, his 'sexual' desire for his father would place him in the position taken by the mother in the primal scene, a position understood as one of submission, of castration – for what is now plainly evident to the fascinated child is both the presence of the father's penis and the absence (the lack) of penis on the body of the mother. The dream thus portrays for the young boy the dreadful consequences of receiving sexual satisfaction from his father and, in the process, his desire for his father is transformed into fear – into his wolf phobia. This is the explanation, Freud argues, for the associations the analysand makes between his dream and two other wolves from his childhood: the first, an illustration from a children's book of a wolf standing upright, striding along, claws stretched out and ears pointed with which his older sister terrorised him whenever possible; the second, a fairytale told to him by his grandfather in which a wolf whose tail has been pulled off by a tailor attempts, with the assistance of several other wolves, to enact a revenge upon the tailor in a nearby forest.[5] When the tailor places himself high in a tree and out of reach of the pack of wolves, the tailless wolf volunteers to position itself at the base of a pyramid of wolves who climb upon each other's backs to reach the trapped victim. Freud argues that the patient makes the connection between his nightmare and these wolf representations because the latter duplicate the latent meaning of his dream: the first association (the picture of a wolf standing erect) is a thinly veiled reference to the now menacing father figure, the father as castrator; the second, with its tail-less wolf used as a base or backside upon whom the other wolves mount, recalls the mother's position as both beneath the father and castrated.

Primal mise-en-scène

> I've had experiences where I've had a moment's flash – it seems like a memory. And it comes with a fantastic feeling of happiness, but I can't for the life of me think *where* that thing occurred. The *feel* is so real, but I can't remember when that would've been. And they're such small fragments, they don't give me enough clues to know whether they really did happen.[6] (Lynch in Rodley 1997: 13)

I shall return to certain aspects of Freud's case history in due course. For now, let me simply add that, although Freud continued to struggle (in *From the History of an Infantile Neurosis*) with the possibility that the primal scene was a real occurrence which his patient has actually witnessed, it is in this same period that he advanced the notion that the primal scene is a fantasy. Indeed, along with the fantasy of castration and the fantasy of seduction, it is, he claimed, a primal fantasy, an original fantasy or fantasy of origin in which the individual is confronted with such fundamental enigmas as: the origin of the individual (primal scene), the origin of sexuality (seduction) and the origin of sexual difference (castration).[7] This suggestion – the primal scene as primal fantasy – is first made in 'A Case of Paranoia Running Counter to the Psychoanalytical Theory of the Disease' where the scenario of parental coupling is re-activated through the ear. The female patient, during a rendezvous in her lover's apartment, hears the sound of knocking or ticking coming from a space in the room partly obscured by a heavy curtain. The delusional paranoia that ensues is the result of the patient's fantasies of the primal scene, stimulated, Freud suggests, by this auditory sensation (Freud 1915: 261–73).[8]

This discussion of the aural dimension of the primal scene brings us to *Blue Velvet*. Indeed, Michel Chion takes the centrality of the auditory component of Lynch's work so far as to suggest that the film-maker constructed his primal scene as the visualisation of an event originally overheard:

> The scene seems to arise from an archaic acoustic impression which endows it with the kind of troubling vagueness that can inspire bizarre theories. A child who overhears the sexual intercourse of adults on the other side of the wall might imagine, for instance, that the man's voice is muffled not because he is speaking against the woman's mouth or body, but because he has stuffed a piece of cloth into his mouth. (Chion 1995: 94)[9]

The speculative quality of Chion's claim should not lead us to overlook the fact that it is a severed ear found lying in the grass that inaugurates the process of detective work which places Jeffrey Beaumont (Kyle MacLachlan) in the closet of Dorothy Vallens (Isabella Rossellini) – thus allowing him to witness, with the sudden appearance of Frank Booth, Lynch's version of the primal scene. We should also not forget the metaphoric import that Lynch himself gives the ear as a passageway from one realm to another (from reality to dream? from innocence to knowledge?). I allude here, of course, to the scene in which the film-maker dissolves from a shot of Jeffrey on his way to Detective Williams' house, to an extreme close-up of the ear into whose cavity the camera slowly penetrates.

Not only does the scene that Jeffrey observes through the louvres of Dorothy's wardrobe accurately fit Freud's general description of the way the act of parental coitus would be perceived by a small child (for example, as an act of sadistic aggression on the part of the father against the mother), it also conveys all that is compelling yet frightening, hypnotic yet utterly grotesque, about this inexplicable event in the eyes, and ears, of its enraptured witness. Recall these images: our wide-eyed young hero, hidden, transfixed, while Dorothy throws her head back in rapture and Frank, aka Daddy-Baby-Sir, comes 'home' with scissors, oxygen mask and a tightly clenched fist. As Laura Mulvey writes, 'This scene, in all its permutations, is acted out with such extraordinary and shocking violence and eroticism that it is truly suffused with horror and the attraction of a fantasy scenario. The scene oscillates' (Mulvey 1996a: 142). It is in addition no small feat that Lynch manages to place us, the film's spectator, in the same position as Jeffrey, in the same state of motionless acuity – our eyes and ears pricked; horrified, yet unable (or unwilling) to remove our eyes from the screen. This episode not only spectacularly evokes the primal scene, it also conjures the two other fantasy scenarios identified by Freud as the primal fantasies – namely, the fantasy of seduction and the fantasy of castration. These fantasies are not interchangeable, but they often become interrelated or co-existent for the inquisitive subject. This is something *Blue Velvet* makes dramatically clear. Within the confines of Dorothy's living space,[10] Jeffrey Beaumont is confronted with each of the primal fantasies in all their enigmatic force; not in strict succession but continuous fluctuation. He is threatened with castration (Dorothy wielding a kitchen knife) and is presented with the woman as castrated (Frank brandishing a pair of scissors between Dorothy's legs). He is seduced by the overwhelming, overripe sensuality of Dorothy Vallens ('Do you like me? Do you like the way I feel? See my breast? You can feel it. My nipple is getting hard – you can touch it'), as well as by the intrigue, the sheer ferocity, of the primal scene itself. Indeed, it is as much the spectacle as a whole as any component or figural element within it which can be said to provoke Jeffrey Beaumont's epistemophilic drive, his desire to attain knowledge, to give answer to the mysteries unfolding before his eyes.[11]

According to Laplanche and Pontalis, 'In fantasy the subject does not pursue the object or its sign: he appears caught up himself in the sequence of images … the subject, although always present in the fantasy, may be so in a desubjectivised form, that is to say, in the very syntax of the sequence in question' (Laplanche and Pontalis 1986: 26). In Lynch, this syntax includes the *découpage* of the primal scene with its shifting register of desire: its rhythmic alternation between shot scales and characters viewed principally in isolation (shots of Frank and Dorothy partly obscure one or the other, such as the tracking shot which rotates around the latter's back as Frank turns on his oxygen machine); the use throughout of a widescreen frame which both decentres and disperses the coordinates of spectatorial attention. As John Belton has noted, this framing technique allows the film-maker to explore and extend a tension between the lateral and axial dimensions of the composition such that there is the effect on the viewer of a 'simultaneous graphic pull across and into the frame' (Belton 1992: 199). Lynch's preference (here and elsewhere) for a wide-angle lens allows him to exploit the 'emptiness around his characters' (Chion 1995: 51) – an emptiness which is, paradoxically 'filled' with latent meaning or dread.

One detail of this primal scene, which adds immeasurably to its tone of comedic horror, is the intoxicant machine that Frank employs as he prepares to ravage Dorothy Vallens, and it provides another intriguing corollary with the Wolf-Man case history. Freud reveals that one of the Wolf-Man's neurotic character traits when he was a small boy was the performance of a curious ritual 'when he saw people that he felt sorry for, such as beggars, cripples or very old men'. This involved the compulsive inhaling and exhaling of breath: 'He had to breathe out noisily, so as not to become like them; and under certain conditions he had to draw in his breath vigorously' (Freud 1918: 17). Freud explains that, since 'breath' is the same word as 'spirit' in his patient's native tongue (Russian), this compulsive breathing was related to the idea of the boy breathing in the Holy Spirit while breathing out evil ones. But that is not all: his breathing out 'at the sight of pitiable-looking people' begins at the point when his mother takes him to a sanatorium to see his hospitalised father: 'he looked ill, and the boy felt very sorry for him' (1918: 67).[12] The father is thus the prototype of the pathetic types whom the child wishes not to be like, and wishes to breathe *out*. Yet, at the same time, this ritualised breathing is also linked to the father's exertions during the primal scene, that is, 'the heavy breathing was an imitation of the noise he had heard coming from his father during the intercourse' (ibid.). In other words, it is simultaneously an identification and disidentification with a figure that is both invincible and deficient. What is evident here is the Wolf-Man's perception of the father not merely as the striding, castrating wolf, but also as the wolf whose tail has been so inconsiderately or nonchalantly yanked off (hence, castrated). Leo Bersani has suggested that what the child perceives during the primal scene is not merely phallic prowess on the part of the father but also a strange incapacity or vulnerability. He asks, could not the phantasy of the father's violence during the primal scene (as it is remembered or reconstituted in dreams and memories) be a reversal, a transposition, of what the child originally witnessed – could it not be a defense 'against what frightens him in the [father's] vulnerability?' (Barsani 1995: 31). Indeed, Freud says as much, although without following its consequences through, when he points out that there remained a 'counter-current' in the patient which placed the father in the role not of castrator but as castrated 'and as calling, therefore, for his sympathy' (Freud 1918: 87). The seed of this interpretation, moreover, comes from a detail that the boy witnesses during the primal scene:

> During the copulation in the primal scene he had observed the penis disappear … he had felt compassion for his father on that account, and had rejoiced at the reappearance of what he had thought had been lost (1918: 88).

In other words, the child (mis)perceives the father's act of penetrating the mother's 'wound' as an act of castration enacted by the figure of the castrating mother, in the name of some as yet inexplicable pleasure for both of the participants.

Vulnerability and a fear of vulnerability seem to be the driving force behind Frank Booth's compulsive behaviour as well. For what do all his fetish items, his various props of intoxication – not only the oxygen mask, but his glass of Pabst! Blue! Ribbon!, his Roy Orbison cassette, his little swatch of blue velvet that he tenderly strokes – suggest except an instability and vulnerability toward power? The mysterious drug that he inhales implies that even Frank needs to be coerced into being the castrating Father, the strutting wolf, the substitute phallus. This quality of 'impotence' has been observed by several of the film's critics. Michael Atkinson, for instance, writes that

> though he stands as one of the most horrifying characters in film history, he is nonetheless torturously, miserably human. In Lynch's and Hopper's hands, the most appalling acts of debasement and viciousness have a edge of sad struggle to them, as if Frank is striving toward a satisfaction he can never attain – like an abandoned infant. (Atkinson 1997: 45)

Slavoj Žižek argues that the film's primal scene is 'staged, deliberately theatrical' and he reads this theatricality as the feigning of 'a wild sexual act in order to conceal the father's impotence from the child'. He adds, 'instead of a son witnessing parental coitus, we have the father's desperate attempt to convince the son of his potency' (Žižek 1994: 120–1). It is exactly this mixture of power and impotence that characterises the father in the primal scene: he is both castrator and castrated, dangerous and impotent. Indeed, does not one entail or explain the other? 'Frank is a ... he's a very dangerous man', Jeffrey informs Sandy. And he *is* dangerous, yet also oddly touching and precarious. This is what makes a later exchange of dialogue between Jeffrey and Frank so strangely resonant. Taking Jeffrey for a 'joyride', Frank notices Dorothy making eye contact with Jeffrey in the backseat. He pulls the car over to the side and turns to face him. The interior car light goes on as Frank barks, 'Fuck, what are you looking at?' Jeffrey answers 'Nothing.' Frank momentarily pauses – his brow creases – then says 'Don't you look at me, Fuck' (or: *don't look at me fuck*). He adds in a whisper, 'I shoot when I see the whites of the eyes.' And yet we might recall that when Frank is required to shoot-to-kill near the climax of the film he again needs to fortify himself, to prop up the phallus with assorted amulets, including the cherished piece of cloth which he drapes over the gun like a protective sheath.

Jeffrey's cognition of the 'father' as an object both of pity and horror is succinctly expressed in the dream he has following his extended visit to Dorothy's apartment. At the beginning of this sequence, Lynch dissolves from a visually and aurally distorted shot of Tom Beaumont in his hospital bed, hooked up to a life-support system (the distortion smears the father's face across the screen as his gaping mouth intones 'Jeffrey'), to a slow-motion image of Frank during the primal scene, silently raging. The sound from the earlier shot continues and intensifies, becoming more metallic and tortured as Frank howls into the night. The next image, a dissolve to a candle flickering and blowing out in the wind, ends in pitch-black and we hear Frank state, 'Now, it's dark.' Words of comfort, but to whom? The constellation of shots which follows is equally suggestive: (1) an extreme close-up of Dorothy's face laying diagonally across the frame (her impossibly lush lips form these words: 'hit me'); (2) a straight cut to Frank in close-up lurching a fist toward the camera; (3) a straight cut to Jeffrey raising his head off the pillow as though jolted into consciousness by the preceding shot. What is underlined here is both Dorothy's status as devouring sadistic presence ('hit me,' in this instance, is pure demand) and Jeffrey's (unconscious) fascination with her position in the primal scene. As Atkinson points out, what is implied in the link between shots (2) and (3) is that Jeffrey in his dream places himself, or finds himself placed, on the receiving end of Frank's 'violence': 'Jeffrey sees *himself* for a moment as Dorothy, pummeled by Frank' (Atkinson 1997: 50). (Atkinson's 'pummeled' could scarcely be more apt.) Of course, Jeffrey comes to tell Sandy a somewhat different version of the events that he has endured. Which one should we believe?

Fantasmatic Transactions

> *Jeffrey* (to Sandy):   You're a neat girl.
> *Sandy* (to Jeffrey):   So are you.

When superimposed over the libidinal intensities of the primal scene, the Oedipus complex is meant to function like an optical grid for the intelligible distribution of positionings in space: passivity and activity, femininity and masculinity become clearly distinguished as opposed positions or modalities of being. It is, moreover, only when these distinctions are settled that the spectatorial affects of the scenario can achieve (for the male child) their 'proper' ordering: identification with the active masculine figure, *or* desire for the passive feminine one. But unconscious fantasies, precisely because they are not constrained by the ego and its repressive functions, are contrary to such a representational system. As Laplanche and Pontalis suggest, there is in such scenarios an 'absence of subjectivisation, and the subject is present *in* the scene' (Laplanche and Pontalis 1986: 22). The subject participates without being in control of the staging of the fantasy. Thus, for instance, in the fantasy 'A father seduces a daughter ... nothing shows whether the [female] subject will be immediately located as *daughter*; it can as well be fixed as *father*, or even in the term *seduces*' (ibid.). In other words, the subject may identify with the daughter or the father or the act itself, and these positions are not fixed: the subject oscillates possibilities, or, more precisely, the subject experiences the fantasy as the oscillation of these possibilities.[13] It is this lack of fixity that, as we have seen, characterises the primal scene for the Wolf-Man: not only can he *not* finally determine who is castrated and who is castrator, he also cannot settle his own relation to, or within, this spectacle. The positions of spectatorial oscillation evident in the Wolf-Man's heavy breathing are brought to the fore in an analogous fashion in his intestinal problems as an adult. We might say that there is a similar tension between the analysand's desire to *retain* and to *expel*.[14]

The permutation of roles and attributions, positions of identity and desire, are everywhere evident in the texture of Lynch's narrative. It is replete with characters jostling to inhabit or to vacate such positions as father, mother and son. Indeed, is this not made explicit in Frank's wild alteration between 'Daddy' and 'Baby'? Is this not crystallised in the film's most dumbfoundingly poignant statement: 'Mommy, Baby wants to fuck. Baby wants blue velvet'? And when Baby begins doing with

Mommy exactly what Baby has requested, the piece of blue velvet which dangles from Dorothy's robe, and that she places gently into his mouth, comes exactly to signify, as Brunette and Wills have suggested, 'the imaginary of an umbilical plenitude', (Brunette and Wills 1989: 153) thus evoking the primal fantasy of intra-uterine existence, of returning to the safety and warmth of the mother's womb. This is only the most blatant example of the exchange of roles, of sites of pleasure, among the film's characters (not to mention, the film's spectators). Dorothy's triadic plea 'Hold Me – Hurt Me – Help Me' confers upon her a series of positionings which confuse and excite Jeffrey exactly because he does not know whether she is a helpless victim (castrated) or whether she is the aggressor (the castrator) whom he needs to revoke, whom he needs to flee in order to save himself. She is the Mother and the 'Blue Lady'. In Frank's nomenclature, she is 'Mommy', 'Shithead' and 'Tits'.

Jeffrey, the film's protagonist, and the principal Lynch surrogate, is just as prone to this vacillation.[15] He is not only the son in the literal sense (Tom Beaumont's son), but he also finds himself positioned in this role with Detective Williams,[16] with Frank Booth, and, of course, with Dorothy Vallens. But she, tellingly, does not call him 'Donny', the name of her small boy, but 'Don', the name of her husband, Donny's father. Moreover, when Dorothy says 'Don' her pronunciation of the word makes it indistinguishable from *Don't*, and, thus, Dorothy seems to bar the way for the son's approach even as she simultaneously provokes him – calling out in the night the name of her husband, her lover, the father of her child.[17] It could not be more *à propos* that Frank links his desire to Jeffrey's: 'You're like me.' They have both been the husband, the lover, the abuser of Dorothy. They have both been the child, the little boy, longing to secretly retain the mother's love. Frank's castration of Jeffrey in the joyride sequence (the latter made 'pretty, pretty' with the aid of Dorothy's red lipstick) momentarily places Frank in the position of menacing Father to terrified son but we should not forget that what Frank wants here primarily is to eliminate Jeffrey, the good neighbor, so that he might again be both Daddy and Baby, one after the other.[18] Chion describes this moment of extreme intimacy between Jeffrey and Frank thus:

> It is both terrifying (you belong to me, you resemble me, we are alike) and paternal (whatever happens, I will love you and I will never leave you). This is 'spoken' as a symbolic father and, if it is appropriate to speak here of homosexuality, it is a homosexuality of a primitive sort, different from the kind that develops later ... He tells Jeffrey he loves him, not with a homosexual love but the way a father loves his son, just as Jeffrey was seduced as a son by Dorothy. And it is as a son that Jeffrey will return his father's love letter in the form of a bullet between the eyes. (Chion 1995: 96)

It is the latter act that precipitates the film's *dénouement* which, as we know, is practically a verbatim account of the Oedipal trajectory: the male child's rite of passage from infantile desire and conflict (the covetous longing for the mother; the hatred for the paternal figure who bars the child's unlimited access to pleasure) to mature, law-abiding heterosexual subject. As Mulvey notes, '[Jeffrey] has ... through his struggle with the villain and victory over him, inherited the place of the father and the father-in-law. He has moved into the position of authority, associated with the patriarchal function, and the Law' (Mulvey 1996: 141). He does so, moreover, by giving up his unhealthy attachment to the mother figure and displacing his affection onto a more appropriate substitute figure, that is, Sandy, Detective Williams' daughter. The flagrance with which this Oedipal resolution is evoked leads some viewers to forget that the film's narrative structure is, in fact, circular rather than linear.[19] This structure is underlined not only by the beetle clasped in the beak of a beautiful, mechanical robin (returning us to the film's initial descent into the Beaumont's front lawn), and by the repetition of picture postcard shots of Lumberton at the beginning and closing of the film, but also by the undulating blue velvet curtains through which the images of Lumberton first emerge and then dissolve. This movement into or out of the recesses of space is, of course, a fundamental Lynchian motif. Recall, not only the camera penetrating the interior of a severed ear, but also Sandy's emergence from the burrow of night. Indeed, it is an axiom of Lynch's universe that if we carefully inspect the exterior of things, the texture of existence – sometimes just by sitting and waiting, being very still – we will discover another dimension of reality, another layer of pleasure: a depth which rises upon the surface, a vertical axis which bisects horizontality and vice versa. Thus, the finale of *Blue Velvet* – by which I mean not the shots of Jeffrey Beaumont safely ensconced in the family kitchen, but rather the image of velvet curtains rustling in anticipation – is less the exhaustion of pleasure, the reconciliation of desire to the law, than its momentary abeyance.[20] As Dorothy informs us before the fade to the final image or texture, 'I still can see blue velvet through my tears...'. So can we.[21]

Notes

1 Freud's analysis of the Wolf-Man lasted for four-and-a-half years, from 1910 to 1914. He completed the writing of the case history in the winter of 1914–15 but its publication was delayed until 1918 as a result of the First World War. See Freud 1918: 7–122.

2 I might point out here that Lynch himself remains noncommittal on the influence of psychoanalysis on the conception of his film. Whenever he is pressed to give an exact meaning or intention to *Blue Velvet* he invariably falls back on the explanation of artistic 'intuition'. Among the visual clues strewn throughout the text there is a cinematic allusion which, as far as I know, has never previously been mentioned: when Sandy and Jeffrey converse over the telephone near the end of the film, and Sandy unconsciously clutches her breast, we notice that the movie-star poster which adorns her bedroom wall is of Montgomery Clift – not the young, beautiful Montgomery Clift but the post-car accident Clift, the aged, alcoholic Clift who was chosen by John Huston to star in the director's 1962 film *Freud: The Secret Passion*.

3 In other words, the recognition of the primal scene is belated. The psychoanalytic

axiom that it takes two traumas to make a trauma applies just as well to the primal scene: the force of the original event is evoked retroactively through a second one that fills in the blank spots or spaces of the first traumatic message.

4   He is 'seduced' at the age of three-and-a-quarter by his older sister who plays with the boy's genitalia. This provokes the child's first series of sexual researches, and a succession of objects upon whom the young boy attempts 'seduction', including his old nursemaid, a servant girl named Grusha, and his beloved father. His infantile attempts at seduction (which include urinating on the staircase of his home) lead to threats of punishment (or castration).

5   The patient's contribution of these two details would, in psychoanalytic terms, confirm the accuracy of the analyst's hypothetical construct. The patient's addition of new elements and new stimuli to the initial constructions of the analyst demonstrates the truth-value of the initial postulate. For more on this see Freud 1938: 257–69.

6   This is Lynch's response to the question 'Given that you draw on a past to such an extent in your work, is it sometimes hard to access memories and events from childhood?'

7   Laplanche and Pontalis, wishing to distance themselves from the extremes of Freud's biologisms, suggest that these scenes are 'primal', not in the sense of being primeval (traces of a phylogenetic heritage) but in the sense of having been fundamental to the subject and the constitution of his/her sexuality (Laplanche and Pontalis 1986: 8). In his more recent work Laplanche has argued against the notion that there are three original fantasies. More heretically, he has suggested that the Oedipus and castration complexes are merely *secondary* elaborations of the content of the primal unconscious; they are merely the subject's provisional or initial attempts to give answer to the content of the enigmatic signifiers that persist in their unconscious (Laplanche 1989: 89–151).

8   Freud makes the astonishing claim that this clicking sound actually emanates from the patient's interior: the sound she hears is actually the beating of her clitoris (in the present and/or in the primal scene).

9   Later in his monograph, Chion conjectures that the scene was inspired by something Lynch himself has overheard: 'Lynch dreamed of creating a character who would see what he (Lynch) had only overheard, but because Lynch remains faithful to the truth of his impressions, he present us with a scene which, from a visual standpoint, does not say much more than what hearing alone would allow us to imagine' (Chion 1995: 170).

10 The decor of Dorothy's apartment contributes effectively to the film's temporal hesitation between the past and the present. When Jeffrey looks out of the closet on to the wide expanse of Dorothy's apartment he appears to be glancing backwards, into the recesses of his (infantile) past. This effect is derived in part by such visual touches as the 'unplant-like snake plants' which litter her Deep River apartment and which Michael Atkinson points out were 'cheapy fashionable' in the 1950s (Atkinson 1997: 35). This temporal uncertainty is often characterised as an example of the film's 'postmodernism', but the imbrication of the past

and the present is central to psychoanalytic thought. It should also be fairly clear by now (after numerous Lynch interviews and profiles) that the past that is evoked in *Blue Velvet* is not some vague, non-historical version of the past but Lynch's own childhood and maturation period. For example: the idyllic images of Lumberton which open and close the film are the artist's memories of his childhood in Boise, Idaho and Spokane, Washington; the bulk of popular songs which appear on the soundtrack were released in 1963, the year that Lynch turned 17 (see Lynch in Rodley 1997: 8–10).

11 This is not the only appearance of the primal scene or primal fantasy in Lynch's *oeuvre*. Indeed, his work appears to be littered with such remnants. Here, I will simply point out two of my favorites. First, the primal scene that opens *The Elephant Man* (1980): the inaugural image is an extreme close-up of the eyes and mouth of John Merrick's mother seen in a photographic portrait. It is followed by a fantasy sequence (but whose, exactly?) of her being 'raped' by an enraged elephant whose fierce cries fuse with the grinding sounds of industrial machinery. At the end of the attack there is a moment of calm as we watch the slow discharge of a billow of smoke. Second, Henry's encounter with the Beautiful Girl Across the Hall in *Eraserhead* (1977). Here the primal scene is inverted. As they 'copulate' in a milky-white substance at the centre of Henry's bed, the Beautiful Girl Across the Hall is repulsed by the sight of the little baby lying on top of a nearby table. (As though it were the mother and not the child asking 'What is this that I am seeing?' 'What does it want from me?') The climax of their encounter – their descent into a pool of liquid, her hair suddenly floating free, disembodied – suggests, like Lynch's other primal scenes, the perspective of a child confronted with an event which it does not (or cannot) fully comprehend.

12 We might recall here Jeffrey's first sight of his father in the hospital. Atkinson writes, 'The image of nightmarish hospital gadgetry matters more than the reality of illness or treatment, which is precisely how a child would perceive the scene' (Atkinson 1997: 23).

13 No essay of Freud demonstrates more clearly the extraordinary variety of roles and positions that the de-subjectivised subject takes vis-à-vis unconscious fantasy than 'A Child is Being Beaten' (Freud 1919: 177–204). For a discussion of this essay in the context of film theory see Rodowick 1991: 66–94.

14 There is obviously insufficient space here to work out systematically this line of thought. Let me simply point out that through a complicated series of interlocking arguments, Freud demonstrates (sometimes unwittingly) that the Wolf-Man's chronic bowel problems are expressive of his simultaneous fear/desire for castration and that this is manifested in his resistance/desire to shit. (See Freud 1918: Sections VII and VIII.)

15 As Lynch tells Rodley, not only does he feel particularly close (or similar) to the Jeffrey character but MacLachlan also played Jeffrey as Lynch's alter ego: 'Kyle buttoned his shirt up because he saw Jeffrey as me and he just took on certain things' (Lynch in Rodley 1997: 140–1).

16 The scene in which Jeffrey asks Williams what it is like to be a detective and the latter answers Jeffrey's 'It must be great' with 'It's horrible too' is a variation of a 'birds-and-the-bees' talk between parent and child.

17 Brunette and Wills were the first (and, as far as I know, the only ones) to draw attention to the way that Rossellini's accent makes Dorothy's 'Dons' sound like 'Don'ts' – or is it the other way round? (Brunette and Wills 1989: 167). Rossellini's vocal intonations have also misled some viewers, Brunette and Wills included, to hear the word 'Madeleine' when Dorothy is on the phone with Don. Actually, what she is saying is 'Meadow Lane': 'You mean Meadow Lane?' This question follows immediately upon her inquiry into the son's status: 'How's Donny?' It is in Meadow Lane that Frank consummates his joyride – a hail of kisses and a blow of fists – with Jeffrey.

18 Elizabeth Cowie, who also draws upon the work of Laplanche and Pontalis, comes to a similar conclusion regarding the oscillation of subject positions in Max Ophuls' *The Reckless Moment* (1949): 'the diverse positions father, mother, child, lover, wife, husband … are never finally contained by any one character' (Cowie 1984: 101). Unlike Cowie, however, I am not attempting to suggest that this analysis of *Blue Velvet* is emblematic of the fantasmatic nature of cinematic narrative and cinematic spectatorship in general, although it may serve an explanatory role in regards to Lynch's body of work.

19 Not Mulvey though. She writes, 'the last shot of the film [sic] shows mother and son, happily reunited in their ideal dyad, waiting for the whole process to begin all over again' (Mulvey 1996a: 147–8). For an engagement with Slavoj Žižek's discussion of the equivalence between circular narrative form and the circularity of the psychoanalytic process see Greg Hainge's chapter in this volume.

20 This is a paraphrase of several points that Rodowick makes regarding the logic of the Oedipus complex that he opposes to the 'uncanny recurrence' of fantasy. As he argues, the persistence of fantasy speaks to the subject's desire to restage its origins and to have them conclude otherwise (Rodowick 1991: 84).

21 I would like to thank Richard Allen, Joe McElhaney and Erica Sheen for their useful comments on earlier drafts of this paper.

CHAPTER FIVE

Blue Velvet Underground: David Lynch's Post-Punk Poetics

Nicholas Rombes

I don't really understand the word 'irony' too much.
  – David Lynch

Not a ghost bloodied country
All covered with sleep
Where the black angel did weep
Not an old city street in the east
  – from 'Black Angel's Death Song' by The Velvet Underground

Henry in *Eraserhead* – he's a punker. Can't you see it? The skinny tie, the spiked hair, the wild eyes. He's a punk rocker. He's Johnny Rotten!
  – Anon.

Eraserhead Carter: Punk President

It was an unexpected moment in my Introduction to Film Studies class, the students having just watched *Blue Velvet* (1986), a film I was teaching for the first time. A fair number of students had not seen it before, and when the film ended there was a palpable mix of awe and anger that, in the ensuing discussion, crystallised around

Punk icon? Henry (Jack Nance) in *Eraserhead*

Blue Velvet's moments of intense emotion, such as the scene in the car outside the church where Sandy describes her dream of the return of the robins in wide-eyed awe. Most of the class read it as a defiantly ironic moment, a mock Frank Capra-esque satire, a send-up of misplaced innocence, a parody of 1950s car-romance melodrama. On that day, thoseof us who read the film's evocation of innocence as sincere – who read Sandy's confession of her dream as an alternative that the film frames with seriousness and love – were outnumbered and eventually had to concede to the lie that *Blue Velvet* was, in fact, a subversive exposé of a kind of sham past, an exposé whose cultural logic is similar to 'Nick at Night' or other forms of ironic deconstruction.[1]

Why David Lynch? And why this film? Because Lynch's work confounds the orthodoxies of postmodern irony even as it has become a canonical representative of that irony, playing the serious so seriously that audiences assume the films must be parodic, as in Roger Ebert's notorious attacks on what he has called the 'sophomoric humour and the cop-out of parody' in *Wild at Heart* (1990) or the 'cleverness of Lynch's ironic style' and 'neat little in-jokes' of *Blue Velvet* (Ebert 1990; 1986). Or, as Paul Attanasio of the *Washington Post* reported after seeing *Blue Velvet*, it was 'all flattened with fake nostalgia', as opposed, we might assume, to authentic nostalgia (Attanasio 1986). Contrast these mid-1980s readings to more current revisionary assessments of Lynch's films, such as those of Salon.com's Charles Taylor, for whom the film is not about 'ripping the veil off of suburbia' but rather 'wanting to hold on to its reassuring safety' (Taylor 2000), or Martha Nochimson, who suggests that the 'mechanical robin is often misread as a burlesque of Jeffrey's and Sandy's contentment' (Nochimson 1997: 119).

I would like to suggest that to appreciate the problem of Lynch's sincerity-in-irony, we need to frame his work not only in relation to film history and theory, but also in relation to punk, a cultural movement which spawned not only, and most famously, do-it-yourself amateur music, but also a do-it-yourself amateur president, Jimmy Carter. 1977, the year of *Eraserhead*'s release, was the *annus mirabilis* of punk rock, and the *Variety* headline that announced *Eraserhead* registered the kind of reprehension that characterised mainstream responses to punk: 'Dismal American Film Institute exercise in gore/Commercial prospects nil' (see Sklar 1994: 353). For if 1976 saw the release of *Horses* and *Radio Ethiopia* by Patti Smith, *Blank Generation* by Richard Hell and the Voidoids, *The Ramones* by the Ramones, 1977 saw *Never Mind the Bollocks* by the Sex Pistols, *The Clash* by The Clash, *Pink Flag* by Wire, *Plastic Letters* by Blondie and *The Idiot* by Iggy Pop.

The gross disjunction between sincerity and irony, between depth and surface, that characterised these releases was itself the product of an earlier, detached aesthetic whose emergence in the late 1960s is perhaps most clearly signalled by The Velvet Underground's first album *The Velvet Underground and Nico*.[2] Released in 1967, produced by Andy Warhol (who also provided the cover banana painting) the album lurched between the lilting Mamas and Papas-esque ballad 'Sunday Morning', the dissonant, avant-garde, free jazz of 'The Black Angel's Death Song' and the S & M-infused 'Venus in Furs'. It is not that the topics in themselves were dangerous, rather that the smash-cut juxtaposition of sunshine and gloom made it difficult to read the sunshine songs as sincere. Contextualised in this raw savagery, chirpy songs like 'Sunday Morning' (which opens with the lyrics 'Sunday morning brings the dawn in') and 'There She Goes Again' are transformed from innocent numbers about love to parodies of West Coast, counter-cultural peace-and-love dirges, culminating with 'Heroin' ('When I put a spike into my vein/And I'll tell you things just aren't the same'). Thus, songs that on first hearing seemed complicit with mid- to late 1960s flower-power anthems, subsequently became complicated by their placement next to S & M 'love' songs, thereby framing the whole album listening experience as an ironic one.

This ironised reading – a reading that suggests that the happy, upbeat mood of tracks like 'Sunday Morning' are in fact cynical parodies of sincerity – is itself a product of what David Foster Wallace has called 'the ironic tone' of television, a medium whose rapid-fire editing and juxtaposition of high and low, 'real' and simulated, created an ironised audience in the 1950s and 1960s (Wallace 1992: 62). As Robert Ray has shown, television unwittingly deconstructed the traditional Hollywood genres (and the ideologies inherent in those genres) by recontextualising the viewing experience in a way that demystified the previously mystical experience of watching and 'losing' oneself in film in a darkened theatre. Shown on television, interrupted by commercials and other household distractions, the sacred, unironic genres (the western film, the gangster film, the screwball comedy, and so on) became increasingly visible as narrative products whose skeletal formulas emerged in the jumble of the television medium. 'In the spring of 1963', suggests Ray, 'a television viewer could watch as network videotapes of the Birmingham race riots led directly into "Cheyenne", "Laramie", "Mr. Ed", "Ozzie and Harriet", or "Wagon Train", depending on the network and the night. Inevitably, that viewer's attitude toward conventional versions of America's mythology became increasingly ironic' (Ray 1985: 266).

Irony, which exploits 'gaps between what's said and what's meant, between how things try to appear and how they really are' (Wallace 1992: 65) emerged into the language of mainstream American pop culture at a time when Vietnam, the Pentagon Papers scandal and Watergate had already begun to demythologise and destabilise the old transcendental narratives of American exceptionalism, nationalism and patriarchy. If The Velvet Underground and Andy Warhol were the first to throw into bed together the popular and avant-garde in order to exploit the gap between 'how things try to appear and how they really are', then it was punk that commodified them into a genre that would sell (rock'n'roll), and it was punk that – along with television – articulated, framed and formalised the ironic stance that would filter into the cultural mainstream. Mainstream Punk and New Wave groups like the Ramones, Television, Talking Heads and especially Blondie wrote songs that resurrected past 'innocent' forms from the 1950s and 1960s, forms that they distorted through manic speed and the juxtaposition of the profane and sincere. The Ramones very often sounded like The Beach Boys (complete with swelling harmonies, simple lyrics, and so forth.) sped up times ten, except that their songs were about sniffing glue and lobotomies rather than surfing and girls. Blondie often sounded like the girl groups of the early 1960s. But when The Shangri-Las had asked 'Is she *really* going out with him?' without the slightest trace of irony in the opening seconds of 'Leader of the Pack' in 1964, by 1976 Blondie opened their song 'X Offender' with teen melodrama: 'I saw you on the corner. You looked so big and fine. I *really* wanted to go out with you.'[3] Debbie Harry's voice is all throaty, mock-sincerity at the beginning of a song that turns out to be about a sex offender; a song that becomes a postmodern cut-up of old forms and the discredited rhetoric of romance. Critic Lester Bangs identified this early, suggesting that 'the music [of Blondie] seems to have no really strong emotions in it, and what emotions do surface occasionally, what obsessions and lusts, are invariably almost immediately gutted by fusillades of irony, sarcasm, camp, what have you, ending up buried' (Bangs in Marcus 1993: 106).

Consider also Lou Reed's meta-interview with John Holstrom in the pages of the very first issue of *Punk* magazine in January 1976:

Punk:	What does an interview mean to you?
Lou:	Nothing. They don't mean shit. They do not sell records, they don't mean shit and I don't fuckin care. I mean anyone can...
Punk:	Why do you do them, then?
Lou:	Just to find out what people like you are up to, y'know, what

you think I'm supposed to be doing, y'know, what's being sold the most, that's what. I mean being on the cover of what's your name don't mean shit ... I mean, you know, if I didn't have people like you around I'd have to pay somebody – find somebody in the streets, say 'Hey, what's happening?' [...]

Punk:	Do you feel?
Lou:	Ah, with my hands, man – what kind of question is that? ... I don't feel at all ... I try to act like I can and really can't. Ed McMahon, y'know can't do either, y'know – he's that guy on Johnny Carson.
Legs:	I think he's great!
Lou:	Isn't he great? I would trust him right down.
Legs:	I think if Ed McMahon ran on the same ticket with Monty Hall this country would be in great shape!
Lou:	That's a cheap little hippy remark. That's bullshit.

(Holmstrom 1996: 11–12)

The exchange fluctuates between sincerity and irony, as, for instance, Ed McMahon is at first discussed in terms that seem sincere (a kind of populist alternative who can be 'trusted' in the era of Nixonian, poisoned politics) but which just as quickly give way to sarcasm. This rhetorical shift – the jump-cut between sincerity and irony – is precisely the logic upon which a whole range of post-punk social formations are built, and which has framed audience reception to Lynch's work. For Lynch's use of what we might call the aesthetics of the punk form, his 'return to the past' with a difference – what Fredric Jameson has called *Blue Velvet*'s 'simulated replay of the 1950s' (Jameson 1991: 295) – is not mediated by an obvious, built-in interpretive frame of reference. Like *Taxi Driver* (1976), released the year before *Eraserhead*, Lynch's work from the 1970s and 1980s is 'incoherent' – to borrow a phrase from Robin Wood's analysis of *Taxi Driver* (Wood 1986: 46–55) – because the juxtaposition of profane and sacred, tender and brutal, light and dark, might work in the service of unmasking, of satire, of subversion, or they might not. Certainly Lynch himself is loath to talk about his work as subversive or ironic. If anything, he frequently returns to the notion that rather than functioning as an element of critique, the 'dark' sequences in his films simply serve as contrasts to the 'light elements': 'This is the way America is to me. There's a very innocent, naïve quality to life, and there's a horror and a sickness as well. It's everything' (Lynch in Rodley 1997: 139). Thus, moments of heightened emotion or melodrama in Lynch's films – such as Sarah Palmer's reaction to news of her daughter Laura's death in the pilot episode of *Twin Peaks* (1990) – tend to be uncomfortable, because post-punk American audiences are conditioned to 'read' such instances (especially in the work of artists) as subversive, ironic, cynical. 'The most frightening prospect, for the well-conditioned viewer', writes Wallace, 'becomes leaving oneself open to others' ridicule by betraying passé expressions of value, emotion or vulnerability ... the crime is naïveté' (Wallace 1992: 63). It helps to explain, I think, why my students either tend to rally around Lynch as a great subversive satirist, or else dismiss him as a sentimentalist, a reactionary whose *Blue Velvet* is little more than the dark subtext to a Frank Capra film. Especially when read against the more pronounced parody of the Coen Brothers (particularly *Blood Simple* (1984) and *Raising Arizona* (1987)), the calculated aloofness of Todd Solondz, and the deconstructing, mock nostalgia pleasures of John Waters in such films as *Hairspray* (1988), *Cry Baby* (1990) or *Serial Mom* (1994), Lynch must be up to the same unmasking.

1980s Deathkit: One Part Evil...

Irony as a form of critique had moved from a subcultural position in the 1960s and 1970s into mainstream pop culture by the 1980s, an era typically described (and decried) as socially conservative in current academic discourse. Indeed, the divide between the way things try to appear and how things 'really are' was perhaps at no time more pronounced than during the Reagan era, the era of the image, of the 'authority of the simulacra', of the hyperreal (Gaggi 1997: 59). Recent scholarship links 1980s American cinema to Reagan (is there any other American president who is invoked more in film criticism?) in ways that almost always critique his unreconstructed, Cold War conservatism. Leonard Quart and Albert Auster write of his 'vicious' social policies and his 'philosophy of volunteerism that seemed to owe as much to Frank Capra (a Capra without a social conscience) as to Herbert Hoover' (Quart and Auster 1992: 128). They go on to suggest that his shallow, 'film-based political vision' finally gave America 'a president who not only embedded, but was deeply committed to, all the crack-brained fantasies and empty rhetoric peddled by Hollywood ever since it became the centre of America's popular culture' (ibid.). Likewise, Michael Ryan and Douglas Kellner refer to a 'dangerously antidemocratic corruption behind the veneer of high-sounding patriotic platitudes' and go on to speak of the 'very clear plight of the homeless poor, whose numbers swelled during this period of public meanness' (Ryan and Kellner 1988: 297). More recently, Susan Jeffords has written of Reagan's 'pro-technology militarism', a militarism driven, in part, by a fear – which Jeffords claims had more to do with science fiction fantasy than reality – of Communist destruction of human freedom (Jeffords 1994: 106, 105), while Emanuel Levy characterises American films of the 1980s as 'strongly reaffirm[ing] the centrality of the nuclear family' (Levy 1999: 152).

Central to a reading of Lynch's films from this era as Reaganite texts is an understanding of the resuscitation of 'evil' as a social imaginary during the 1980s. One could argue that it took Reagan to re-introduce evil into the American national consciousness as a potentially real, identifiable thing rather than as a materialist social construction as it was imagined in the rhetoric of the Great Society, where, for instance, poverty is the product not of sin but of unjustly configured distributions of wealth and power. This notion is perhaps best crystallised in Reagan's famously Cold War-retro speech to the House of Commons in June 1982 on the 'evil empire':

We see totalitarian forces in the world who seek subversion and conflict around the globe to further their barbarous assault on the human spirit. What, then, is our course? Must civilisation perish in a hail of fiery atoms? Must freedom wither in a quiet, deadening accommodation with totalitarian evil?

And later in that same speech:

The British people know that, given strong leadership, time, and a little bit of hope, the forces of good ultimately rally and triumph over evil. (Reagan 1982: 1, 4)

The words bubble up from some deep Puritan past, re-introducing a serious and non-ironic vision of evil into a postmodern political culture that would prefer to think of the word evil only fenced in with quotation marks. In Reagan's discursive universe, evil is the real McCoy that finds its expression – its expression only – in social forces such as fascism or communism. For Reagan, in other words, social and political 'problems' are only expressions or reflections of the larger and far more sinister underlying problem of evil.

That good eventually triumphs is finally more a verdict of Fate than human ingenuity; when scrutinised too closely, evil vacates into the details of history, details that never held as much attraction to Reagan as the larger narrative they told. 'I cannot help but feel,' he said in a speech on the Cold War in 1990, 'that there was some divine plan that placed this continent here between the two great oceans to be found by people from any corner of the earth' (Reagan 1990: 5). This Winthropian, non-ironic vision of American exceptionalism is paradoxical because while it is, on the one hand, so hostile to American intellectualism, it is, at the same time, symptomatic of a larger postmodern condition – what might be termed nostalgia with difference. Reagan's invocation of the past ('there was some divine plan') is made impossible and embarrassing when, in the postmodern present, the past itself is revealed to be a story, a narrative – shifting, subjective and relational – and nothing more. The postmodern question is no longer, 'which history is true', but rather, 'which history do I choose?' Difference is not a symptom, but a condition of postmodern culture.

And if one of the hallmarks of postmodernism is its 'fragmentation of time into a series of perpetual presents,' as Fredric Jameson has suggested, then Reagan is America's first postmodern present, arriving late on the already fading scene – at once invoking the past in a way that mixes up history and movies, the real and the fantastic, image and substance, representation and simulation (Jameson 1996: 202). He is, as Howard Hampton has noted, our first Hollywood president, our movie-star president, emerging from the entertainment industry and entering political culture, erasing the boundaries between them, obscuring the real and the not real (Hampton 1993: 38).

One could argue the familiar, that Lynch's *Blue Velvet* projects a similar, ahistorical fantasy-landscape: what seems to be a contemporary 1980s setting is haunted by signs from the past – an old 1940s car gliding past, the *Rebel Without a Cause* tension between the teenagers (some dressed straight out of the 1950s), the scenes of Jeffrey's mom watching old *noir* movies on the living room television, the melodramatic soundtrack. Jeffrey is drawn into a mystery and into 'secrets' that the adult world seems matter-of-factly deadened to. When he finds the human ear severed by scissors in a field and takes it, in a bag, to Detective Williams, the Detective opens the bag, looks at the ear, and simply says, 'That sure looks like a human ear, doesn't it?' The fact that in the film, adults of the official world (parents, police, etc.) are deadened to the horrors around them, is what helps make the film almost comically bearable. In one scene included in the shooting script but not in the theatrical release, Jeffrey enters the living room as a doctor is giving his mother an injection of medicine: 'That will take care of you, Frances, for another week,' the doctor tells her. Jeffrey's problem is that he is not numbed to the evil; he takes no medicine for that. Instead, he comes face to face with evil's brute face and comes back for more. The only adult from this camp who acknowledges the compelling terrors of secret evil is Detective Williams. 'I'm just real curious, like you said', Jeffrey tells him. 'I was the same way when I was your age', the detective responds, 'I guess that's what got me into this business.' 'It must be great', says Jeffrey. 'And it's horrible too', replies the detective, providing only a glimpse into the brutal nature of the world that lures Jeffrey. *Blue Velvet*, in this reading, is a conservative text because it evacuates evil from a social context, personalises it, and abstracts it into the old, familiar transcendental binaries of self vs. other, innocence vs. experience.

It is a world where secrets and mysteries *do* exist; a world that so uncannily conflates past and present, image and reality, dream and wakefulness, that a social register of explanation seems absurd. Economic conditions, politics, the effects of population, laws, the presence or absence of social services, peer pressure, unresolved childhood problems – in short, the stock-in-trade of cultural film critics who deconstruct Reagan-era cinema as veiled 'social problem' films – these issues do not figure in the lyrically unmotivated dark stretches of the film. Lynch's films – especially *Blue Velvet* and to some extent *Lost Highway* (1997) – offer an encrypted retreat from the social, even as they confront its perverse symptoms head on. Many other films of Reaganite cinema, on the contrary, are encoded conflicts of a public and ultimately political sort: *Star Wars* (1977) as political conflict of empire; *Raiders of the Lost Ark* (1981) as returned-to historical conflict; *Aliens* (1986) as economic conflict of corporatism and also gender, etc. *Blue Velvet*, however, enacts a very different sort of tension difficult to read on the interpretive grid used most often by contemporary cultural film theorists in that it appears to be socially unmotivated. 'The film excavates a topography of the fantastic', suggests Laura Mulvey, 'of an underworld, out of a social setting which appears to repress its very possibility' (Mulvey 1996a: 152).

After spending time in the dark, underneath world of drugs and sexual violence, Jeffrey asks his girlfriend, Sandy – who also goes with him into this world, but only part of the way – 'Why is there so much trouble in this world?' Sandy's initial response – 'I don't know' – is followed by her story of her dream:

I had a dream. In fact, it was the night I met you. In the dream there was our world and the world was dark because there weren't any robins, and the robins represented love. And for the longest time there was just this darkness. And all of a sudden thousands of robins were set free and they flew down and brought this blinding light of love. And it seemed like that love would be the only thing that would make any difference. And it did. So I guess it means there is trouble until the robins come.

There is an overarching opposition in the film between the robins (in Sandy's dream and in one of the film's closing images of a robin with a bug in its mouth) and the bugs (in scenes such as the opening sequence, in Jeffrey's disguise as an exterminator to gain entrance into Dorothy's apartment and in the shooting script version which has Jeffrey's house infested with termites). This opposition, which culminates with the victory of the robins over the bugs and the restoration of order, casts the film's essential conflict in larger, socially unmotivated terms. Lynch himself has spoken many times of the attraction to secrets and mysteries: 'I love mysteries. I love not knowing about certain things because in the mystery I feel more than what would be there if it was explained to me' (Lynch in Hickenlooper 1991: 97). His comments on this matter are similar to comments by Flannery O'Connor, a writer who is comparable to Lynch in her presentation of grotesques amidst the normalcy of everyday life. In 1958, in a personal letter about politics, O'Connor wrote: 'The Liberal approach is that man has never fallen, never incurred guilt, and is ultimately perfectible by his own efforts. Therefore, evil in this light is a problem of better housing, sanitation, health, etc. and all mysteries will eventually be cleared up' (O'Connor 1978: 302–3). In *Blue Velvet* the 'problem of evil' is both petty (the criminals in the movie are small-time and stupid) and profound (Jeffrey's interest in what at first appears to be a simple kidnapping leads him into a difficult examination of the dark recesses of his own soul). Its gleeful, horrible foray into the American nightmare is profoundly Reaganesque – it has none of the dour, serious, bunker-mentality of the Carter years, and certainly none of the ideology of responsibility or village-ism (reflected most blatantly in *Independence Day* (1996)) of the Clinton era. Jeffrey's or Agent Cooper's 'aw-shucks' sincerity in the face of unspeakable monstrosities and violence can, if forced, be read as some kind of Quentin Tarantino-esque hip, postmodern irony, but the film is never as excessively self-aware as a Tarantino film. And this is precisely what is so curious, and ultimately significant, about *Blue Velvet*. If the postmodern glories in its own ironic artificiality, throwing itself back to the past to resurrect it with a knowing, cynical difference then Lynch's work offers a glimpse of what possibly lies ahead, after postmodernism. Lynch's films fully enact, rather than reflect, the postmodern, absurd extremes of sex, violence and decay, but with none of the high seriousness of Modernism, nor the ironic, 'in-crowd' detachment of postmodernism that began to hold sway over a lineage of the New American films beginning with Arthur Penn's *Bonnie and Clyde* (1967). The violence of Lynch's films is real, shocking and dangerous – yet it is still only a front for a greater and more mysterious disruption, a disruption that can only be met, in the language of *Blue Velvet*, by the return of the robins. The film's secret and daring question, how to account for evil in a world that no longer recognises it, is both playfully and seriously asked. Aware of two registers for asking these questions – with high seriousness or high cynicism – *Blue Velvet* and other films such as Michael Mann's *Heat* (1995) and Joel Coen's *Fargo* (1996), opt for both and neither, thus showing us an early glimpse of a sensibility emerging out of the postmodern.

The problem with a reading of *Blue Velvet* as either in league with, or ironically distanced from, the forms of nostalgia it invokes is the assumption that irony, or its lack, is today any measure of a film's level of critique. By remaining open to both possibilities, *Blue Velvet* – like David Fincher's *Fight Club* (1999), which is accessible as either a proto-fascist fantasy or else as a progressive social satire – move beyond postmodern parody and irony and instead recognise that, in an already-deconstructed culture of reality television, *The Simpsons* and self-reflexive television commercials, irony and parody no longer function as sharp weapons of critique because they are already everywhere. Thus, I would map out the 'problem' with orthodox Lynch criticism as follows: critics attempting to do the cultural work of situating Lynch's 1980s films assume that such films are complicit in the reinforcement or subversion (or, more likely, something in between) of the era's dominant cultural norms, and that Lynch's films can be properly excavated for their ideological content against the backdrop of 1980s cultural repression. In attempting to read the films through this 'finalistic' interpretive lens, critics, such as those cited above, arrive at the problem of Lynch's irony, or lack of it, and either read Lynch's work as participating in the reactionary nostalgia of the Reagan era, or else subverting it via a satirical, mock-nostalgia sensibility. And so the argument goes: if Lynch's films are ironic, they are subversive (a good thing), but if they are not ironic, they are complicit (a bad thing). Jonathan Culler and others identified the problem with this kind of path-dependent, institutionalised, over-determined film criticism long ago, with David Bordwell claiming that 'we need no more diagnoses of the subversive moment in a slasher movie, or celebrations of a "theoretical" film for its critique of mainstream cinema' (Bordwell 1989: 18). If Lynch's films do not offer an apparatus by which to demystify or reify the Reagan era, then what they do provide, perhaps, is a sensibility that offers an alternative to the binary sincerity/irony reading paradigm that has held sway since the punk era.

An Alternative Reading

I would like to approach the problem of irony in an already ironised culture by suggesting that it is in the juxtaposition of realist, 'classical' Hollywood tropes and open, abstract forms that irony is constructed by post-punk viewers conditioned to be suspicious of sincerity. In other words, Lynch's films embed their traditional narratives (boy tries to save girl, etc.) in an avant-garde cinematic tradition that most movie-going Americans are unfamiliar with, resulting in readings of Lynch as satirist or ironist, someone who is deconstructing American myths as opposed to someone who is simply exploring them in a cinematic language that has a history. A. L. Rees notes that early Hollywood 'rejected the methods of modern art in favour of a nineteenth-century realist aesthetic based on the well-rounded story and on closed rather than open forms of narration' (Rees 1999: 10). And, although linkages have often been made between Lynch's work and that of Fellini, Herzog, Tati and Wilder (especially Wilder's *Sunset Boulevard* (1950)), his work bears a striking resemblance to Maya Deren's avant-garde films, especially *Meshes of the Afternoon* (1943), which use the classical Hollywood genres and paradigms (i.e. detective story, romance) only to explore them via abstract, open and visually experimental passages. (At one point, for instance, the main character, played by Deren, confronts two other versions of herself at a table.) Deren's film 'meshes' elements of cause-and-effect, continuity-based classical narrative (for instance, who is the robed figure Deren follows throughout the film?) and formally abstract, disorienting sequences, such as Deren's attempt to climb the stairs as the camera – positioned at the top of the stairs – 'throws' her from side to side as it tilts violently from left to right.

Whereas Deren's films were self-conscious avant-garde texts (part of a cinema movement which openly articulated a creative alternative to commercial, mimetic Hollywood cinema), Lynch's films nest their experimentalism in more traditional Hollywood narrative conventions, and it is this disparity that leads to readings of his work as ironic or parodic. While *Blue Velvet* may be 'the most influential and crucial film of its decade' (Atkinson 1997: 11), I would like to suggest that it is in his most critically underestimated film, *Twin Peaks: Fire Walk with Me* (1992), that Lynch meshes the avant-garde and classical modes in disorienting ways that move beyond the orthodox postmodern logic of irony and parody, a logic which, according to Linda Hutcheon, involves a 'rummaging through the image reserves of the past in such a way as to show the history of the representations their parody calls to our attention' (Hutcheon 1989: 93). For if *Twin Peaks: Fire Walk with Me* is Lynch's most formally radical film until *Lost Highway*, it is also the one that most violently marries the logic of the classical Hollywood style and non-representational cinema. Where *Lost Highway* ultimately rejects the realist mode (although of course it is possible to provided an over-determined, Freudian reading of the film which neatly decodes its narrative logic), *Twin Peaks: Fire Walk with Me* lurches violently between its avant-garde set pieces and its sources in the conventional Hollywood and television genres of teen romance, soap opera, science-fiction and family tragedy.

What if – *Twin Peaks: Fire Walk with Me* asks – we take these moments, not as parodic, but sincere; and what if we break the 'codes' of Hollywood storytelling, but not in a self-conscious, subversive way, since the forms have already been demythologised and denaturalised? Television has done it for us, as Wallace has shown, through a now decades-long strategy of commercials that parody their own shallowness, their own attempts to sell you something. Although the filtering process is alive and growing on the internet, it still allows for relatively unmediated access to vast and vastly different types of information, and the process of accessing that information speedily through simple mouse clicks further accentuates the constructedness of those information patterns. Yet if in popular cultural forms this kind of rapid juxtaposition yields a kind of cynical irony (i.e. pick your website to get the version of the news you want – it is all just a story), in Lynch's films the aesthetics of juxtaposition point beyond this logic. In *Twin Peaks: Fire Walk with Me,* the most startling example of this is the 'moving picture' sequence where Laura 'enters' the framed photograph on her wall and thus moves – with two selves or a divided one? – between two alternate places. Although framed as a dream, the sequence proceeds with a kind of realist logic: Laura gets out of bed to look for Bob in the hallway. As she opens her closed bedroom door and moves into the doorway she stops, looks back into her bedroom and sees herself in the picture on the wall, standing in the door in the picture. In terms of representation, the scene is impossible, and it demands a kind of reading that accepts its contradictions. That is to say, in order for the film to 'work', we have to abandon a reading position that tries to explain how one visual or narrative mode ironically 'comments' on another (i.e. *Blue Velvet*'s sadomasochism comments on the film's Hardy Boys aesthetic in an ironic way) and instead accept both the avant-garde and the normative together. The scene is strikingly reminiscent of Deren's similar experiments with doubling and spatial dislocation, especially in the silent *At Land* (1944), where, in the opening sequences, Deren emerges from the ocean (its waves rolling backwards in reverse motion), climbs an enormous piece of driftwood, and finds herself crawling simultaneously through the underbrush (exterior) and a enormous banquet table, around which people sit oblivious to her presence. Like Laura Palmer, she crosses and exists in multiple spaces simultaneously, and gazes upon herself as she does so.

Dick Laurent is Dead

It has been my argument that Lynch's films were among the first to move beyond postmodernism's ironic, parodic appropriation of historical genres and narrative conventions, and that to this day readings of Lynch as 'ironic' persist because irony has become the dominant form of reading in a culture that recognises narrative (historical, political or otherwise) as mere performance. And while this form is persistent, especially in hyper-mimetic reality-TV shows such as CBS's *Survivor* and MTV's *The Real World*, which encourage an ironic, campy identification with characters who wear their identities as badges – the 'gay' character, the 'ethnic' character, the 'slut' character, etc. – there are nonetheless hints of a new sensibility that deconstructs narrative without recourse to irony or parody. It turns up in movies like Spike Jonze's *Being John Malkovich* (1999) which acknowledges the constructedness not only of identity, but of genre as well, shape-shifting between romance, drama, fantasy, without the self-satisfied, distant, ironic positioning that characterises classic 1980s postmodern films such as David Byrne's *True Stories* (1986), released in the same year as *Blue Velvet*. This 'beyond postmodern' sensibility is also evident in films such as Vincent Gallo's *Buffalo 66* (1998), whose deconstructing tendencies function without parody: its happy ending is not a knowing wink at happy endings, but rather an sincere invitation to an actual happy ending.

And if, in music, punk and new wave helped shape an ironic audience, and if grunge recontextualised the macho rock star into defeated, sexually ambivalent parody, and hip-hop's sampling/pastiche prioritised social context over text, then newer groups pillage genres and types without the self-consciousness of postmodern bands like Talking Heads or Nirvana. Bands like The Neutral Milk Hotel and The Magnetic Fields and The Flaming Lips, for instance, shift gears in just one song from folk to gospel to punk to speed metal to psychedelic without the slightest trace of parody. If postmodern rock flaunted its own performance as Performance ('Bowie's breakthrough album, *Ziggy Stardust and the Spiders from Mars*, was the first postmodern record: a sequence of songs about a mythical pop star', suggests Jon Savage (1992: 72)), then the new post-deconstructive forms – both in film and music – are more interested in pillaging old styles and genres not to demystify the Old Forms, but rather to build unstable narratives.

And *Lost Highway* is another such key narrative, one whose radicalness is not structured via juxtaposition (i.e. *Blue Velvet*'s innocence vs. experience), but rather through an integration of historical modes and genres into the narrative fabric itself, so that Fred Madison's transformation into Pete Dayton does not serve to provide the kind of contrast between, say, *Blue Velvet*'s Jeffrey and Frank. In the script, one of the scenes that was shot but cut from the movie involves Fred Madison in his death-row prison cell listening to the execution of a fellow inmate, Sammy, and the pre-execution banter between Sammy, fellow inmates, the guards and the warden. The deleted scene adds a kind of 'psychological realism' dimension to the film, helping to explain Fred's psychosis, breakdown and transformation into Pete as the result not only of possible guilt over the supposed murder of his wife, but also of outright terror. But the deletion of the scene (significantly, Lynch retained a few seconds in the form of the blue 'electrocution light' on the ceiling of Fred's cell) deflects attention away from the 'whys' of Fred's metamorphosis and towards the fact of metamorphosis itself. (One of Lynch's unproduced projects is an adaptation of Kafka's *Metamorphosis*, which Lynch says he has 'moved ... to the 1950s – '55 or '56' (Lynch in Rodley 1997: 216).) The script makes it clear that Fred actually becomes Pete in a way that is worth quoting at length:

> *Fred brings his shaking, tortured hand to his forehead. He pulls his hand down across his face squeezing it as it goes. As his hand passes over his face, Fred's features are removed leaving a blank, white mass with eye sockets...*
> *Fred's blank face begins to contort and take on the appearance, feature by feature, of Pete Dayton.*
> *Fred Madison is becoming Pete Dayton.*
> (Lynch and Gifford 1997: 48, 49)

This sequence hints that the transformation is at least in part self-created – an act of will, as Fred in effect erases his own face and identity. In Kafka's *Metamorphosis*, Gregor Samsa immediately recognises and articulates his own transformation because he literally sees the effect of his transformation, asking 'What has happened to me?' While Gregor can ask that question with at least the certainty that he has changed into something and that he recognises what he was before his transformation, for Pete what was 'before' remains out of reach. Significantly, Pete's first words are not 'What am I?' but 'Where am I?' suggesting that his dislocation might be one of space as well as personality. And it is precisely this upon which the film turns, and points beyond postmodernism's now routine and orthodox demythologising of identity, out of which films like Ridley Scott's *Blade Runner* (1982) and other canonical postmodern films emerged. For in *Lost Highway*, dislocation involves not simply identity (who am I? am I human?) but space as well: Pete might not only be someone else ('Who else could I be?' he asks Sheila) but someplace else, too. The film does not frame Pete's situation as parodic, and it resolves his crisis through a narrative device that does not 'solve' anything at all, but rather loops the process all over again, ending with the same line that began the script ('Dick Laurent is dead'). And the movie's cruel joke is that while the unknown voice that speaks the line into the Madison's intercom at the beginning has been identified as none other than Fred Madison himself, this information does not really explain anything. Solving the mystery has not solved the mystery, after all.

Judith Mayne has suggested that in classical Hollywood film, the 'importance of the subject in narrative is that all of the meaningful oppositions, crises and resolutions are addressed to a subject, i.e., positions of stability and coherence are assigned within the narrative. Put another way, narrative structures are not meaningful unless certain positions are taken up by the spectator' (Mayne 1993: 25). I would argue that Fred's/Pete's crisis is really an audience crisis, and that Lynch's narratives are structured in such a way as to complicate the viewing subject's position as voyeur, making identification itself fraught with contradiction. Whereas the postmodern text, according to Hutcheon, relies on parody and 'ironic quotation' to both legitimise and subvert 'that which it parodies' (Hutcheon 1989: 93, 101), it often does so within a narrative framework that is still coherent and stable and that still makes clear what is being parodied. This is especially true of orthodox postmodern films, such as *Blade Runner*, *Fight Club* or Terry Gilliam's *Twelve Monkeys* (1995), that raise interesting epistemological questions within a narrative framework that is heavily invested in the very classical epistemologies they subvert. Thus, both *Blade Runner* and *Twelve Monkeys* (and even Andy and Larry Wachowski's *The Matrix* (1999)) can be read by audiences as social problem films whose narrative disruptions and innovations call attention to themselves to such an extent that they come to be seen as strategies rather than ways of being. They cannot take their own deconstructing tendencies for granted because the whole point of deconstruction is to unmask the natural, to make visible the invisible. And it is to this end that irony and parody work, providing the audience a safe position (yet one that *seems* to be dangerous) from which to critique. In postmodern film, especially, the social dimension, the object of critique (i.e. commodification in *Fight Club*; slavery in *Blade Runner*; surface culture in Mary Harron's *American Psycho* (2000), surveillance culture in Steven Spielberg's *Minority Report* (2002)) is signalled through a narrative self-consciousness (direct-to-camera addresses in *Fight*

Club, for instance) that is finally a safe, familiar strategy, in a do-it-yourself culture where looking at the camera has become simply yet another storytelling method. Multinationalism, corporate greed, hegemonic social practices, nostalgia, bourgeois values and genre itself (especially in Wes Craven's *Scream* films (1996, 1997 and 2000)) are thus objects of critique in movies whose narrative cleverness (i.e. the dead narrator in Sam Mendes' *American Beauty* (1999)) finally provides the spectator a safe position from which to join the film in critique.

For a culture that has already absorbed these parodic practices (and here Wallace's essay on commercial television's postmodern aesthetics is useful), irony seems to be lurking everywhere, even in Lynch's films, which, as I have tried to show, are not really ironic at all. Like *Being John Malkovich* or Jonze's *Adaptation* (2002), whose narratives work against parody and satire even as the films can be read this way, *Lost Highway*'s subversion lies in the fact that it does not provide audiences with a comfortable, ironic position from which to make coherence from its incoherent, contradictory narrative. In Lynch's most extreme films – *Blue Velvet, Wild at Heart, Lost Highway* and *Mulholland Drive* (2001) – narrative dislocation is not simply recuperated via irony and comfortable social critique. Rather, they respect what the audience already knows: that their narratives are *already* deconstructed. In this respect it is strangely fitting that *Mulholland Drive* opened in the USA in October 2001, the month after the terrorist attacks in New York City and Washington, DC. Although it is easy now to mock those who declared 'the end of irony' in the wake of the attacks, *Mulholland Drive*'s fevered but sincere dream-logic is in many ways open to this fresh, after-postmodern era, an era symbolically born in the destruction of 9/11. Dependent upon audiences' willingness to deconstruct the mythologies of identity in a land so saturated with the fictions of Hollywood, in many ways *Mulholland Drive* addresses and points beyond the crisis of postmodernity articulated by Wallace and others: how to recover sincerity without losing the critical edge that irony provides. Although in Lynch's film the beautiful, innocent Betty is only a figment of Diane's dream, Lynch is not ironically debunking anything here, but rather recognising the chaos of contradictions – the peace and the violence, the fact and the fiction, the desire and revulsion – that go into the making of any self. These contradictions are promises that, at its best, punk recognised, and that the art of David Lynch fulfils.

Notes

1 'Nick at Night' refers to night-time programming on the Nickelodeon cable network, which runs repeats of American sitcoms from the 1950s through to the 1980s (these include *I Love Lucy, Gilligan's Island, The Brady Bunch* and *Three's Company*). The shows are packaged and promoted in a style that veers between sincere nostalgia and camp irony (with such promotional taglines as 'Don't I get enough reality in my life? No mad cows, rat eating, or home wrecking. TV land ... for TV satisfaction ... guaranteed').

2 The Velvet Underground, *The Velvet Underground and Nico*. Verve V/V6-5008.

Original release, March 1967, reissued Polygram Records 1996.

3   Blondie, 'X Offender'. Originally released as Private Stock single PS45 09 July 1976. Reissued in 1993 on *Blank Generation: The New York Scene (1975–8)*, Rhino Records.

CHAPTER SIX

Laura and Twin Peaks: Postmodern Parody and the Musical Reconstruction of the Absent Femme Fatale

John Richardson

> At the end of the series, I felt sad. I couldn't get myself to leave the world of Twin Peaks. I was in love with the character of Laura Palmer and her contradictions: radiant on the surface but dying inside. I wanted to see her live, move and talk.
>   – David Lynch in Rodley 1997: 184

> Have you ever dreamed of Laura as your wife at the policeman's ball? You'd better watch out ... or you'll end up in a psychiatric ward. I don't think they've ever had a patient who fell in love with a corpse!
>   – Waldo Lydecker to Lt. McPherson, *Laura* (Otto Preminger, 1944)

David Lynch's sentiments undoubtedly echo those of many followers of the cult television series *Twin Peaks* (1990). The motivation behind this desire to see Laura Palmer 'live, move and talk' may well vary amongst viewers; the wish to see her alive and well, however, to flesh out the bones of the elusive portrait of the character provided in the pilot and subsequent 29 episodes, does appear to have been a common feature of many viewers' experiences.[1] And yet, when this wish was finally granted in the feature film prequel, *Twin Peaks: Fire Walk with Me* (1992), the result for many viewers and critics was a conspicuous lack of fulfilment (Lavery 1995b: 3;

10–11). Clearly, more than the mystery of how she was murdered and by whom, a large part of what made *Twin Peaks* tick in dramatic and specifically audio-visual terms was precisely the tantalising and apparently unbridgeable distance created by Lynch between Laura and the viewing and *listening* subject – a distance created and sustained by the fragmentary visions *and sounds* of the female protagonist provided, which, in the words of Michel Chion, 'serve[d] everyone as a prop for their own projections and fantasies' (Chion 1995: 144–5).

Here I will look at the role of music and sound in the construction of these projections and fantasies, particularly in the pilot episode of *Twin Peaks*. Another aim is to elucidate the role played by allusions to other films and genres as a means of channelling the interpretative strategies of the viewer-listener. Arguably, the most significant intertextual point of reference in the series is to Otto Preminger's film, *Laura* (1944). Numerous other relevant touchstones have been identified, including Stanley Kubrick's *Lolita* (1962), *noir* classics such as Alfred Hitchcock's *Vertigo* (1958) and Billy Wilder's *Sunset Boulevard* (1950), as well as the audio-visual and narrative conventions of television soaps. Here, though, I will concentrate on the Preminger film, and more broadly on the sub-genre to which it belongs, that of *film noir*, as I believe these to be the most illuminating points of reference when considering the reconstruction of the character of Laura Palmer in music and sound.

In his seminal study on Lynch, Michel Chion makes little of these allusions, although somewhat paradoxically much of his writing seems concerned with unpacking them (1995: 113–14).[2] While the following discussion contests Chion's position, it is not my wish to reduce *Twin Peaks* to a small number of intertextual allusions. On the contrary, by invoking relevant intertexts and by doing so from a critical distance, marked in this case as postmodern, the series affirms its irreducible difference with respect to these genealogical touchstones. However, as David Lavery notes, the recognition of salient intertexts does appear to have been a determining feature of the reception of the series:

> a large part of the series' appeal to aficionados … was tracking its intertextual, allusionary quotations: the many actors and actresses reborn from the never-never land of old TV and movies; the red herring evocations of old movies; allusions to previous Lynch movies; numerous inside jokes; cameos by Lynch … Frost … and even Lynch's son Austin. … These and many other facets of *Twin Peaks* invited fanatic, cultic participation, generating discourse about discourse. (Lavery 1995b; 6)

One of the more successful attempts to account for intertextual allusion in postmodernist art is Linda Hutcheon's influential study on parody (Hutcheon 1985). According to Hutcheon, parody is a form of bitextuality wherein the 'source' and 'new' texts are allowed to coexist, always asserting their difference, and yet rarely, as might be the case in earlier forms of parody, 'coming to blows' – with the latter in some way 'subtracting' from the former. Hutcheon arrives at this definition by reconsidering the etymology of the Greek word *parodia*. The sememe 'para', she observes, can be translated as 'beside', suggesting accord or intimacy, in contrast to more conventional definitions which translate it as 'counter' or 'against', thereby implying opposition or antagonism (Hutcheon 1985: 32). Some sense of 'critical distance' is usually implied between the parodied text and the new, however, which is often characterised by irony. But irony, Hutcheon argues, can be playful – it does not only denigrate. Postmodernist parody, involving both 'complicity and distance', a simultaneous 'respectful homage and ironically thumbed nose' (Hutcheon 1985: 32, 33), is, I would contend, the dominant mode of representation in *Twin Peaks* and it is a far more illuminating concept in this context than the Jamesonian notion of 'pastiche', defined as 'blank parody, parody that has lost its sense of humor' (Jameson 1983: 114).

Here we will see ample evidence of bitextual parodic dialogue between source and new texts. This essay begins with a broad discussion of the conventions of *film noir*, with particular attention paid to one of its key elements, the presence of a *femme fatale* character. After a general discussion of how these conventions might inform constructions of character and narrative in *Twin Peaks*, I will proceed to a close examination of a key source text, Preminger's film, *Laura*, in relation to one specific episode of the series, the pilot, which I consider to be a distillation of the series.

Twin Peaks as film noir parody

Twin Peaks resembles, and at the same time parodies, *film noir* conventions in several ways. In fact, it fulfils all of the criteria for the sub-genre as identified by Christine Gledhill (1978: 14–19). First, it is based on an investigative narrative structure in which a male detective embarks upon a moral quest in search of a rational explanation to the irrational (largely feminine) world into which he has been plunged by his quest. Occupants of this world include *femmes fatales* and other, less interesting women cast in the role of victims. (In *Twin Peaks*, as in some examples of *film noir*, these roles are combined.) Second, it features both flashbacks and the use of voice-over: Agent Cooper's taped conversations with Diane (for example 00.35.00 [hours.minutes.seconds]) can be considered to parody the conventional *film noir* voice-over. Third, *Twin Peaks* features numerous shifts in point of view 'where a single woman is seen from several viewpoints – either by different characters (as in [Preminger's] *Laura*) or at different moments in time', producing 'a fractured, incoherent image' (Gledhill 1978: 17). Fourth, the characterisation of the heroine of *Twin Peaks*, like its classic *film noir* model, incorporates various role- and character-switches behind which the true personality of the *femme fatale* remains shrouded in mystery; this is in contrast to the male protagonist's identity, which is invariably more coherent and stable. Finally, *Twin Peaks* resembles *film noir* in certain aspects of its distinctive visual style. It is true that confusion of the categories 'good' and 'evil', an emphasis on betrayal (of various characters by Laura), the extreme violence of the *Twin Peaks* underworld, the apparent promiscuity of Laura, and the numerous complex twists in the plot of the series place it firmly in

Lieutenant McPherson (Dana Andrews) and the image of Laura (Gene Tierney) in *Laura*

the domain of the contemporary and bring to mind the category 'neo-*noir*' (see Cobb 1999: 207–13). However, the extensive use of parodic allusion in *Twin Peaks*, resulting in a distinctive combination of complicity and distance, serves to differentiate the series from films such as Paul Verhoeven's *Basic Instinct* (1992), in which playful bitextual strategies are arguably less explicitly in evidence, although parody does seem to be a dominant strategy in more recent 'neo-*noirs*' such as Quentin Tarantino's *Pulp Fiction* (1994).

Twin Peaks, therefore, while standing at a parodic distance from *film noir*, makes clear reference to all its defining characteristics. Resemblances in plot between *Twin Peaks* and *Laura* are not, therefore, 'superficial', as Chion contends, but quite substantial. The plots of both are about detectives who become romantically attached to an absent female protagonist whilst investigating her murder. Both women are stereotyped as *film noir femmes fatales*, in neither case unambiguously, and music plays an active role in reinforcing conventions associated with this category. Moreover, in both cases static portraits of the women (in *Laura*, a painting; in *Twin Peaks*, a photograph) are prominent, and become the canvas onto which characteristics of the dead protagonist's personality, reconstructed (or imagined?) by the detectives in the course of their investigations, are projected. In *Twin Peaks*, there are numerous sub-plots, in keeping with its status as a soap opera (albeit a parody), but the main plot is concerned with the relationship between Laura Palmer and Agent Cooper. In the Preminger film, Laura returns to life; in *Twin Peaks*, she does not. Had she done so, however, it would no longer be accurate to speak of an allusion, but of a direct appropriation of a key source text.

Laura Palmer as femme fatale parody

As for Laura Palmer (Sheryl Lee) herself, Chion describes her as a 'mixed-up, small-town, high-school girl' (Chion 1995: 114), but clearly she is more than this. The poignancy of the 'Homecoming Queen' photographic portrait of Laura, seen on numerous occasions in the series and during the closing titles of each episode (with the exception of the pilot), inheres in the fact that this image of the girl bears little resemblance to almost everything Agent Cooper finds out about her in the course of his investigation. The contrast is most evident in Cooper's encounter with Laura at the end of the pilot (00.42.08). Here Laura's appearance and behaviour are very much in keeping with the role occupied by the *film noir femme fatale*. She appears in a low-cut, black velvet evening dress with a high split, and she is lavishly adorned with a necklace similar to those worn by the *femme fatale* stars of both *Laura* and *Vertigo*; both sonically and semantically she is an enigma, and she exudes an air of sexually self-aware sophistication that is impossible to reconcile with the school-girl portrait. This aspect of the construction of her character invites comparison with Kubrick's *Lolita* (as noted by Chion 1995: 115), although the resemblance is fairly superficial due to Lynch's character's unrealistic precociousness: in this scene, Laura Palmer is cast as a mature adult, not as a child mimicking adult behaviour as is most definitely the case in *Lolita* (Nochimson 1995: 151). Above all, it is the enigmatic quality of Laura, a characteristic not ordinarily associated with adolescents, which connects her most closely with the *femmes fatales* of *film noir*. As Richard Dyer puts it,

women in *film noir* are above all else unknowable. It is not so much their evil as their unknowability (and attractiveness) that makes them fatal for the hero. To the degree that culture is defined by men, what is, and is known, is male. *Film noir* thus divides the world into that which is unknown and unknowable (female) and, again by inference only, that which is known (male). (Dyer 1978: 92)

Laura Palmer (of *Twin Peaks*, but not *Twin Peaks: Fire Walk with Me*) is in many ways the paradigmatic unknowable woman. This unknowability is most obviously exemplified visually in the use of static portraits, which serve as *idées fixes* in both *Twin Peaks* and *Laura*, and which undoubtedly raise more questions than they answer concerning the characters of both of these women. There are clear musical and sonic parallels to the use of this technique, as I will explain.

To be sure, the use of portraits in both *Twin Peaks* and *Laura* reinforces the patriarchally marked dichotomy that casts men as active/mobile and positions women as passive/static objects of the male gaze. This is not the whole story, however. Notwithstanding recent critiques of the gaze as exclusively male and the recipients of its attention as exclusively female, the character of Laura Palmer appears to re-write conventional gender positions, deflecting and returning the objectifying gaze in several key scenes.[3] In these scenes, Laura seems to be looking at us – albeit as though from another world. This is most evident in the interrogation sequences with Agent Cooper, where a home video is shown to witnesses in which Laura is witnessed in a state of self-absorbed – one might even say ecstatic – motion, thus deflecting the gaze, which demands a passive, motionless object (00.48.38; 00.54.13). Moreover, towards the end of this sequence, Laura approaches the camera and seems to look right through its lens at Agent Cooper and beyond him to the viewer (00.50.00; 00.56.15). Here there would appear to be some possibility of positive identification and self-empowerment for the female spectator. Adrienne McLean (1993) has argued that women are similarly empowered in *film noir*, most notably in the song and dance numbers of films such as Charles Vidor's *Gilda* (1946). Like Rita Hayworth in *Gilda*, Laura dances in these sequences, and her constant, impulsively playful motion suggests a sense of agency and, above all, pleasure that is all the more striking because of her reduction to the status of static object in the remainder of the series.

The darker, more menacing side of the *femme fatale* is also invoked in these sequences, however. Laura's return of the gaze is reminiscent of the opening credits of *Vertigo*, where, to the accompaniment of Bernard Herrmann's spiralling arpeggios, the eye of a woman becomes a kind of dehumanised, irrational whirlpool into which the male protagonist and (by identification) the viewer are irresistibly drawn. The same admixture of enigmatic self-empowerment and aggressive dehumanisation is present in both of the above examples and has similar implications in each case.

Such ambivalence typifies perceptions of the *film noir femme fatale*. Janey Place speaks for many feminist film critics when she asserts that while *film noir* is without question a male fantasy that reinforces a fundamentally phallocentric viewpoint, it is 'one of the few periods in film in which women are ... intelligent and powerful, if destructively so, and derive power, not weakness from their sexuality' (Place 1978: 35). Furthermore, she observes that the cinematic language of this sub-genre is 'so highly stylised and conventionalised that the final "lesson" of the myth [that such women are dangerous and should be punished or domesticated for their perceived transgressions] often fades into the background and we retain an image of the erotic, strong, unrepressed (if destructive) woman' (1978: 36). But is this the case with Laura, whose death and conspicuous absence from the greater part of the series would seem to overshadow any visions of her as 'strong' and 'unrepressed'? And is the parodic distance implied between source and new texts always sufficient to refract the ideological underpinnings of the former relating to the didactic content of the plot, or are there moments when characterisation in Lynch's series adds little, in the way of contemporary critical perspective, to the intertexts that are its building blocks? It is necessary to listen to as well as to look at the character in order to paint a more complete portrait of her, as it is ultimately in music and sound that she is made to 'live, move and talk'.

The Musical Representation of Infatuation – Two Instances of Monothematic Scoring

Arguably all of the music in *Twin Peaks* is related in some way to the character of Laura Palmer. I am going to restrict the present discussion, however, to the music which relates most directly – in a limited sense, leitmotivically – to this character, including:

(i)   the music heard at the beginning and end of each episode called 'The Twin Peaks theme';

(ii)   the romantic theme referred to by Lynch and composer Angelo
        Badalamenti as 'Laura's theme'; and

(iii)   the diegetic song based on the melody from 'The Twin Peaks
        theme', called 'Falling'.

So saturated is the soundtrack with this music, all of it closely related thematically, that one might almost refer to the entire soundtrack of the series as monothematic, a term Roy Prendergast employs in his discussion of David Raksin's music to Preminger's *Laura*. Themes not related to the three Laura themes generally have an improvisatory or colourist flavour ('Audrey's Dance', 'Dance of the Dream Man', 'Night Life in Twin Peaks'), and they are usually interrupted at some point by one of the more overtly melodic Laura themes (for example, 'The Bookhouse Boys' and 'Dance of the Dream Man').[4]

In Preminger's *Laura*, the music participates in the construction of character by drawing on conventions familiar to the audience from their experience of the music of other films and more general musical codes: for example, the association of jazz with poverty and depravity, and of classical music with respectability and high social standing.[5] All of this was in keeping with the artistic aims of the director Otto Preminger, who reportedly characterised the leading lady as 'a whore', to which composer David Raksin claims to have replied 'by whose standards?'[6] But more important than characterisation is the role repeated hearings of the theme play in the structure of the film. The music quite literally turns up everywhere. At first diegetically, on a record left in the apartment of the apparently deceased leading lady, which the detective is told was one of Laura's favourites (00.13.10). The theme is heard again diegetically in a restaurant (00.15.50), before it eventually crosses over into the subjective world of the detective and his antagonist, when it is heard non-diegetically to accompany both the flashbacks of Waldo Lydecker and the fetishistic fantasies of Lieutenant McPherson as he peruses Laura's apartment and belongings (00.21.00; 00.41.38). The music plays an important role, therefore, in conveying the infatuation of both of these characters (most of all, the detective) with the (at the time) totally unreciprocating (indeed, almost *irrelevant*) woman named Laura. To his credit, Raksin imparted to Laura's theme an elegiac tenderness that perfectly captures the main affective thrust of the film – the detective's amorous intent towards his unattainable (and, initially, unknowable) object of desire. Although it is stylistically dissimilar to Laura Palmer's themes, it does share certain structural characteristics; most notably, a descending diatonic line in the melody (B, A, G), a widely recognised signifier of lament in Western music since the renaissance (see overleaf).[7] What composer Angelo Badalamenti refers to as the 'falling' section of 'The Twin Peaks theme' is based on the same musical affect.

Laura Palmer's music is every bit as ubiquitous as that of her 1940s namesake. Or, as the Man from Another Place puts it in the final scene of the pilot episode, Twin Peaks is a place where 'there's always music in the air', suggesting perhaps a similar obsessive tendency. But, in order to understand more fully the semiotic workings of the music and its attendant associative formations, it is necessary to

Laura, Laura's theme

examine more closely each of the themes associated with the character in relation to the specific audio-visual instances in which they become anchored to meanings that constitute the main narrative infrastructure for the entire series.

'The Twin Peaks theme'

The first and arguably the most memorable use of music is 'The Twin Peaks theme', heard during the opening and closing credits. Several associations are fostered during these sequences which help to establish certain pervasive archetypes upon which the series is steadfastly grounded. The first of these involves a blurring of the conventional nature/culture dyad. The very first shot is of a bird (00.00.00), which viewers familiar with the final scene of *Blue Velvet* (1986) will recognise as an ironic symbol of idyllic well-being in small-town America (George 1995: 111). In the film, the bird's movements are obviously mechanised, drawing attention to the hackneyed artificiality of the film's too-good-to-be-true happy ending. In this context, Lynch does not go quite so far in signalling ironic intent, but awareness of the resonance of this scene with this earlier instance might suffice to indicate that this is the case. This segues into a shot of the Twin Peaks sawmill (00.00.03), thus establishing the timber industry as pivotal to the divine order of the rural community. Shots of machinery in the sawmill are strongly aestheticised through partial synchronisation with the music (00.00.12). Indeed, the machinery takes on an anthropomorphic quality, at the same time imparting to the organic world a substratum of mechanical certainty, of black-and-white reassuring truths, and of stability and continuity – much as the ironically, because excessively, stalwart character of Agent Cooper brings to mind similar qualities. But these qualities, the music tells us, are grounded not in the present day but in late 1950s North America, a time of rapid economic growth which witnessed the explosion of a youth culture whose impact has conditioned many aspects of Lynch's contemporary and mythological artistic universe. But there is something unnerving about this machinery that seems to have a life; intimations of a terrifying power that is fully manifested in the electrical noises heard through-out the series and at the end of the closing credits of each episode. This sonic idea is reiterated on many levels throughout the series, most notably in numerous electrical disturbances that are invariably associated with the presence of evil and are both visually and audibly indicated. A discrepancy that signals ironic distance between the opening sequence's idyllic vision of nature and industry in harmony and these more unsettling effects, is indicated also in the music, which invokes the 1950s but does not quite succeed in taking the listener to that era. The twangy retro-guitar sound (in fact, significantly, synthetically produced) of the first section of the theme music (00.00.00) is a little too clean, and a little too stereotyped to successfully capture the innocence and integrity of authentic 1950s youth culture.

The second section of 'The Twin Peaks theme' comprises an over-the-top build-up to a cadence featuring a rising diatonic line that eventually weaves its way to its utopian goal, a strong cadential resolution onto the tonic (00.00.12). The romantic nature of the melody is confirmed in its orchestration for strings, but also in the lyrics of the song version of the theme. Performed diegetically in the pilot episode, this section of the melody culminates on the line 'Are we falling in love?' – the word love coinciding with the return to the tonic (00.00.36; 01.12.45).

Twin Peaks, 'falling' motif

The third and final section of the theme is arguably the most semantically pregnant. Here a repeated four-note diatonic descent, which lingers tantalisingly on the supertonic (the second degree of the scale) before eventually resolving to the tonic, is clearly recognisable as the same lament trope encountered in Raksin's music to Preminger's *Laura* (see Example 2). In the song version, the word 'falling' is extracted from the previous section (the line 'falling in love'), and this is repeated several times on its own. Falling is a recurrent motif of the opening sequence, but also of the entire series. In the visual images accompanying this section, the first shots of a waterfall are shown and subsequently of river water descending, presumably towards the lake in which Laura Palmer's body is found (00.01.40).[8]

'Laura's Theme'

An elaboration of the final two sections of 'The Twin Peaks theme' is found in what Lynch and Badalamenti refer to as 'Laura's theme', which is possibly a lightly-veiled allusion to Raksin's theme of the same name. This music sounds when Laura Palmer's body is identified, and coincides with the first mention of the character by name (00.07.35). It is linked leitmotivically to her from this moment on – most notably in instances when her portrait is shown, such as the closing credits of each episode.

The extended 'falling' section of the theme is heard when Leland Palmer drops a telephone after hearing of his daughter's death (00.14.13). Here the downward panning of the camera along the length of the phone cord provides a visual parallel to the irrevocable descent of the melody. Chion makes a pertinent observation regarding the symbolic significance of the telephone cord in scenes such as this. When discussing two examples from French cinema, he notes that 'there is a relationship to be pointed out between the vocal connection, umbilical cords and telephone cords' (Chion 1999: 62). This is a nurturing connection, which due to the tenuous nature of the link is easily ruptured. So, as Laura Palmer's mother screams out in grief and her father allows the telephone receiver to fall from his hands, the umbilical connection is severed and both the idyllic vision of the Palmers' nuclear family and the picket-fenced innocence of small-town North America are torn asunder. Aside from this symbolic association with the deceased protagonist and, implicitly, her family, as well as the loss of innocence implied by her death, the 'falling' section of the theme is linked indexically to the decline of industry in the Twin Peaks region following the murder. The fall of Laura, therefore, takes on a significance broader than the tragedy of the death itself, representing both the decline of Twin Peaks and of rural America.

Kathryn Kalinak has noted that the use of this theme is incongruous in the scenes in which it is heard, romantic music being 'inappropriate' in scenes where audiences would expect to be horrified or shocked. While I would agree that a kind of defamiliarisation is effected by the 'hyper-stylised, excessive quality of the score' (Kalinak 1995: 89), this is not achieved by the use of anempathetic techniques (see Chion 1994: 8–9). The use of 'Laura's theme' in moments of emotional excess is not a radical departure from convention; in the context of television soap-operas, it is *all too* conventional – wherein lies its parodic force. Kalinak seems to acknowledge this in the final sentence of her essay, where she notes: 'Music ... is "too" everything in *Twin Peaks*: too insistent, too excessive, too loud, too disorientating, too familiar, and ultimately, too irresistible' (1995: 90–1).

As an example of anempathetic audio-visual relations, Kalinak provides several examples of 'Laura's theme' becoming divorced from the character whose name it bears. Examples of this include romantic encounters between James (Laura's 'legitimate' boyfriend prior to her murder) and Donna, and between James and Madeleine. In the first instance, however, the couple are discussing a golden heart that belonged to Laura, while the second encounter is with a double of Laura played by the same actress, Sheryl Lee. Although physically absent, Laura makes her presence felt in both scenes. A third example takes place after Audrey's unsuccessful attempt to seduce Agent Cooper. Here, Kalinak writes, we are encouraged 'to interpret Audrey's behavior as somehow tragic or pathetic and Cooper's behavior as gallant and noble' (1995: 90). This is a valid observation, although in terms of point of view as articulated in the music, a significant additional layer of meaning can be identified. The presence of the theme at this moment intimates that the main reason Cooper has no interest in Audrey is his growing infatuation with Laura. The musical text imparts this knowledge, just as the music heard when Lieutenant McPherson searches Laura Hunt's apartment leaves little doubt about his growing attachment to the woman he has been summoned to investigate. On the surface, Agent Cooper seems relatively immune to the emotional excess of 'Laura's theme', but already at the end of the pilot we see and hear him falling prey to the heartrending appeal of the character and her music.

'My arms bend back at the elbows' – Defamiliarisation through Technological Mediation

So how is this desire of Agent Cooper's (Lynch's alter-ego?) to see Laura Palmer 'live, move and talk' articulated in sonic terms? As suggested in the opening paragraph of this essay, much of the allure of Laura Palmer inheres not in what we know about her, but in what it is seemingly impossible to find out. So while the romantic piano theme undoubtedly becomes associated leitmotivically with perceived personal traits of Laura, and conforms closely to the sweeter-than-sweet photographic image of her, we have seen already that the excessive nature of the theme, the excesses of the characters' reactions to her death, and the camera's constant homing in on the photographic image of her all serve to call into question this version of reality. All of these are strategies of defamiliarisation, which encourage the viewer to take a critical step backwards. This step guides the viewer away from the 'face value' of events – which positions Laura unequivocally as a mixed-up small-town girl and high-school sweetheart. It also, however, nudges the viewer towards the domain of parody, which, as Hutcheon has shown, does not cancel out the source meaning but simply adds to it a corrosive parallel substratum.

The vision of Laura fashioned is fragmentary, internally inconsistent and unfathomable. We catch glimpses but never do we get a sense that we are seeing and hearing the whole picture. The presence of excessive, and therefore parodic, gestures in the music is one way of creating instability, of implying that this version of Laura is not the whole truth and thus creating a vacuum where knowledge concerning Laura ought to be. Not all of the sonic techniques employed by Lynch and his collaborators are, strictly speaking, musical, however – or perhaps as the Man from Another Place, or indeed Roland Barthes, might tell us, the sensuous sonic surfaces of *Twin Peaks* can be perceived as *nothing but music*.[9] In Lynch's work in television and film, as in many other multimedia artforms that have been labelled postmodern, the surface textures of the sound, its sensual materiality, are explored to such an extent that conventional narrative substance is eclipsed. Barthes writes of 'the grain of the voice' (Barthes 1977b), and Jameson has made much of a perceived turn towards surfaces, a new depthlessness, in recent artistic production (Jameson 1991: 6). It is easy to see Lynch in this light, but attention to exterior pleasures should not lead to neglect of interior ones, since invariably there is some degree of reciprocity between the two.

Distancing by means of attention to surface textures is conveyed perhaps most obviously in connection with the character of Laura in her voice. In a sense (or, to be more accurate, *in sense*), Laura Palmer is mute. She does have her own way of talking, however: backwards. In scenes reminiscent of the cinematic experiments of Jean Cocteau, Agent Cooper converses with Laura in several surrealistic encounters in the mythological Other space referred to as the Black Lodge, which, significantly, is curtained in red. The most noteworthy of these encounters occur in the pilot (00.42.08) and the final episode of the series. In these scenes, Sheryl Lee and the other actors spoke their lines and acted backwards when recording their parts. These clips are then played back in reverse making them just about comprehensible to the attentive listener; with the use of subtitles they are made fully comprehensible, in contrast to Agent Cooper's speech which is normal. The result is a fairly obvious defamiliarisation technique which draws attention to the production apparatus in true Brechtian style, but, more obviously, sets Laura Palmer and the other inhabitants of this world apart from the 'normal' world of the main storyline.

In Preminger's *Laura*, sounds associated with the title character are manipulated in a similar way, and arguably to similar effect. Here, though, it is the piano and not the human voice that is mechanically treated. In a key scene in the film, when McPherson is searching Laura's apartment and first comes under her spell, an elaborate (if primitive, from today's standpoint) process of physically turning off the microphone for the initial attack of the piano chords and combining this sound with sections of recorded piano played in reverse was employed, resulting in a markedly otherworldly effect (Prendergast 1991: 66–77). The ghostly 'distance' from which this Laura's theme is apprehended due to manipulation of the source sounds provides a sonic parallel to the apparently unbridgeable distance between the detective and the woman he is investigating, and engenders in the listener a desire to bridge this distance and to apprehend the untreated source sounds – and thus to approach the living, breathing Laura. This process resembles those discussed by Chion under the category of the *acousmêtre*, wherein the disembodied cinematic voice exerts a powerful, or magical, influence over characters in the diegesis who come into contact with it (Chion 1999: 17–29). The power of this voice inheres in its ability to cross boundaries, which can be attributed to the fact that it is not bonded to a visual source within the diegesis. In the Black Lodge, however, Laura is visible and can be heard; the relationship between visual and auditory material is merely strained, not severed. Denis Smalley's concept of 'source bonding' might shed further light on the affective impact of this technique (Smalley 1997). Source bonding describes an interpretive strategy whereby the listener intuitively attempts to relate sounds to their real or imagined sources, making use of his or her previous experiences and cultural conditioning regarding the make up of the sonic world.[10] Here, however, the stakes of crossing the divide between manipulated and source sounds are raised by the location of an elusive object of desire at the source. Not only does the listener desire to see and hear Laura due to the machinations of the plot, but because it is his or her predilection as a listener to attempt to reconstruct the voice in its unmediated guise. The two strategies, dramatic and rhetorical, reinforce one another.

The dislocated voice of Laura Palmer can be heard in another context. In a tangible sense, the voice of Julee Cruise, who lip-synchs to the song 'Falling' in a markedly unconvincing diegetic performance in the Roadhouse in *Twin Peaks* (01.12.01), becomes the surrogate voice of Laura Palmer. Due to the presumably intentional non-realism of this scene and the electronic manipulation of the singer's voice through the use of a heavy reverb, Cruise sings from a distance that clearly parallels the distance between the Other world that Laura Palmer has *fallen* into and the primary diegetic world of the other characters. The lyrics of the song 'Falling' (written by Lynch) reinforce this impression since they can easily be understood as representing Laura's point of view. The second verse of the song is as follows:

Don't let yourself be hurt this time
Don't let yourself be hurt this time
Then your kiss so soft
Then your touch so warm
The stars still shine bright
The mountains still high
Yet something is different
Are we falling in love?

The first line, if recognised as articulating Laura's subject position as related to events in the diegesis, seems to reflect upon the incestuous abuse of the character which culminates in her murder. References to sensual experience undoubtedly reinforce the image of Laura as sexually active in addition to the more banal primary level of signification implying romantic attachment. These references could implicate any number of male characters; several are identified as Laura Palmer's actual or potential partners, including her father and, perhaps most significantly given his obsessive interest in Laura, Agent Cooper. Yet the reference to a 'touch so warm' is unsettling in light of the fact that the character whose (surrogate) voice we are hearing is dead. 'Something', which seems to elude the singer of 'Falling' and its subject, Laura, is indeed 'different'; and as the scene I turn to next illustrates, this difference, and the distance it implies, is indicated in Laura's real, as well as her surrogate, voice.

As already discussed, the allure of the *film noir femme fatale* is that she is unknowable – so elusive is she that any attempt to bridge the divide between her and the rational world of the male detective is apparently predestined to fail. Yet it is precisely the impossibility of piecing together the fragments of the narrative mystery and of the various, apparently incongruous, aspects of her character, combined in no small measure with her implied sexuality, that make it impossible for the luckless detective to turn away from his epic quest. Humpty Dumpty's *femme fatale* incarnation has fallen off the waterfall – as evidence of this trauma, Laura Palmer's arms 'bend back at the elbows' – and with it the detective's, and perhaps the viewer's, predilection to attempt to put her back together again.

Yet, in *Twin Peaks* the pieces do not fit. More than that, the puzzle can be recognised as a puzzle – as artefact, a rhetorical construct. The combination of conspicuous distancing techniques and numerous obvious (and more esoteric) intertextual allusions makes it hard to say with any certainty what *Twin Peaks* is *about*. Superficially, the story tells of a paradoxical *femme fatale*/'family girl' compound who comes to woe in part because she was abused as a child, but also, it is implied, because of her independence vis-à-vis the patriarchy linked to her dangerously heightened sexuality. In studies of such roles in *film noir*, a subtext has been identified relating to the paranoia of patriarchal society in the United States in the post-Second World War years (Kaplan 1978: 3). But *Twin Peaks* can hardly be reduced to this explanation; it is, on one level at least, a parodic, anti-realist narrative *about* such narratives.

This would seem to result in something of an interpretive impasse, which might, however, be side-stepped by bringing into play poststructuralist theory pertaining to the voice. In her influential study, *The Acoustic Mirror: The Female Voice in Psychoanalysis and Cinema* (1988), Kaja Silverman draws on the ideas of Chion, Julia Kristeva and others in theorising a form of discourse in recent cinema that invokes the Lacanian 'imaginary'. Located by Kristeva within the self-enclosed, quasi-mythic domain of the *chora*, the Lacanian imaginary serves as a reconstitution through language of the subject (Kristeva 1980a: 133–9). Not surprisingly, the vehicle par excellence for this reconstitution is posited by Silverman and others to be the mother's voice, or, by extension, any sonic experience which invokes the imagined plenitude of early childhood; ultimately, in utero experience (the enclosed nature of the *chora*, among other things, suggests imagined female interiority) (Silverman 1988: 101–40). Regarding the possible driving force behind this construction, Alice Kuzniar writes:

> In *Twin Peaks* it is not surprisingly the woman's voice that is particularly fetishised and separated from the rest of her body, functioning as a surrogate for what remains hidden from view and thereby generating a powerful longing for a more complete revelation ... the voice pledges metonymically to signify Laura's body, about whose drug and sexual abuse the *Twin Peaks* addict pruriently wants to learn more. (Kuzniar 1995: 123)

The metonymic extension of the voice does not stop there, however, and in considering further the affective implications of invocations of a maternal pre-symbolic, it should be noted that many theorists conceive of this subjective 'place apart' in markedly equivocal terms. Whilst the notion of the *chora* as maternal sanctuary has enjoyed currency in much of the literature, Kristeva and Chion point also to its oppressive or destructive side – a nightmarish experience of loss of control, subjective annihilation within an all-encompassing phallic feminine (Kristeva 1980a: 206; Chion 1999).[11] It is this fantasy that is enacted in the Red Room of Lynch's Black Lodge and the events that take place within its curtained confines. This claustrophobic Other space can easily be recognised as a primarily, although not unequivocally, dysphorically encoded *choric* construct. Here Laura Palmer whispers to Agent Cooper in incoherent tones (00.46.48) – not quite dead but certainly not alive. Here her strangely dislocated utterances captivate at the same time as they repel, and entice as they seem to ward-off the listener-viewer. Intimations of this space are offered also in the performances of Cruise, which, to be sure, challenge dominant modes of representation, but also offer a haunting parodic vision of a strongly feminised musical and cultural mainstream whose insipid, almost non-human, naivety seems to serve as a warning.[12] When it comes to interpretations of *Twin Peaks*, however, it is probably best to steer clear of unequivocal and univocal answers. Just as Laura herself is subject to the pulls and eddies of a dark, apparently all-engulfing undertow, so the upbeat optimism of pseudo-1950s rural America finds its distorted mirror image in the limitless nihilism, corruption, anger and perversion of BOB and the proprietors and clientele of One Eyed Jack's. Each is inconceivable without the other.

So just what is it that David Lynch is trying to tell us? If we listen carefully we might just solve the mystery. But, like Agent Cooper, after his discussion with Laura in the Black Lodge in which she reveals the identity of her murderer, we might have trouble remembering what we were told in the morning.

Notes

1   The reception of *Twin Peaks* among female viewers has not been adequately researched. While much has been written on the series by female researchers and critics, research on the *Twin Peaks* discussion group alt.tv.twinpeaks regretfully acknowledges a preponderance of male research subjects, which allows only for speculation as to broader female audience responses to the series. See Jenkins 1995: 60–1.

2   While pointing to a number of clear and obviously intentional references to Preminger's *Laura* in *Twin Peaks*, Chion nevertheless dismisses his findings as tangential to an overall understanding of the series. For Chion, *Twin Peaks* is not an example of *film noir*, as evidenced by the absence of characteristic markers of the genre, such as a central role occupied by a femme fatale character; instead, the series is considered best discussed in its own terms, as the authentic and original product of the creative mind of the auteur David Lynch. He writes: 'Too much has been made of the quotes and allusions in *Twin Peaks*. The references to Preminger's *Laura* via a mina bird named Waldo and a veterinarian named Lydecker who jointly form the name of *Laura*'s Pygmalion, and to Hitchcock's *Vertigo* (1958) via Laura's look-alike cousin Madeleine, are no more than the manifestation of a debt towards two well-known films with analogous basic situations. These situations were then incorporated and interpreted differently in each case. The only part of *Twin Peaks* which is clearly modelled on *film noir* is also its weakest section – James Hurley's love affair, in the second series, with a colourless 1940s femme fatale' (Chion 1995: 113–14). This quotation is in line with Chion's approach to avant-garde cinema in his more recent writing, in which he advocates a form of neo-auteurism to combat the excesses of poststructuralist audience-centred approaches, recognising that the construct of the directorial auteur weighs heavily in the reception of contemporary cinema (see Chion 2001). In placing such a strong emphasis on the auteur at the expense of widely recognised cinematic and televisual intertexts, however, Chion risks eclipsing one form of contextual sensitivity with another. A related

concern emerges in his writing on Stanley Kubrick, in which the films *2001: A Space Odyssey* (1968) and *Eyes Wide Shut* (1999) are seen as adumbrating a non-referential aesthetic of 'absolute cinema' (Chion 2001). While it is clear that his usage of this term is not naïve, the problematic nature of the concept of 'the absolute' as illuminated in so much of the recent criticism makes some degree of qualification and explanation of the concept desirable.

3   For a polemical opening statement concerning voyeuristic pleasures in cinema, see Mulvey 1975. More recent criticism (such as Kaplan 1983; Hutcheon 1989: 151) does not hold the gaze to be inherently male, but suggests that both men and women can occupy dominant and submissive roles and highlights the possibility of 'against the grain' readings of even conventional cinematic texts.

4   Titles are taken from the CD, Angelo Badalamenti, *Twin Peaks (TV Soundtrack)*. Warner 7599 26316 2.

5   On the use of jazz in *film noir*, see Porfirio 1999.

6   For more on the background to the music of *Laura* see Royal S. Brown's interview with David Raksin in *Overtones and Undertones: Reading Film Music* (Brown 1994: 283–4). For a discussion of the music to *Laura*, see also Prendergast 1991: 58–68 and Kalinak 1992: 159–83.

7   For more on the background of the lament, historically and in contemporary contexts, see Richardson 1999: 62–8.

8   It is significant that the composer Badalamenti refers to this section as 'the Falling Part' (Givens 2000).

9   For more on the sonic aspects of Lynch's approach to cinema and music/sound-effect ambiguities, see Annette Davison's contribution to this volume. See also Chion 1995.

10   Smalley defines 'source bonding' as the 'natural tendency to relate sounds to supposed sources and causes, and to relate sounds to each other because they appear to have shared or associated origins'. In the following passage, he elaborates: 'The word 'bonding' seems particularly appropriate since it evokes a binding, inescapable engagement or kinship between listener and musical context. The bondings involve all types of sounding matter and sound-making, whether in nature or in culture, whether they arise as a result of human agency or not. Source bondings may be actual or imagined – in other words they can be constructs created by the listener; different listeners may share bondings when they listen to the same music but they may equally have different, individual, personalised bondings; the bondings may never have been envisaged by the composer and can occur in what might be considered the most abstract of works; wide-ranging bondings are inevitable in musics which are not primarily weighted towards fixed pitches and intervals. Bonding play is an inherent perceptual activity' (Smalley 1997: 110). See also Lack 1997: 320.

11   For interpretations of music incorporating these psychoanalytical concepts, see Richardson 1998 and 1999 and Schwarz 1997.

12   On perceptions of the feminisation of culture in modernist discourse, see Huyssen 1986: 44–62.

CHAPTER SEVEN

Twin Peaks, Weak Language and the Resurrection of Affect

Sheli Ayers

I have experience, and I do not mean it jokingly when I say that it is a sea sickness on *terra firma*. The essence of this sickness is such that you have forgotten the true name of things, and so in haste you overwhelm them with arbitrary names. Now quickly, quickly. But scarce have you run away from them, and already you have once again forgotten their names. The poplar in the fields which you named 'the Tower of Babel' – for you did not want to know it was a poplar – sways again namelessly, and you have to name it 'Noah in his cups'.

> – Franz Kafka[1]

Cooper: I think I saw a cottontail rabbit.
Truman: It must have been a snowshoe rabbit.
Cooper: Snowshoe! Snowshoe. Snowshoe rabbit!
> – Mark Frost and David Lynch[2]

The pilot episode of *Twin Peaks* (1990) endows Special Agent Dale Cooper with two complementary traits: connoisseurship and a propensity to name. As he drives into Twin Peaks for the first time, Cooper tells Diane about the marvellous cherry pie at the Lamplighter Inn, hopes he can find a good hotel – 'a clean place, reasonably priced' – and then adds: 'Gotta find out what these trees are. They're really something.' In the next scene, having asserted his authority in the Laura Palmer murder investigation, he asks, 'Sheriff, what kind of fantastic trees do you have growing around here?' Like Adam re-entering Eden after a long absence, Cooper sets to naming this world. He appears to be just the man to restore epistemological order – a character who stands in for a target audience that prides itself on its own ability to distinguish 'good' (that is, cinematic) entertainment from the dross of network television.[3] Yet soon we discover that, as connoisseur, Cooper is more avid than discriminating. All coffee is 'damn fine coffee' provided that it has not been brewed with a fish, and the pie at the Double-R Diner turns out to be just as incredible as the pie at the Lamplighter Inn. We also learn that names divide and multiply in the linguistically volatile spaces of *Twin Peaks*. Values are displaced continually; they cannot hold. No sooner have we named them 'Douglas firs' than the trees sway again, namelessly.

The sickness described by Kafka and manifested in *Twin Peaks* could be diagnosed as allegory. Walter Benjamin distinguished allegory from the Romantic symbol. Unlike symbol, anchored directly in the divine, allegory is language in and of ruin. Benjamin suggests that allegory arose from the need to resignify the gods of antiquity. Once the communal values of the gods were displaced, they became the site of allegorical graphomania. In an endless process of recoding, the allegorist resigns the object once-but-no-longer legible. Sign is heaped upon sign to create a palimpsest; no single meaning can prevail. Symbol was born in the humanist dream of a natural language; allegory, by contrast, is language forsaken and unmoored. Through negation, it gestures toward redemption as the end of historical and linguistic anomie (Benjamin 1977a: 160–6).

Following a signpost set by Gianni Vattimo, one might say that if symbol makes 'strong' metaphysical claims, then allegory – as a condition of continual exchange – represents its 'weak' counterpart.[4] As weak language, allegory institutes the reign of arbitrary signs. Nonetheless, it remains thoroughly contaminated with metaphysics: the profane allegorical world yearns toward the redemption that it excludes from the frame of representation.[5] From dead language, allegory resurrects feeling.

As allegory, *Twin Peaks* moved toward this resurrection of affect, immersing viewers in a multi-layered, melodramatic world in which feeling could be reborn. I agree with Jim Collins' observation that the tonal variety of *Twin Peaks* ultimately encouraged an 'empathetic response' rather than 'ironic distance' (Collins 1992: 346). On the whole, however, critical analyses of *Twin Peaks* have tended to emphasise techniques that supposedly prompted viewers to stand at a superior remove from the kitsch contents and soap-operatic tonalities of the series. Terms such as 'parody' and 'pastiche' describe what, in the view of these critics, made *Twin Peaks* a paradigmatic postmodernist text. Some critics blamed the failure of these techniques of distantiation for the commercial and artistic decline of the series in its second season.[6] I will leave aside the task of charting the commercial failure and early cancellation of *Twin Peaks* in order to reevaluate its aesthetic form.[7]

According to Fredric Jameson, pastiche is the 'blank parody' of postmodernism (Jameson 1991: 17). As an eclectic jumble of cultural signs relieved of their historical referents, pastiche signals what Jameson famously called 'the waning of affect' in postmodernity. Yet, the process by which *Twin Peaks* recycles cultural materials goes beyond simple eclecticism. This process bears an affinity to Walter Benjamin's theory of allegory. It develops analogically and cumulatively – by historical correspondence rather than historical causality. Lynch's surrealism, like Benjamin's allegory, continuously refurbishes 'dead' cultural materials. In the Arcades Project *convolut* devoted to Baudelaire, Benjamin writes of the allegorist's ruminations over arbitrarily cut puzzle-pieces of knowledge:

> Through the disorderly fund which his knowledge places at his disposal, the allegorist rummages here and there for a particular piece, holds it next to some other piece, and tests to see if they fit together – that meaning with this image or this image with that meaning. The result can never be known beforehand because there is no natural mediation between the two. (Benjamin 1999a: 368–9)

Pastiche refers to the abstraction of cultural materials, but the process of rummaging and puzzling through the 'indiscriminate mass of dead lore' belongs to allegory. Operating in a world in which names perpetually come unfixed, Cooper uses allegorical correspondence as a forensic method; for this reason, he proves to be the ideal detective for the allegorical Blue Rose cases (the FBI code name for investigations associated with the Black Lodge). His quirky connoisseurship, which initially appears to wink ironically to an audience capable of identifying kitsch as kitsch, eventually emerges as a prerequisite for the investigation. Cooper's *empathy for things* – for this is what his connoisseurship signifies after all – destabilises the boundary between subject and object. Ultimately, and rather unexpectedly considering what we know about the show's target demographic, Cooper's connoisseurship fails to vouchsafe any attempt on the viewer's part to maintain a position of superiority in relation to that which the series represents, or to the televisual medium itself.

Cooper's devotion to things (including the human body as a thing) signals the deep formal structure of *Twin Peaks* – neither parody nor pastiche, but rather allegory. Through a surrealist dream logic, this passionate living-room allegory explores an uncanny cycle of consumption: the Golden Circle of Appetite and Satisfaction described by MIKE the One-Armed Man and represented by Cooper's gold ring.[8] Using television not only as a medium but also as a figure in its own allegory of consumption, the series mirrored the domestic space of its viewers as a space of melodramatic pressure – a space where the body, crowded on all sides by things, perpetually risks invasion by kitsch. The overall effect of the series was cumulative; over time, *Twin Peaks* became a palimpsest through which initiated viewers experienced a sincere emotional engagement.

Twin Peaks borrowed heavily from both televisual and cinematic genres: soap opera and melodrama, police procedural and *film noir*. At times the series may have called the viewer's attention to these recycled conventions; however, it did not do so in a way that prevented his or her emotional involvement. The self-reflexivity and abstraction that characterise allegory appear as symptoms of the sickness of allegorical language, a condition that ultimately produces, by means of a reversal, the resurrection of passion through mortified cultural materials. This tendency was not immediately obvious in *Twin Peaks*. It was only as the series performed the displacements through which its objects accumulated significance, in the manner of a palimpsest, that allegorical emotion came into its own.

My position is here at odds with the critical consensus, which interprets *Twin Peaks* as encouraging the viewer's emotional distantiation through a self-consciously ironic stance. For instance, David Lavery argues that

> *Twin Peaks'* cultic appeal certainly lay in its visual inventiveness, its distinctive televisual look. The series frequently invited viewers to 'desuture' themselves, through self-conscious awareness, from the ordinary seducements of TV, and in so doing to confirm cult membership. (Lavery 1995b: 5)

In other words, *Twin Peaks'* innovation consisted in its translation of a cinematic technique into televisual terms. Using the suture/desuture dialectic – derived by psychoanalytical film theory from Lacan – Lavery suggests that *Twin Peaks* turned the televisual medium back upon itself in a canny, cinematic manner.[9] The 'desutured' viewer awakens to the formal construction of the narrative, experiences a weakening of narrative identification and ascends to the more rarefied pleasures of formal play. Lavery suggests that through self-conscious cinematic techniques *Twin Peaks* realised a previously unexploited potential for desuturement in the medium of television; as a cinematic hybrid, *Twin Peaks* encouraged a kind of critical coming-to-consciousness in televisual form. This claim serves a dual purpose: it suggests that *Twin Peaks* encouraged viewers to break free from the suturing of classical Hollywood cinema, and it simultaneously elevates the series above the weaker seducements of televisual distraction. In this way, Lavery perpetuates an attitude of contempt toward the televisual medium in general through the example of *Twin Peaks* as auteur television.

Invitation to Love, the soap opera that some of the Twin Peaks residents watch,[10] might be cited as an unambiguous example of the kind of formal distantiation to which Lavery refers. As a self-conscious gesture that plays upon the degradation of the feminised serial form of the soap opera, *Invitation to Love* alerts the viewer to the melodramatic conventions of *Twin Peaks*, thereby allowing him or her to maintain the superior position of the self-conscious consumer. Yet, Lynch conceived of *Invitation to Love* not as an ironic device but as a fully developed parallel world charged with subconscious energies.[11] Even though *Invitation to Love* comes off as a spoof, Lynch's alternate reading indicates a conceptual, formal unity that is essentially allegorical. Analogy links *Invitation to Love*, *Twin Peaks* and the viewer's own family room as a series of receding spaces. Irony stabilises the relationship between these interpenetrating spaces, rendering the analogical structure safe to a certain degree; nonetheless, this structure implicates the viewer and draws him or her into the text. By giving the television a role within the text, *Twin Peaks* works at the boundary that separates textual space from the viewer's own domestic space as the site of consumption. That this structure generally tends toward immersion – not, that is, toward distantiation – becomes increasingly clear as the series accretes significance.

Allegory accumulates. Meaning precipitates from the saturated allegorical text in the crystalline flash of the oxymoron: fire/ice, good/evil, visible/invisible.[12] Through accumulation, the world of Twin Peaks divides and subdivides between realms of darkness and light. Passion springs from emotional dissonance, as when Leland's distress inspires a new dance move at a gathering of Icelandic investors (episode 5) or when the romantic 'Laura's Theme' surges above the comic yet genuinely horrifying spectacle of Leland embracing his daughter's lurching casket while Sarah Palmer screeches, 'Don't ruin this too!' (episode 3).[13]

Within the allegorical palimpsest, heightened emotion often accompanies abstraction. Throughout the series, intense colour serves to delineate and link spaces. The glossy blue fabric in the title sequence of *Invitation to Love* contrasts with the red curtains that link the Roadhouse, One-Eyed Jack's and Jacques Renault's cabin to the other-worldly Red Room. The Palmer living-room is cream-corn yellow – a colour associated with pain and suffering ('garmonbozia').[14] The extensive use of natural wood and taxidermy in other spaces – the Great Northern Hotel, the Packard Sawmill, the Sheriff's Office and the Book House – confuses interior with exterior. Over time, these more or less subtle visual cues form a subjective code through which spaces may be distinguished or deliberately confused.

The Johnson house offers an example of how such allegorical complexities develop in *Twin Peaks* over time. The establishing shot of the Johnson house shows that one side has been covered with a semi-transparent plastic tarpaulin. The Johnsons seem to be 'making do' with a missing wall, a fact likely to alert the viewer to their socioeconomic difference from the Palmers, Haywards and Hornes. The plastic tarpaulin might also point circumstantially to Leo Johnson's involvement in Laura's murder. In time, however, another layer of meaning emerges from this image, and the link between the violence that reigns inside this house and the dangerous energies in the surrounding woods becomes more pronounced. In episode 21, Shelly Johnson slices the plastic in an attempt to escape from the murderous Leo, and Leo makes his own escape into the woods through the slit in the plastic. An uncanny force simultaneously emanates from and presses upon this domestic space, and the question of where these acts of violence originate – from within or from without – is never decisively resolved. Finally, as a figure for the television itself, the Johnson house with its permeable 'screen' confounds the distinction between televisual space and actual space – an interpretation that becomes tenable only in the context of the show's second season.

Another example from the second season demonstrates how the attitude of worldly superiority that supposedly distinguished *Twin Peaks* from other soap operas broke down as viewers developed emotional attachments to certain characters. In a comic subplot played out in episodes 15–17, Norma prepares the Double-R Diner for the arrival of a food critic rumoured to be visiting Twin Peaks under the pseudonym of M. T. Wentz. Not recognising the indelibility of the class codes that distinguish their diner from a fine restaurant, Norma and her ex-con husband Hank concoct fancy specials and festoon the diner tables with new tablecloths, flowers and candles. This situation is treated comically until, in a genuinely painful scene, Norma's mother Vivian discloses that she is M. T. Wentz, author of a withering review of the Double-R. In response to her daughter's baffled hurt, Vivian coldly claims that 'some standards must hold'. Suddenly the comic subplot turns to pathos, a turn-about sharpened for initiated viewers who have witnessed Norma's proprietary pride and decency in episode after episode.

This scene from the second season calls for an empathetic response quite unlike the self-conscious formal distantiation that many critics saw as the series' trademark device, and in fact it seems to answer to such criticism. To some degree character development facilitated deeper emotional involvement; yet, I believe this involvement has a more fundamental cause related to the process of allegorical puzzling. The *Twin Peaks* fan became the initiate to a mysterious hermeneutics involving the exchange value of things. According to Marx, 'value ... converts every product into a social hieroglyphic. Later on, we try to decipher the hieroglyphic, to get behind the secret of our own social products' (Marx 1967: 74). Hieratic things populate Twin Peaks, and these things call out to be deciphered. Benjamin shows how the allegorist's attempt to decipher things endowed with an uncanny power produces allegorical form.

Melodrama and the Afterlife of Things

'[T]he world of things,' Benjamin observes, 'towers oppressively over the horizon of the *Trauerspiel*' (Benjamin 1977: 133–4). In *Twin Peaks*, as in the baroque 'mourning play', things weigh down upon characters who – whether through death or through possession – are themselves at risk of becoming things. Allegory embraces what Thomas Elsaesser calls the melodramatic 'aesthetics of the domestic' (Elsaesser 1972, *passim*). Melodrama, according to Elsaesser, feeds off of the '[p]ressure generated by things crowding in on the characters' (1972: 13) in the home or in the small town where hysteria may erupt at any moment. Domestic melodrama complements magical allegory; in both, social relations find expression through a heightened presence of things.[15]

In episode three, the camera pans slowly over Nadine Hurley's meticulously arranged figurine collection, halting on Ed Hurley's deadened expression as he fingers something sparkly and pink. Nadine throws her arms around him. 'Is this a new one?' he asks. 'Yes', she raptly replies, 'Isn't it beautiful?' Ed, who has just promised his sweetheart Norma that he will divorce Nadine, nearly suffocates in Nadine's overzealous embrace. The figurine collection, where cloying sentiment meets martial discipline, expresses the repressive quality of this domestic space and pushes the scene over the edge of melodramatic excess. The camera, moving slowly on a line from left to right, 'reads' the figurines. When it finally comes to rest on Ed's empty gaze we realise that Ed himself has joined the ranks of Nadine's collection. In the context of the first season, this scene is undeniably comic, and some of its humour depends upon the audience's ability to identify the figurines as kitsch. But it also foreshadows the central conflict of the Laura Palmer story, obscurely sensed in Cooper's dream (episode two): the reification of human beings. In fact, one of the figurines we see is the guardian angel with two children, an image that will be closely associated with Laura Palmer and her struggle with the insatiable BOB.

An important shot in episode 14 – the harrowing episode of Maddy's murder, as directed by Lynch – closely resembles the shot of Nadine's collection. A moodily painted moose fills the screen, the words 'Missoula Montana' barely legible in the lower-left corner. Louis Armstrong's 'What a Wonderful World' plays as the camera pans right to show the yellow wall that instantly identifies the Palmer living room. The camera continues to pan across the mantelpiece cluttered with bric-à-brac: a cupid figurine, a few decorative books, a porcelain clock, several framed photos of Laura (including the famous homecoming queen shot). It passes over a settee with an embroidered doily, more white porcelain, knick-knacks, photos and a bushy evergreen, coming to rest on a tableau of Sarah, Maddy and Leland pressed together on a couch. In what could be described as a lurking point of view – possibly BOB's – the shot lingers here with maximum depth of field, the objects in the foreground and the characters in the background appearing in equally sharp focus. A black-and-white photo of blonde Laura appears nearly transposed over brunette Maddy. Again the camera drifts to the right and Leland's old-fashioned record player (still playing the Armstrong song) appears. These objects, like Nadine Hurley's figurines, heighten the emotional claustrophobia of this scene in which Maddy tells Leland and Sarah that she is planning to return to her home in Missoula. Later in the episode, Maddy will die when Leland/BOB rams her head into the Montana painting shown at the beginning of this shot. Here the treatment of set-dressing clearly exceeds the requirements of atmosphere. These objects are uncanny, even demonic.

Another demonic object in the Palmer house is, of course, the ceiling fan above the stairwell. Like the traffic light swinging in the wind, the image of the fan at first seems simply atmospheric – a detail used cinematically to create a strong sense of place. Yet, through precise repetition, the image gains narrative significance. The fan appears in the pilot episode when the viewer knows that Laura is dead, but Sarah still does not. It appears again (with ominously distorted sound) in Sarah's vision of BOB at the end of the pilot, and again when Leland dances with Laura's photograph in episode two. By the episode of Maddy's murder, the fan signifies BOB's presence. In the cinematic prequel *Twin Peaks: Fire Walk with Me* (1992), Lynch uses sound cues, a shot of power lines, and the strange appearance and disappearance of Philip

Jeffries to bolster the idea already established in the series – for instance, through the power outage in the hospital morgue that coincides with the appearance of the One-Armed Man – that the passage between worlds is an electrical phenomenon. Thus an initiated reader such as Martha Nochimson can reasonably interpret the ceiling fan's stillness in Laura's dream in *Twin Peaks: Fire Walk with Me* as a sign of Laura's redemption; however, this interpretation is possible only through an exceedingly complex and cumulative network of correspondences (Nochimson 1997: 187).[16]

The ceiling fan is not the only object in *Twin Peaks* that assumes this demonic aspect. The broken heart necklace initiates a process of doubling, mirroring and exchange. Donna Hayward's transformation into a cigarette-smoking vixen in the second season is linked to a pair of Laura's sunglasses that Donna receives through Maddy. And Cooper's gold ring becomes the material emblem of the Golden Circle of Appetite and Satisfaction linked to the Black Lodge. The magical aspect of such ordinary things arises through the auspices of allegory. Dispossessed BOB is a projection of suburban incest and bourgeois greed – a figure within an American mythology that mystifies violent domestic energies by displacing them onto the figure of the criminalised outsider or 'drifter'. BOB also belongs to the uncanny realm of exchange value, where bodies take their place among commodities: he possesses bodies like a demon and consumes souls like fire; he wrecks Leland, abandoning the shell of his body; and he codes his dead victims with letters and leaves them wrapped in plastic.

Who can BOB, MIKE and the other spirits of the Black Lodge be if not the reflection of used-up things, the sometimes vengeful spirits of dead commodities? 'We lived among the people', MIKE tells Cooper. 'How do you say, convenience store? We lived above it' (episode two). As a mobile collection of things subject to abstraction and exchange, *Twin Peaks* recalls once more the words of Marx: 'A commodity appears at first glance a self-sufficient, trivial thing. Its analysis shows that it is a bewildering thing, full of metaphysical subtleties and theological capers' (Marx 1967: 71).

I do not wish to suggest that *Twin Peaks* functioned, either by intent or in effect, as a historical materialist critique. However, I do suggest that, through *Twin Peaks'* secular allegory, an experience of historical transformation takes the form of an untidy collection of cultural materials, an aesthetics of the domestic replete with 'metaphysical subtleties and theological capers'. Death-as-reification becomes the object of Cooper's contemplation and the means of Laura's redemption.[17]

The theological capers of BOB and MIKE are related to the fate of the natural object – the end of what Benjamin calls 'aura': recluse Harold Smith's attempt to cultivate orchids in his hothouse apartment ends with a suicide note: 'Je suis l'âme solitaire'; live animals (for instance, Sarah Palmer's hallucinated white horse) appear in enclosed spaces as totems; a gaudy owl lamp in the Briggs' house doubles the mysterious owls in the woods; and the ubiquitous hunting trophies reach an extreme form when Windom Earle arranges his murder victims in elaborate emblematic tableaux. Taxidermy represents the condition of the natural body in allegory; in taxidermy, death is united with kitsch.

Benjamin recognised the commodity (the kitsch object in particular) as a hollowed-out and transformable space, the space of endless reinscription. It is the restless space of the modern dream, inhabited by a host of things. According to a brief essay entitled 'Dream Kitsch: Gloss on Surrealism' (1927), the Surrealists are

> less on the trail of the psyche than on the track of things. They seek the totemic tree of objects within the thicket of primal history. The very last, the topmost face on the totem pole, is that of kitsch. It is the last mask of the banal, the one with which we adorn ourselves, in dream and conversation, so as to take in the energies of an outlived world of things. (Benjamin 1999b: 4)

What strange resonance these words create with the objects we have been tracking! In what way does *Twin Peaks* move the viewer from detached superiority toward an immersive involvement with kitsch? How, in other words, does *Twin Peaks* resurrect affect from abstraction? Reading on, we find a clue:

> What we used to call art begins at a distance of two meters from the body. But now, in kitsch, the world of things advances on the human being; it yields to his uncertain grasp and ultimately fashions its figures in his interior. The new man ... is a creature who deserves the name of 'furnished man'. (1999b: 4–5)

The body itself is susceptible to the invasion of things, and it is precisely this problem that the heightened melodrama of *Twin Peaks* explores. In the figure of Leland Palmer, above all, kitsch has moved into the body and taken up housekeeping.

Celeste Olalquiaga illuminates the different degrees of affective engagement with religious kitsch in the late twentieth century. The first degree of religious kitsch concerns those items sold explicitly for devotional use, such as novena candles and statues of the Catholic saints and martyrs. Consumers of these devotional objects include both the 'believers', who do not identify them as kitsch, and 'aficionados' who do identify them as kitsch but who derive a vicarious emotional charge from them. The second degree of kitsch concerns what Olalquiaga calls 'neo-kitsch': novelty items sold at specialty stores catering to the knowing consumer. The third degree is artistic or hybrid kitsch, which invests religious iconography with 'either a new or foreign set of meanings' (Olalquiaga 1992: 4).

Clearly, some viewers came to *Twin Peaks* for neo-kitsch. Those who stayed to form a kind of cult membership were more likely to be the kitsch aficionados. Indeed, *Twin Peaks: Fire Walk with Me* seems to complete the process of emotional immersion, demanding a degree of belief in the fate of Laura Palmer that surpassed the comfort level of many of the series' original viewers. As secular allegory that refurbishes cultural materials, *Twin Peaks* most closely resembles the hybrid form that Olalquiaga identifies as the third degree of kitsch. Although the series supported different degrees of emotional engagement throughout its run, it lost a certain ironic detachment as it became heavy with accumulated meaning. For those initiated viewers who stayed with the series, *Twin Peaks* enabled a general movement away from 'ironic enjoyment from a position of enlightened superiority' and toward 'a safe release into sentimentality' (1992: 45).

The death of Leland (episode 14) exemplifies this kind of release through the sentimental spectacle of deep tenderness between men. Abandoned by BOB, Leland weeps. He tells Cooper that he first encountered BOB when he was a boy: 'He opened me and I invited him and he came inside me.' BOB and MIKE hungered for 'others that they could use like they used me.' As the romantic 'Laura's Theme' builds, Leland gasps, 'Oh God have mercy on me. What have I done? What have I done? Oh God, I loved her. I loved her with all my heart.' Cradling Leland's head in his lap and caressing his hair, Cooper gently guides Leland

> into the light ... wherein all things are like the void and cloudless sky, and the naked, spotless intellect is like a transparent vacuum without circumference or centre. Leland, in this moment know yourself and abide in that state. Look to the light, Leland. Find the light.

In death, Leland returns to divinity and finds *l'aura*. The scene calls upon a popular Western conception of death as ascendance to the light, a hint of Eastern religion and a large dollop of romanticism. Only kitsch spiritualism can answer the unrestrained sentimentality of kitsch grief, kitsch love. Cooper openly weeps as Leland dies – an indulgence of feeling beyond narrative motivation. (We have never even seen Cooper and Leland engage in a personal conversation.)

The pathos of the scene is heightened by the choral grouping of Harry Truman and forensic expert Albert Rosenfeld, characters whose relationship until this episode has been characterised by adversarial posturing. This compassionate Albert sharply contrasts the Albert of episode three who called Truman a 'hayseed' and who attempted to open Laura Palmer's skull in front of a group of mourners. With his evident disdain for everything in 'this burg', the early Albert had stood out as the figure of urban sophistication in a world of domestic kitsch. While other characters – most notably Leland Palmer, Donna Hayward and Josie Packard – undergo comparable shifts in temperament, these shifts are all motivated in some way. The abrupt transformation of Albert, however, receives only a cursory and unconvincing explanation (he is a closet pacifist); it serves melodramatic emotional tone at the expense of plot and action.

The scene of Leland's death offers an emotional climax and resolution to the Laura Palmer murder investigation. The episodes that follow supply Cooper's tragic backstory and a fundamentally conventional love interest and rivalry. They also show Sheriff Truman's grief over Josie Packard, and the development of an increasingly corny friendship between Truman and Cooper. Despite a proliferation of weird events, these situations are played straight, without any notable attempt to mark distance from soap conventions. In other words, *Twin Peaks* took viewers – at least those who stayed from beginning to end – through a passage from self-conscious and ironic kitsch consumption (neo-kitsch) to a less self-conscious emotional involvement.

The resignification of cultural material, emblematised in the Blue Rose murders, resurrects affect through a process of abstraction. BOB does not merely kill his victims; he inhabits them, reifies them and recodes them. As Christine Buci-Glucksmann has observed, Benjamin's allegory of modernity circulates around and through the double figure of the prostitute and the angel (Buci-Glucksmann 1994: 224). As the ultimate human commodity, the prostitute-body becomes in modernity the site of exchange value par excellence. *Twin Peaks: Fire Walk with Me* emphasises the reinscription of the female body in the scene of dancing Lil, the codified female body as kitsch. Gordon Cole (David Lynch) arranges this tableau for the benefit of Special Agent Chet Desmond and Forensic Specialist Sam Stanley following the murder of Teresa Banks. It is a stylised version of the murders themselves, in which the commodified female body appears as the site of subjective allegorical signification and puzzling.

In allegory, there is no natural bond between the object and its name, or the name and its meaning. Benjamin draws an analogy between the volatile process of signification in allegory and the volatile price of the commodity in a system of exchange. Both are processes of abstraction:

> The modes of meaning fluctuate almost as rapidly as the price of com-modities. In fact, the meaning of the commodity is its price; it has, as commodity, no other meaning. Hence, the allegorist is in his element with commercial wares. As *flâneur*, he has empathised with the soul of the commodity; as allegorist, he recognises in the 'price tag', with which the merchandise comes on the market, the object of his broodings – the meaning. The world in which this newest meaning lets him settle has grown no friendlier. An inferno rages in the soul of the commodity, for all the seeming tranquility lent it by the price. (Benjamin 1999a: 368–9)

The arbitrary relation between the image and its meaning in baroque allegory has, as its modern analogue, the arbitrary relation between the commodity and its price. The fire within the commodity arises from the vertiginous displacements of exchange value. Far from causing affect to wane, exchange value initiates new modes of passionate communication full of 'metaphysical subtleties'.

Gianni Vattimo suggests that modern philosophies such as phenomenology and Marxism succumb to metaphysics all the more catastrophically in their effort to overcome metaphysics. In contrast to the 'strong ontology' of Marxism, with its romance of use value, Vattimo's accomplished nihilism requires a 'weak thought' through which Western philosophy becomes resigned to exchange value and to metaphysics (Vattimo 1988: 22–3). One could say that the allegory or 'weak language' of *Twin Peaks* enabled a resurrection of affect through the refurbishment of dead cultural materials. In so doing, it played with and upon the distinction between televisual and cinematic media. One of the most striking innovations of the series is that it took television seriously as a site of consumption – a domestic altar where recycled culture may be reinvested with subjective values.

Twin Peaks: Fire Walk with Me opens with a 'snow show': a screen filled with blue static. The camera pulls back, a woman screams 'No!' and the screen of what we now identify as a television is smashed. *Twin Peaks* helped to destroy the boundaries between media. Assigned the task of inoculating network television with cinema, it ultimately contaminated cinema with television.

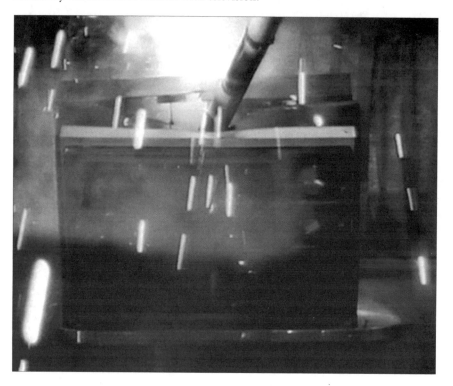

Notes

1   Quoted in Rickels 1988: 244.
2   The pilot episode of *Twin Peaks*.
3   The US broadcasting network system differs from broadcasting systems in Europe and elsewhere in that – like American radio – it was built and operated by the private sector and funded primarily with advertising revenue. Three large, competing networks composed of local affiliate stations dominated the industry until the 1980s, when the growth of cable systems, the advent of Rupert Murdoch's Fox network, and the rise of video sales significantly reduced their market share. According to Les Brown, the networks' combined share of prime-time viewing fell from 90 per cent in the 1970s to less than 60 per cent

in 1990. See Brown 1998: 147. Thus, *Twin Peaks* debuted as a remedy for ABC at a time when all three networks saw drastic attrition of viewership with no end in sight. According to Miriam Horn, 'ABC executives never expected *Twin Peaks* to score with a mass audience. But it did hope its high artistry might recover a demographic group largely lost to network TV: upscale young urbanites with large amounts of disposable income' (Horn 1990: 56). For a more extensive analysis of this demographic group and the way in which the *Twin Peaks* marketing campaign and press appealed repeatedly to concepts of connoisseurship and auteur cinema, see Collins 1992: 342–5. See also Henry Jenkins' fascinating analysis of the *Twin Peaks* interpretive community on the internet, '"Do You Enjoy Making the Rest of Us Feel Stupid?": alt.tv.twinpeaks, the Trickster Author, and Viewer Mastery', in Lavery 1995a: 51–69. Participants in this online news group frequently reiterated an identity of sophisticated viewership based on their appreciation of *Twin Peaks* as programming outside of the cultural mainstream.

4 Vattimo's 'accomplished nihilism' incorporates Heidegger's notion of the *Ge-Stell* ('the universal imposition and challenge of the technological world') as it coincides in postmodernity with *Ereignis* ('the advent of Being in which every appropriation occurs only as a trans-propriation') (Vattimo 1988: 26). Without a highest value or foundation, value itself is liberated in all of its 'vertiginous potentiality' (1988: 21). For Vattimo, postmodernity is not a historical period that follows modernity but rather the culmination of the *Ge-Stell/ Ereignis*, in which the nature of reality as fable becomes visible. Accomplished nihilism acknowledges this fabulousness; it performs 'weak thought' in which transcendent, metaphysical values are continually displaced in the process of generalised exchange value (1988: 26–30).

5 'As those who lose their footing turn somersaults in their fall, so would the allegorical intention fall from emblem to emblem down into the dizziness of its bottomless depths, were it not that, even in the most extreme of them, it had so to turn about that all its darkness, vainglory and godlessness seems to be nothing but self-delusion. … Ultimately in the death-signs of the baroque the direction of allegorical reflection is reversed; on the second part of its wide arc it returns, to redeem' (Benjamin 1977a: 232–3).

6 On *Twin Peaks* as a prime example of postmodernist self-consciousness, see the essays in Lavery 1995a.

7 For an excellent critique of the unspoken aesthetic assumptions behind the critical pronouncements on the 'failure' of *Twin Peaks*, see Dolan 1995.

8 In episode 16, MIKE relates that he and BOB achieved a 'golden circle of appetite and satisfaction' through killing. Cooper sees a correspondence between this remark and his own gold ring, which the Giant took in episode eight. The Giant returns Cooper's ring later in episode 16 when Cooper identifies Leland as Laura's murderer.

9 See Lavery 1995b.

10 The seven references to *Invitation to Love* in the first eight episodes form an

interesting profile of its viewership. The women who watch *Invitation to Love* include Shelly Johnson, Lucy Moran, Nadine Hurley, and (possibly) Norma Jennings, all of whom are identified as working-class. These women are sharply distinguished from the female characters who more closely approximate typical serial drama heroines and who inhabit almost completely separate spaces and story lines, for example, Catherine Martell, Josie Packard and Blackie O'Reilly. The men who watch *Invitation to Love* (Leland, Dr Jacoby and the comatose Leo Johnson) all do so in states of extreme grief or emasculating disability.

11 See Nochimson 1995: 75–6. According to Nochimson, Lynch related in a personal interview that he was surprised to discover that Mark Frost had made *Invitation to Love* into a broad parody of soap operas – something Lynch had never intended.

12 For a related discussion of Benjaminian allegory as the language of passion, see Buci-Glucksmann 1994.

13 See Kalinak 1995. I agree with her claim that Badalamenti's score often seems to contradict visual cues, but I disagree with her precisely when she claims that such moments 'function ironically or parodically … to effect a kind of distantiation' (1995: 89).

14 The Red Room subtitles in *Twin Peaks: Fire Walk with Me* translate 'garmonbozia' as 'pain and suffering'. The word has no known origin; however, attempts by *Twin Peaks* fans to decipher it by sounding it out backwards – deriving phrases such as 'I sob, no more rage' and 'I saw Windom Earle' – demonstrate the strong kinship between allegorical puzzling and the hermeneutics of conspiracy.

15 My analysis of melodrama in *Twin Peaks* cannot do full justice to the simultaneous influence of *film noir*; however, I am indebted to Jesse Engdahl for showing me that melodrama and *noir* represent different sides of the same repressive social order. Some *Twin Peaks* storylines, like the Norma-Ed-Nadine triangle, play out on the side of melodrama; others, like the Cooper-Audrey romance, play out on the side of *noir*. Generally, however, the series is a true hybrid.

16 Nochimson argues that when Laura takes the hieroglyph ring from the Man from Another Place in *Fire Walk with Me*, she is already redeemed. One of the signs of this redemption is that, after taking the ring, Laura is relieved to see that the ceiling fan in the hallway by her bedroom is 'inert'.

17 See Christy Desmet, 'The Canonisation of Laura Palmer' in Lavery 1995a, 93–108. That *Twin Peaks* finally subsumes Tibetan Buddhism and Native American animism under a Judeo-Christian rubric of sin, death and redemption should alert us to the powerful presence of secular myth.

CHAPTER EIGHT

'In Dreams…': Gender, Sexuality and Violence in the Cinema of David Lynch

Jana Evans Braziel

CAPITOL IS AN ARTIST WHO MAKES DOLLS.
MAKES, DAMAGES, TRANSFORMS, SMASHES.
ONE OF HER DOLLS IS A WRITER DOLL.
THE WRITER DOLL ISN'T VERY LARGE AND
IS ALL HAIR. MANE HAIR. RAT FUR. DIRTY
HUMAN HAIR. PUSSY.
                    – Kathy Acker (1990; 1994: 20)

Femininity in modernity has become very much a question of hypervisibility.
                    – Mary Ann Doane (1991: 14)

Postmodern film director David Lynch – variously called a 'psychopathic Norman Rockwell' (Woodward 1990), 'Jimmy Stewart from Mars' (Mel Brooks in Kämmerling 1990) and the 'Wizard of Odd' (Gilmore 1997) – paradoxically fuses and fragments images from 1940s glamour films and photography, black-and-white *film noir*, small-town Americana, graphic violence, mutilated bodies and mythic icons (such as blue velvet, picket fences, Dorothy Vallens' red shoes, the crimson lipstick of Frank Booth and Marietta Fortune, flowing curtains, and the conflagration of cigarettes, flesh and entire buildings). From his earliest to his most recent films, Lynch has both fascinated and repulsed audiences. His visual style, influenced by artists Francis Bacon, Jackson Pollock and Edward Hopper, balances narrative with non-representational images.[1] The effect is a startlingly beautiful, if bizarre and sometimes horrifying, montage of sights, sounds, bodies, lights and movement that denaturalises the parameters of space and time, and conventions of embodiment, violence, sex, desire and gender. Moving these elements away from traditional terrains of meaning, Lynch's films deterritorialise desire, provocatively refiguring gender and sexuality in ways useful for feminist and queer thought. In addressing this process of deterritorialisation, this essay responds both to feminist critiques of Lynch and to feminist recuperations of his work.

Lynch's films treat feminine corporeality as a site of visual and linguistic subversion. Although they often seem to be aggressively heteroerotic, if not heterosexist, they also expose the violence of heterosexual codes through a zone of excess, a feminine erotic economy that I define below as *femm(e)rotics*. While *Blue Velvet* (1986) and *Wild at Heart* (1990) are integral to my analysis, *femm(e)rotics* also propels the cinematic chaosmos of *Lost Highway* (1997). Combining Deleuze and Guattari's schizoanalysis (1987) with the feminist and queer theoretical explorations of materiality in Elizabeth Grosz (1995) and Judith Halberstam (1999), I outline a zone for heterogeneous mappings of desire, corporeality and even the deterritorialisation of violence itself.

Femm(e)rotics, (Faux) féminin, male femininity

Feminist reception of David Lynch's films has been extremely critical, especially in terms of his depictions of femininity, masochism and the female body as sites of graphic violence. Lynda Bundtzen (1988), Cynthia Fuchs (1989) and Jane Shattuc (1992) have denounced *Blue Velvet* as a sadistic male fantasy in which woman is cast as masochistic object of desire. By contrast, Martha Nochimson argues for a feminist revaluation of Lynch's films, explaining that her vision stems from 'a distinctly feminist dissatisfaction with what Hollywood films generally present as reality, particularly regarding the representation of masculinity and femininity' (Nochimson 1997: 1). Allowing herself to let go of 'presuppositions about realism in Lynch's representation of women', she regards Lynch's films as a loosening of 'Hollywood's straightjacketing of gender identity': 'Lynch denaturalises and deglamorises the usual Hollywood definition of control over the individual female and over everything associated with femininity' (1997: 2, 12).

However, in her efforts to recuperate Lynch's films for feminist ends, Nochimson reinforces traditional conceptualisations of femininity and masculinity. She argues that Lynch's films establish connections between femininity and the subconscious – 'forces beyond rational control' – and that, conversely, masculinity and masculine desires are associated with logic, a destructive 'will-to-control', and with 'male' characters. For Nochimson, the *feminine* is defined by receptivity and the *masculine* by control or domination. Characters such as Ben in *Blue Velvet* (Dean Stockwell) and the Mystery Man in *Lost Highway* (Robert Blake) represent a 'masculine alienation from femininity', the 'reduction of the feminine to a masculine performance of softness and receptivity' (1997: 113). She reads these characters as 'male projections of interior malignity' onto Dorothy Vallens (Isabella Rossellini) and Renée Madison (Patricia Arquette) (1997: 214). She also argues that Frank Booth (Dennis Hopper) fetishises Ben's artificial femininity 'as much as he loathes not only women but also what is humanly open and sympathetic' (1997:113). For Nochimson, Ben is pure artifice: 'His performance is the icon of non-being – a man who makes the gestures of femininity, and who opens his mouth and does not sing' (1997: 114).

Although Nochimson allows for masculine-to-feminine transgender traversal, such a reading assumes an ontology of gender: a *real* femininity (as opposed to mere 'gestures') that opens *her* mouth and *really* sings. Conversely, Michael Moon reads Ben's lip-synched version of Roy Orbison's 'In Dreams', and Frank's mimed version later during the joyride, as illustrative of the mimetic nature of fantasies and erotic desires:

> When Lynch has Frank mouth the words of the song a second time [Ben having done so, to Frank's anguished pleasure, back at the whorehouse a short time before], this time directly to a Jeffrey whom he has ritually prepared for a beating by 'kissing' lipstick onto his mouth and wiping it off with a piece of blue velvet, it is as though Lynch is both daring the viewer to recognise the two men's desire for each other that the newly discovered sadomasochistic bond induces them to feel and at the same time to recognise the perhaps more fearful knowledge that what most of us consider our deepest and strongest desires are not our own, that our dreams and fantasies are only copies, audio- and videotapes, of the desires of others and our utterances of them lip-synchings of these circulating, endlessly reproduced and reproducible desires. (Moon 1991: 146)[2]

Rather than reading Frank's response to Ben's words, 'in dreams you're mine', as homophobic repulsion, as do a number of critics (including Nochimson and Kenneth Kaleta), Moon reads Frank's response as one of 'anguished pleasure'. The mimetic reproduction of desires is also present in the blue velvet, used to smear the lipstick around Jeffrey's open mouth; the blue velvet mirrors, and fractures (as if through a broken mirror), the gagging of Dorothy by Frank as they fuck, and as Jeffrey watches from the closet. Lynch's films are – to borrow the words of film, disability and cultural studies critic Susan Crutchfield – 'overtly concerned with mimesis ... with the relationship of contact to copies, and specifically the violent relationship to photographic and filmic copies of objects and experiences' (Crutchfield 1999: 275).[3] On the joyride, Frank looks at Jeffrey and says, 'You're like me.' As Judith Butler (1990) argues about sexual performativity, such voyeuristic (and oral) mimesis has no origin or original: copies are copies of copies – simulacra – as Moon suggests. I shall return to this point later in the essay.

Nochimson asserts that Frank's donning of lipstick, like Ben's performance of Orbison's 'In Dreams', signals 'a reduced and circumspected form of energy ...

Ben (Dean Stockwell) lip-synchs to Roy Orbison's 'In Dreams' in *Blue Velvet*

visually representing a psychology of maimed masculinity arising from depleted identification with boundless female energy' (Nochimson 1997: 115). In contrast, Jeffrey Beaumont (Kyle MacLachlan) exhibits genuine femininity through his openness, receptivity and vulnerability: 'Frank cannot absorb Jeffrey into his perverse fantasies in which vulnerable femininity disappears into a series of stereotypical gestures and the masculine will engulfs everything' (ibid.). Nochimson's readings of male masculinity (Frank), 'artificial' femininity (Ben) and (even) 'genuine' male femininity (Jeffrey) are thus constrained by essentialist definitions of gender: femininity is/as ineluctably receptive, vulnerable, passive; masculinity is/as intrusive, impenetrable, aggressive and abusive. Where this approach privileges gender over sex, sex acts and sexuality, a theorisation of *femm(e)rotics* destabilises gender by valorising or privileging sex, sex acts and sexuality.

Like Judith Halberstam, who resists the notion that masculinity is the ineluctable 'social and cultural and indeed political expression of maleness', and who argues that 'masculinity must not and cannot and should not' be reducible 'to the male body and its effects' (Halberstam 1999: 1), I hope here to reframe the interrelations of sex/gender/desire and femininity. Just as Halberstam has resisted essentialist perspectives on masculinity, my own theoretical approach resists the notion that femininity is the ineluctable 'social, cultural and indeed political expression of femaleness'. I argue instead that femininity cannot be reduced to female bodies, their anatomical parts or multiple affects. For Halberstam, masculinity 'becomes legible as masculinity where and when it leaves the white male middle-class body' (ibid.). Within heteronormative structures masculinity maps itself transparently onto maleness. By contrast, feminity as a violent erotic economy – or as a *femm(e)rotics* – is hyper-legible and quintessentially artificial, its legibility heightened in spaces and bodies that diverge from an idealised female anatomy. Two such sites within Lynch's films are corpulent flesh – the fat prostitutes at Ben's apartment in *Blue Velvet*; Marietta (Dianne Ladd) and the Texas-style porn stars in *Wild at Heart* – and male femininity – *Blue Velvet's* Frank, Ben and Jeffrey. These bodily sites not only 'mark the process by which … [femininity] becomes dominant in the sphere of idealised [or essentialised] femaleness, but also discombobulate its symptomatic anatomy as cultural, not natural' (1999: 2).

My work, then, is informed by Halberstam's work on masculinity, and I extend her ideas to a theorisation of femininity.[4] I define *femm(e)rotics* as a dynamic refiguring of femininity that displaces it from its traditional and exclusive relation to female bodies and opens new sites for bodily pleasures, desires and identifications. *Femm(e)rotics* supplants an essentialist masculinist economy with one of virtual femininity, shifting from identification to erotics.[5] In Lynch's films, such nomadic spaces are in creative motion; they operate according to a *femm(e)rotic* economy. Characters such as Frank, Ben, Jeffrey, Dorothy Vallens, *Wild at Heart's* Lula (Laura Dern), Marietta, Johnnie (Harry Dean Stanton) and Juana (Grace Zabriskie), or *Lost Highway's* Renée and Alice (Patricia Arquette), and the Mystery Man all violently refigure femininity as artifice, surface and orifice. Such bodily realignment creates a virtual field for rethinking corporeality, gender, sexuality and desire.

Within the violent economy of a Lynchian *femm(e)rotics* femininity is *not* to female as masculinity is to male. Its feminine force erodes the heteronormative aligning of sex/gender/desire, creating transgendered and transsexual spaces – nomadic 'desiring machines', to use Deleuze and Guattari's term – for the corporeal circulation of desire. Like male masculinity in Halberstam's work, female femininity figures as a hermeneutic, and at some points as a *faux-féminin* (Laura

Dern's portrayal of Sandy Williams in *Blue Velvet,* for instance) that destabilises *femm(e)rotic* desire. Within Lynch's films, volatile bodies and violating desires mark what Butler defines as a *process of materialisation*.

Volatile Bodies, Violating Desires

In *Bodies that Matter: On the Discursive Limits of 'Sex',* Judith Butler suggests that bodies are not fixed objects of thought. Bodies, she writes, 'indicate a world beyond themselves ... [a] movement beyond their own boundaries, a movement of boundary itself'. This 'movement of boundary' is 'central to what bodies "are"' (Butler 1993: ix). Such a statement offers a provocative theoretical frame for thinking about bodies, movements and boundaries in Lynch's films. Butler's conception of matter is not a pre-discursive given, but rather 'a process of materialisation that stabilises over time to produce the effect of boundary, fixity and surface we call matter' (1993: 9). However whilst Butler's process of materialisation is both discursive and performative, it emphasises restrictive, interpellated norms over the creative movements of energy, force and desire – creative movements that are integral to the textual, visual and spatial fields of Lynch's films. The queer writings of Elizabeth Grosz and the schizoanalysis of Deleuze and Guattari offer more creative and affirmative theories of materiality.

Grosz writes that 'puncturings and markings of the body do not simply displace or extend from already constituted, biologically pre-given libidinal zones; they constitute the body in its entirety as erotic' (Grosz 1995: 139). Skin defies the demarcations of interior and exterior: it is both inside and outside. It is contiguous with sub-epidermal layers of flesh; it is the sensate and bodily surface through which we dwell in our bodies and in our worlds. Orifices also defy dichotomisation: inside, outside. Or, as Deleuze notes in *Le Pli (The Fold),* they are not invaginations, but folds: highly charged erogenous zones that are interior/exterior (Deleuze 1988a; 1993). In Lynch's films, skin with its multiple folds, surfaces, orifices and pores is a field for erogenous energies, forces and desires that constitute the body as body. If gender normativity is heterosexually defined through codified anatomical difference – cunts and cocks – as folds they can also be unfolded, refolded, surfaced, resurfaced, inscribed, reinscribed. Skin can be violently marked, with wounds, scars or blood, but also with clothes, lipstick or vomit. It is an enfolded, convoluted site for transgressive deterritorialisations of the corporeal. Violatory acts that traverse skin (Frank's brutal kissing of Jeffrey; Marietta's dishevelled lines of lipstick) deconstruct the essentialised body, marking it as a zone of intensity (to use another of Deleuze and Guattari's terms), a shifting locus for multifarious, nomadic reconstructions of the body.

Deleuze and Guattari also offer provocative deformations of essentialised notions of body, sex and desire. Proposing a theoretical project in which desire is understood as machinic, social and schizoanalytic rather than psychological, subjective and neurotic, their *Anti-Œdipe (Anti-Oedipus)* inaugurated a forceful dismantling of Lacanian thought (Deleuze and Guattari 1969; 1983a). Lynch's films have been pervasively interpreted from a psychoanalytical perspective. According to Steven Shaviro, 'psychoanalysis remains the sole and ubiquitous horizon of "serious" (read: academic) discourse on film', especially for interrogations of 'desire and politics, gender and sexuality, culture and ideology in the movies' (Shaviro 1993: 13, 4). But the Lynchian aesthetic, with its fragmented desires, bizarre erotic entanglements and abstract non-representationality seems more schizoanalytic than psychoanalytic. In *Anti-Œdipe*, Deleuze and Guattari forcefully extend desire beyond the Freudian family, specifically examining the links between Oedipalisation and capitalism as a *machine-désirante*, 'desiring machine'. (1969; 1983a). Whereas capitalism deterritorialises the state apparatuses of feudal or hierarchical structures, it also reterritorialises desire as a commodity form – an Oedipal dynamic that situates desire in the psychoanalytic subject. Desires are thus fragments of social machines; bodies are spaces of forces, energies and desires; they are 'bodies without organs' (Deleuze and Guattari 1980; 1987).

For Deleuze and Guattari, the psychoanalytic model reduces all desire to the 'polymorphous pervert' of the castrated Oedipus who ignores all desires that do not conform to Oedipal model – such as *fellatio*. The schizoanalytic model shifts desire away from organised erotogenic zones to intensities along a disorganised, intense corporeal spatium, the *Corps sans Organes (CsO)* ('body without organs', BwO). Unlike the phallocentric Lacanian desire, for Deleuze and Guattari desire passes in intense waves or lines across the 'body without organs'. It displaces corporeal organisation based on centre/margin. No one organ is given erotogenic primacy or invested with the power of psycholinguistic structuring: 'desire is revolutionary because it always wants more connections and assemblages. But psychoanalysis cuts off and beats down all connections, all assemblages – it hates desires, it hates politics' (Deleuze 1993: 79).

And so to the *femm(e)rotic* desires of Lynch's films – desirous connections, not director's cuts...

David Lynch's Femm(e)rotics: Becoming-Woman

Thus, drawing on the work of Halberstam, Butler, Grosz and Deleuze and Guattari, I will now analyse the Lynchian *femm(e)rotics* in *Blue Velvet* and *Wild at Heart*. My analysis focuses on two elements from these films – bodily (de)formation and corpulence, as illustrated in specific scenes from each film. The key scenes from *Blue Velvet* are the 'This is it' scene at Ben's apartment and the joyride. From *Wild at Heart*, I focus on Marietta's bodily-psychic breakdown in her bedroom and the 'pornographic' scene in Big Tuna, Texas. In all of these scenes, the body is violently marked, and this marking initiates a violent process of gender deformation. The joyride scene from *Blue Velvet* shows Frank erotically, if also violently, beating and violating Jeffrey Beaumont. The bedroom scene from *Wild at Heart* screens Marietta – in white satin gown and pink hair bow, garish signs of femininity 'proper' – unravelling emotionally and physically after her betrayal of Johnnie. In both scenes, lipstick marks the bodies with a violent *femm(e)rotics* that deterritorialises normative identifications of gender. The red lipstick – traditionally neat contained lines on the lips of women – exceeds its boundary and constitutes a transvestic, gender performative 'colouring out of the lines'.

Lynch's films further deterritorialise corporeality through the disruptive excess of corpulence, as seen in the 'This is it' scene at Ben's and the courtyard in Big Tuna – that is, femininity *out of bounds*.[6] Here, corpulent bodies (like injured or mutilated bodies) mark a satirical and violent zone of excess.[7] In contrast to the slim, traditionally sexy bodies of Lula/Peanut and the myriad Creole women in the Louisianan brothel, *Wild at Heart* presents Marietta as a woman who is rapidly spilling over towards boundlessness. Marietta marks her wrists with red lipstick. While this act can be read as a violent, metaphorical suicide, it also enacts or catalyses a machinic surfacing of infolded flesh that opens the body to its own dissolution. As orifice, the lips, open and violent, disarrange inside/outside. As Marietta covers her whole face with lipstick, the boundaries for eroticism and gender become blurred and obscured. Painted red, her lips accentuate feminine beauty and artifice. Painted red, her face displaces feminine beauty through a hysterical orificing of the entire countenance. Painted red, it becomes an erogenous zone spreading like wildfire to re-mark the terrains of femininity and corporeality, desire and body. Lips deterritorialise face; face deterritorialises body. Orifices surface. Surfaces orifice.

After talking to Johnnie on the phone, Marietta violently vomits into the toilet, and the white silk robe falls open, revealing her naked thigh spread corpulently over the floor in a shot that lasts for several seconds. Until this scene, her body has been contained and draped in close-fitting skirts and dresses that girdle her body from overflowing, but the bare thigh represents the body exceeding its bounds, the point of departure for a corporeal line of flight.[8] This fleshly unfolding deforms the hetero-alliances of gender, sex and desire. This fleshly unfolding disorients the viewer's gaze, as Marietta's body seems to open up and spill over from the inside out. Her thigh, half-covered with white satin gown as if skin, protrudes from her groin, meat-like and raw: it suggests the interiority of exposed flesh, denuded and open, as if flayed. The exterior surface hints profanely at grotesque cut flesh. Its unfolding marks it as once folded, interior, unexposed. Exteriority over-exposed thus creates the simulacrum of an interiority violated. Marietta confounds bodily coding and anatomical sense; she confounds gender. Her vomit – marks or markings of inside/outside and self/other, not quite subject, not quite object, but rather, in Kristevan terms, abject (Kristeva 1980b) – also establishes a flux and continuum that discombobulate the symptomatic anatomy.

For Marietta, as for other characters in Lynch's films, desire always assembles the 'body without organs'. In his dialogues with Claire Parnet, Deleuze resists the pathologisation of the 'organised' body, theorising the anorexic body as a BwO:

> The anorexic consists of a body without organs with voids and fullnesses. The alternation of stuffing and emptying: anorexic feasts ... void and fullness are like two demarcations of intensity; the point is always to float in one's own body' (Deleuze in Deleuze and Parnet 1987a: 110).

A body exceeding its bounds: Marietta Fortune (Diane Ladd) in *Blue Velvet*

Desires and intensities map deviant bodies without organs, even as they materialise the bodies as bodies. The boundaries between interior and exterior are fluctuating and malleable. Marietta has surfaced, quite literally. As she leans against the toilet, her fingers touch her lips, painted with lipstick, spattered with vomit. Red painted fingernails touch stained lips, re-signifying surfaces of skin as inside, outside, contiguous.

But Marietta has other corporeal others: she is many. Throughout the movie, Lula is haunted by her mother's maniacal cackling, a sound she phantasmatically conflates with the laughter of the Wicked Witch of the West from *The Wizard of Oz* (recall Marietta's 'witchy-woman' black shoes in the bedroom scene). The pervasiveness of this disconcerting laughter increases as Marietta moves toward an unlimited boundlessness. This confluence – her corpulence and her psychotic, malevolent mirth – culminates in the scene at Big Tuna, Texas. Lula and Sailor Ripley (Nicolas Cage) sit talking with several men at a picnic table in the dark, when a man directs their attention towards a noisy trailer unit saying, 'Hey Timmy, what's going on over there in number four where bright lights are on all the time?' to which Timmy responds, 'Them are making a pornographic movie – Texas-style, you want to join in?' Shortly after, three corpulent, barely clad women flow out of the trailer, laughing hysterically and dancing around the courtyard. The women leave without speaking. Denoted only by their corpulence and their laughter, the fat women resist definitive signification. *Wild at Heart*'s corpulent bodies deterritorialise the limits of female corporeality. Excessively and parodically they unmap the long historical association of women with matter, while remapping the (fat) terrains of desire and sexuality – pornography 'Texas-style'. As Laura Kipnis argues, fat *as fat* is pornographic (Kipnis 1996).

Yet other sexually transgressive bodies also inhabit Lynch's cinematic imagination. In *Blue Velvet,* he presents two scenes with corpulent women at the heart of a dissolution of control, a transgression of boundaries. When Frank and his devotees enter Ben's apartment, the men are surrounded by fat chicks – or frumpy whores – who defy traditional standards of beauty. A fat woman dressed in red and black leaves the room, and Dorothy stands speechless among the men. The fat women are similarly mute, but casually traverse the space of the room. When Frank says, 'Let Tits see her kid', Dorothy runs excitedly towards the door and is allowed into the adjoining room. She is thus interior to the scene that follows, but invisible: we only hear her voice. These representations (an absent but audible Dorothy; the visibly present, yet mute fat prostitutes) are diametrical poles of the corporeal and the ethereal that femininity traditionally either incarnates or reifies. Reduced to voice only, Dorothy's thin body is displaced and replaced by these ambulating, dancing, groping women and their unlimited, transgressive corporeality.

In a scene that seems to foreshadow Marietta's cosmetic dissolution in *Wild at Heart,* Frank puts on lipstick before kissing Jeffrey. As he violates the demarcated bounds of gender, a fat woman dances enigmatically on the hood of the car, seemingly oblivious to the scene below, curiously unaware of all boundaries of signification. With her corpulent body, she incarnates the space of erotic traversal, the cartographic area that maps out the transgressive lines of flight for the scene of *femm(e)rotic* desire between Frank and Jeffrey. Although this scene could be defined, following Luce Irigaray's theorisations of *le féminin* and *hom(m)osexualité,* as a narcissistic *hommo-eroticism,*[9] such a definition would assign the forces and movements of desire to gender-normative sites for bodily pleasure and sexual identification. I prefer to define this desire as *femm(e)rotic*. Frank and Jeffrey 'become-woman' through a violent economy of *femm(e)rotic* desire marked by the transvestic infractions of the BwO. The Deleuzean models of the 'body without organs' and 'becoming-woman' offer paradigms for redefining deviant bodies. Within this frame, such deviant bodies are 'desiring machines'; and the body becomes a spatium in *flux* over which intensities flow, desires move and energies pass.

Deleuze and Guattari maintain, ironically, that one makes oneself into a BwO by 'becoming-woman' (*devenir-femme*): 'She never ceases to roam upon a body without organs. She is the abstract line, or a line of flight' (Deleuze and Guattari 1987: 277). According to them, 'all becomings begin with and pass through becoming-woman. It is the key to all other becomings' (ibid.). Feminists such as Luce Irigaray, Alice Jardine, Rosi Braidotti and even Elizabeth Grosz have resisted this Deleuzean concept. Neverthlesss *devenir-femme*, 'becoming-woman', can be read as subversive to normative gender categories. For Deleuze and Guattari, *devenir-femme* inverts Plato's argument in the *Timaeus* that lascivious men become women in their next incarnation as punishment for ill deeds committed in their first life. *Devenir-femme* privileges 'becoming' over Platonic 'being' and subverts Platonic forms through matter, or the *moléculaire* ('molecular'). *Devenir-femme* is in endless flux, multiplicitous and material becoming. Through *devenir-femme*, and – in a hyper-molecular mode – through *devenir-grosse femme*, Lynch's violent *femm(e)rotics* nomadically resist the reterritorialisations of (essentialised) femininity, while reconfiguring points of erotic feminine becoming. It forces characters (and bodies) into molecular becomings through their amorous-sexual, schizo-social and consuming desires.

Historically postulated as the corporeal pole of human existence, or even in some metaphysical discourses as *essentially* non-existent, 'woman' confounds definitions of the self based on body/soul and inside/outside. For Irigaray, 'woman' as a masculinist construct simultaneously burdens the 'demarcation of limit', and overflows into the 'sign of excess' (Hardie 1995: 159). In this context, the intensities and desires of transgressive 'bodies without organs' exceed containment: fat flesh hyperbolises incarnate excess, threatening to overflow the parameters of metaphysical thinking. Drawing on Irigaray's insights, but perhaps in a direction counter to her intentions, I would argue that this 'sign of excess' within the feminine, or *femm(e)rotic* energy, is already other: it is male; it is corpulence; it is Frank or Jeffrey or Sandy or Johnnie as well as Marietta; and it is always already artifice. The feminine, or *le féminin*, operates as an erotics of violence: violent *femmes* unsettle heteronormative configurations of gender, sexuality and desire through a *femm(e)rotics* of 'becoming-woman'. By 'becoming woman', Lynch's characters resist the reterritorialisations of essentialised or bodily-bound desires.

Notes

1 Martha Nochimson explores the influence of postmodern, non-representational art on Lynch's filmic texts in 'Portrait of the Director as a Surfer in the Waves of the Collective Unconscious' (1997: 16–45).

2 This passage by Moon is also quoted in Pfeil 1992: par. 49, n. 7.

3 Crutchfield's unmodified quote reads, 'The slasher film is overtly concerned with mimesis as Taussig describes it, that is, with the relationship of contact to copies, and specifically the violent relationship to photographic and filmic copies of objects and experiences' (1999: 275). The internal citation is to Taussig 1994.

4 In this sense, my work is informed by queer theory and gay historical work on camp, drag and male femininity. For theoretical and historical work on camp, see Newton 1970 and more recently, Meyer 1994.

5 I define this violent erotic economy as *femm(e)rotic* in contrast to Luce Irigaray's theorisations of femininity and sexual difference through the sexual economy of *hom(m)osexualité* (1974 and 1985). Irigaray's theorisations of *le féminin* comprise a feminist response to what she sees as sexual (in)difference within a monosexual economy – *hom(m)osexualité* – based on masculinity and maleness. Although I am sympathetic to Irigaray's feminist theorisations of *le féminin*, her work, in a post-queer era, remains too wed to sexual difference and too grounded

in a heterosexual economics of desire to fruitfully engage nomadic spaces of sex/gender/desire such as those we encounter in Lynch's films.

6   For a discussion of popular cultural constructions of corpulence, see Jana Evans Braziel and Kathleen LeBasco (eds) 2001.

7   Although not the focus of this essay, a performative approach to representations of disabilities within Lynch's films is needed. For contributions to the emergence of disability studies within the field of cultural studies, see Ingstad and Reynolds Whyte 1995, Thomson 1996 and 1997, and Crutchfield and Epstein 2000.

8   This scene could also be disturbingly related to the scene in which Johnnie is murdered by Santos's allies in what appears to be a sexualised, murderous (not to mention sensationally distorted) 'voodoo' ritual. For a critique of Hollywood representations of Haitian and Creole Vodoun, see Dayan 1995. See also Warner 1997.

9   See de Lauretis 1993.

CHAPTER NINE

'Up in Flames': Love, Control and Collaboration in the Soundtrack to Wild at Heart[1]

Annette Davison

People call me a director, but I really think of myself as a soundman.
– David Lynch (in Chion 1995: 169)

A number of critics have suggested that David Lynch inserts himself into his films and television work. In literal terms, he poses as FBI Regional Bureau Chief Gordon Cole in *Twin Peaks* (1990) and *Twin Peaks: Fire Walk with Me* (1992) and as a Spice Worker in *Dune* (1984). Figuratively speaking, he can be read into the character of Henry in *Eraserhead* (1977) (Woods 1997: 34–5), Paul Atreides in *Dune* (1984) (Woods 1997: 63; Rodley 1997: 140–1), Jeffrey Beaumont in *Blue Velvet* (1986) (Woods 1997: 74–5; Rodley 1997: 140–1), Agent Dale Cooper in *Twin Peaks* (Woods 1997: 95; Rodley 1997: 140–1), mechanic Pete Dayton – and potentially also musician Fred Madison – in *Lost Highway* (1997) (Newman 1997: 48–9).

In their views on *Lost Highway*, both Marina Warner (1997: 6–10) and Kim Newman (1997: 48–9) argue that Lynch also inserts his presence into his soundtracks. For Warner, Lynch's foregrounding of the soundtrack in his films 'creates a faceless but insistent double … masterminding the audience response' (1997: 10). In *Mulholland Drive* (2001), Lynch draws more attention than ever to this insistent doubling: here, in the form of a magician at Club Silencio who states (and then demonstrates) that 'There is no band. This is all a tape recording …

It is all an illusion.' The integrity of live performance is subsequently re-affirmed by the following act, singer Rebekah Del Rio; the performer audibly knocks the microphone as she takes up her position on stage. During her impassioned performance of Roy Orbison's 'Crying' (sung in Spanish), we see close-up shots of Ms Del Rio's face which function to persuade us that the performance we are seeing is real – that is, live – rather than recorded.[2] In the middle of the song Ms Del Rio suddenly falls on the ground unconscious, though her vocal performance continues on the soundtrack. The impact of this moment is startling: in retrospect, the magician's – and, arguably, Lynch's – control and manipulation of the soundtrack is foregrounded. In this chapter, I trace a similar case of the director's insertion into his soundtracks as 'faceless but insistent double', along with his figurative insertion into the film's soundtrack via a character, but here in an earlier film, *Wild at Heart* (1990).

The first part of my analysis considers some of the musical and sonic codes used in *Wild at Heart*, and the use of the concept 'music' as a code in itself. The film valorises musical performance and active and bodily response to musical performance. Indeed, it is through Lynch's appropriation of conventions of the Hollywood musical that the character of Sailor (Nicolas Cage) – as temporary member of the band and controller of the soundtrack – is connected to the figure of Lynch, a director with a particularly collaborative mode of production. The second part of the essay focuses on sonic spectacle in contemporary Hollywood cinema that has been made possible through technological developments in sound recording and playback. Such moments offer interruptive pleasures, though these tend to exist in order to exemplify a film's high production values. Lynch's soundtracks go further, however: they generate highly connective structures in terms of both thematic and physical relationships between sounds. I suggest that this too is a result of Lynch's collaborative mode of production, which, while rooted in Hollywood production practice, offers a radical reconfiguration of it.

Music in Wild at Heart

From the opening credits sequence it is clear that the use of music is central to *Wild at Heart*. The sequence is ignited into life by a match. The greatly magnified close-up of the flame seen on-screen is paired with an intensely reverberant and heavily amplified 'aural close-up' of the combustion produced by it. As this sound begins to diminish, the lush romanticism of the orchestral introduction to 'Im Abendrot' from Richard Strauss's *Four Last Songs* (1948) begins – quietly at first – with a winding line played by the upper wind and strings. On-screen, as the music gradually begins to swell, the names of Nicolas Cage and Laura Dern appear on intertitles. With that – and by now the music is really building – the words 'Wild at Heart' speed toward the front of the screen space one after another, from a point on an illusory horizon, growing in size as they do so. The motion of the words is synchronised to the sound of a flame burning, here too, heavily amplified, but without the sound created by the friction of the strike which produces the flame; an explosion without the bang. The amplitude of the sound is linked proportionally to the size of the words; as the words speed toward the front of the screen, increasing in size, so the sound gets louder. Immediately each word has reached the front of the screen space, the sound – now very loud indeed – stops abruptly. At this point, huge swirls of flames engulf the screen. At times, the sound of this great fire threatens to drown out the music, but, ultimately, a balance is maintained. Just as the names of the actors playing the roles of Sailor and Lula are connected in the credits by a single flame, so the bond between their characters in the film gradually becomes associated with the representations of power and strength of both the music and the flames in this sequence.[3]

The *Four Last Songs* were the final works Strauss completed before his death in 1949. The texts and mood of the songs present a serene acceptance of death as a stage on a path towards eternity. 'Im Abendrot' ('At Dusk'), the last of the four, is written in a major key and regularly affirms its tonality. The music opens with a tonic chord from which the upper wind and strings begin a long, slow descent with a meandering line, which, owing partially to the use of drone-like pedals as accompaniment, fails to establish the rhythmic emphasis of a regular metre. The absence of movement in the opening bar (the chord) also contributes to this lack of metre and to the quality of timelessness, or free-falling, which results. This is further compounded by the abundance of notes tied across bar-lines, which creates a general sense of delay in the teleology of the lines. This impression of a suspension of metre during the introduction to the song invites the listener to be suspended alongside the music in its ethereal descent. The happy resignation of the teleology of the descending lines of the upper wind and strings is confirmed by the re-affirmation of the tonic chord (E♭ major) on reaching this destination (bar 20). Michel Chion describes the opening of this music as having an 'extraordinary sense of notes bursting into flower' (Chion 1995: 134); a description which captures well its joyous, passionate and yet also enduring nature.

As mentioned above, the Strauss extract is first presented non-diegetically – that is, outside of the fictional world of the film, which only the film's audience can hear – with the engulfing flames of the opening credits, then later, again non-diegetically, with Sailor and Lula's silent proclamations of love under a red evening sky (literally *Abendrot*) (0.48.59; hours.minutes.seconds). It is also heard as we watch Lula despair at the prospect of losing Sailor to 'black angel' Bobby Peru (1.36.57).[4] Finally, it accompanies Sailor's realisation that he 'should not turn away from love' following his visitation by Glinda, the 'good witch' from *The Wizard of Oz* (Victor Fleming, 1939) (1.54.00).

The strength and passion of Lula and Sailor's love is not only expressed in the lush neo-romanticism of the orchestral introduction to Strauss's 'Im Abendrot', however. It is also present in the speed-metal track, 'Slaughterhouse', by the band, Powermad. This latter song is a loud and grandiose piece of rock music that builds in strength through a combination of the emphatic repetition and variation of thematic figures with percussive interruption.[5] Chion suggests that these very different pieces of music actually provide 'two expressions of the same power of love (the accent should fall on the word "power")' (1995: 135).[6] The slow, bombastic introduction to the Powermad track is first presented when Sailor defends both himself, and Lula, from Bobby Ray Lemon's threats in the opening scene (0.03.07). It is next heard when we see Lula and Sailor making love for the first time after he has been released from Pee Dee (0.06.39). Its next appearance starts with the second, quicker semiquaver section of the song, when Lula and Sailor dance to the band when Powermad perform the song live at the Hurricane (0.16.59). Later, the slow introduction is heard again as we see Marietta's flashback to the scene of Lemon's death, with Sailor (literally) pointing the/his finger toward her (0.25.50), and as we watch Sailor and Lula having sex (0.39.41). The last time the Powermad track is heard – and here again it is the fast section of the song – is when Lula can only find misery on the car radio. Sailor stumbles across 'Slaughterhouse' as he twists the dial, and the two of them dance frantically at the roadside until they are breathless (0.48.31). After they come upon the fatal car crash, following which their situation changes from bad to worse, the Powermad song is never heard again. It is certainly possible to read its absence as signifying the absence of Lula and Sailor's physical relationship, until they are reunited at the end of the film.

Sailor and Lula are portrayed as more receptive to music than any other characters in the film: whether speed-metal or 1950s piano jazz, it makes them dance. The exception here is Mr Reindeer, who, as Martha Nochimson points out, is also associated with music: a simpering, solitary high register violin melody with barely audible accompaniment (Nochimson 1997: 230 (n. 10)). Mr Reindeer does not dance, however: he watches others dance – usually virtually naked women in his employment. We see no evidence that music has any physical or emotional impact upon him. Reindeer's association with music is a superficial one that is not grounded in feelings, but behaves instead as a signifier of bourgeois musical taste. Sailor and Lula, on the other hand, gain release from the evils of the world through music and their bodily response to it. The clearest example of this occurs at the end of a day's driving on the open road, mentioned above. Lula is unable to find any music on the radio: the only stations she can find recount stories of sexual abuse, violence and mutilation. Shots of Lula's despair at having to listen to this 'crap' (as she looks in disbelief at the radio) are inter-cut with shots of the radio in extreme close-up, with her hand twisting the dial erratically. Of the four shots of the radio in close-up, two linger on the radio alone with Lula's hand absent: are we to infer that the radio itself is a force of evil, polluting the air with tales of destructive acts? Lula pulls the car off the road aghast: 'Holy shit! There's not a livin' fuckin' thing!' When Sailor asks her, 'What's wrong peanut?' she climbs out of the car screaming 'I can't take no more o' this radio. I never heard so much shit in all my life! Sailor Ripley, you get me some music on that radio this instant. I mean it!' As Sailor starts to fiddle with the radio dial, the words 'sexual assault', 'mutilations' and 'rape' are again picked out from the various stations. However, as soon as there is a cut to a shot of his hand twisting the dial, Sailor finds a music station. Furthermore, it is playing the (now familiar) strains of 'Slaughterhouse' by Powermad. Sailor and Lula instantly recognise the music of their favourite band and (after Sailor has somersaulted out of the car) begin to dance wildly to it, screaming aggressively, punching and kicking at the air.

Sailor (Nicolas Cage) in his snakeskin jacket

It is also through music that Sailor expresses his most profound feelings for Lula: he sings first Leiber and Stoller's 'Love Me', then Presley and Matson's 'Love Me Tender' in the style of 'E' (Elvis). His performance of 'Love Me' takes place at the Hurricane club, following a fight sequence which also warrants analysis. When Sailor sees someone else try to dance with Lula, he raises his arm to the band: they stop playing instantly. When Sailor asks the man in question to apologise to Lula, he refuses and insults Sailor's snakeskin jacket. The ensuing fracas is introduced, and then accompanied, by the sound of cymbal crashes (played back in reverse) and snare, with Powermad's kit as a possible diegetic source (yet also a distinctly impossible one, given the cymbal sound's manipulation) (0.18.21). The synchrony of these (musical) sounds to Sailor's movements is precise, creating a brief moment of 'mickey-mousing'; a term used to describe a scoring technique by which music is directly synchronised with the action onscreen, and which is otherwise rare in this soundtrack. Immediately after the fight, Sailor asks the band to join him in a song – 'Love Me'. As a result, Sailor begins to be associated with the musicians: he becomes a kind of temporary member of the band, part of a collaborative musical team.

Direct synchronicity between music and image occurs on only two other occasions in *Wild at Heart*: here too it is associated with Sailor and violence. The first instance occurs at the start of the film, with Sailor's defensive attack on Bobby Ray Lemon synchronised to the introduction to 'Slaughterhouse'. Sailor's violent acts achieve almost balletic status here. The other example occurs at the end of the film when Sailor is beaten by a gang in the street to the rhythm of a piece of blues-rock music: both the punches he receives and his subsequent collapse are synchronised with the music (1.51.51). The composition of music to 'mickey-mouse' action on-screen is usually a post-production task: when a final cut of the image exists, the music is composed to synchronise with it. However, in terms of the production on *this* film, it is likely that in these two sequences the action was choreographed to the music.[7] Lynch often has music played through his headphones during production, along with any dialogue being recorded, and he sometimes also has the music played back on-set (Lynch in Rodley 1997: 133). In this way, Lynch has a soundtrack of his own making *in use* during production. Thus, the production of these fight sequences owes more to the conventions of the Hollywood musical (that is, the choreographing of action or dance to music at the production stage) than to the post-production precision of 'mickey-mousing'. This represents a dramatic reordering of production tasks as undertaken in Hollywood since the studio era, in which a film's music and most of its sound effects remain post-production tasks; composers and sound designers often have little or no opportunity for dialogue with the director or other members of the crew at the production stage.[8] Indeed, such complaints are still common among composers and sound personnel who currently work in Hollywood.[9] Furthermore, sound and music are frequently produced wholly separately, which can lead to clashes between sound and music cues at the mixing stage.[10]

Lynch and composer-performer Angelo Badalamenti discuss and play through music before, during and after shooting, though Lynch has revealed that before *Blue Velvet* – the first film on which he worked with Badalamenti – he had been frustrated when it came to his films' scores (Lynch in Rodley 1997: 132–3). Furthermore, he believes that many more directors must also be frustrated by the system, 'because you rarely get to sit down with the composer until late in the game – post-production' (Lynch in Rodley 1997: 127).[11] As far as Lynch is concerned the model of classical Hollywood production practice that developed during the studio era – that is, as heavily compartmentalised – still persists in some quarters, at least in relation to a film's music (though music and sound personnel are no longer on the producing studio's payroll). During the studio era, this extreme specialisation of labour proved highly effective in economic terms. As I discuss below, however, it could also be argued that this mode of production rarely achieved the utopian potential that the vertically-integrated – 'all under one roof' – Hollywood studio structure *could* have supported.

The Soundtrack

> The borderline between sound effects and music is the most *beautiful* area.
> – Lynch in Rodley 1997: 242

Since the coming of sound, Hollywood's high production values have been evinced in its soundtracks. Indeed, for a time in the late 1920s and early 1930s the presence of synchronised sound *in itself* signified high production values.[12] More recently it has been argued that Hollywood soundtracks offer pleasure to the spectator-auditor, due, at least in part, to the high definition sound recording and theatrical playback equipment now available.[13] Developments such as Dolby Digital, Sony Dynamic Digital Sound and Digital Theatre Systems have not only resulted in a much wider range of possible frequency response and a huge reduction in unwanted noise: they have changed the very nature of the soundtrack forever.[14] Chion has commented on the direct correspondence between changes in sound technology and the character of recent soundtracks. He believes that recent Hollywood cinema has been experimenting with, and is in pursuit of, sensation: 'of weight, speed, resistance, matter and texture':

> Recent American productions like John McTiernan's *Die Hard* (1988), Steven Spielberg's *Indiana Jones and the Last Crusade* (1989) or James Cameron's *The Abyss* (1989) have also added to this renewal of the senses in film through the playful extravagance of their plots. In these movies matter – glass, fire, metal, water, tar – resists, surges, lives, explodes in infinite variations, with an eloquence in which we can recognise the invigorating influence of sound on the overall vocabulary of modern-day film language … The sound of noises, for a long time relegated to the background like a troublesome relative in the attic, has therefore benefited from the recent improvements in definition brought by Dolby. Noises are reintroducing an acute feeling of the materiality of things and beings, and they herald a sensory cinema. (Chion 1994: 154–5)

As Chion suggests, improvements of sound definition in recording and playback offer one reason why set pieces that focus on the materiality of things – such as people jumping or falling through glass – have become such a frequent occurrence in recent cinema. Improvements in definition are the result of enhancements in high frequency response which enable greater detail and precision to be heard. Chion also points out that recent cinema sound varies from 'real world' sound in terms of what happens to it when it is amplified. When a sound increases in intensity in the real world, it generally distorts, resulting in changes to its 'nature, colour, resonance' (Chion 1994: 101). In the amplified sound world of the cinema, sounds have as much clarity at extremely high amplitude levels as they do at very low ones. Acoustic verisimilitude is sacrificed in the name of exploiting the technology that is now available, and which includes the spatialisation of sound, for example.[15] Sound has finally caught up with the widescreen spectacle of the image and is able to be 'spectacular' in its own right, at the stages of both production *and* exhibition. Indeed, following Roland Barthes, I would argue that today moments of sonic spectacle offer the spectator-auditor of contemporary Hollywood cinema the opportunity to step out of the narrative to marvel at both the precision of the sound design and the technical capacity of the sound system.

In 'The Grain of the Voice' and *The Pleasure of the Text*, Barthes emphasises the materiality of the signifier as a source of sensual pleasure, in contrast to the conceptual content it signifies (Barthes 1977b; 1990). In the former he writes about the singing of a Russian Cantor, a bass, in which he detects something 'beyond (or before) the meaning of the words ... something which is directly the cantor's body' (1977b: 181). What Barthes detects in the grain of the voice is individual to that body, is singular, unique. Rather than telling us of the specific singer's personality or subjectivity, it speaks of the physical nature of her/his body: 'The "grain" is the body in the voice as it sings, the hand as it writes, the limb as it performs' (1977b: 188). 'Grain' is not simply a reference to a sound's timbre, but to timbre as a signifier (*signifiance*) of the body of the sound's source. In vocal music, Barthes places this potential 'grain' of the voice at the boundary between language and music, but argues that it can also occur in instrumental music. Rather than evaluating a performance on the performer's interpretation of the text's representational meanings and emotions, of their ability to conform to 'constraints of style', Barthes urges us to judge a performance on its ability to realise the body that sources it (1977b: 189). Furthermore, it is our own body – rather than our conscious (or unconscious) self or subjectivity – that recognises such embodiments in texts and experiences *jouissance*.

In *The Pleasure of the Text*, Barthes distinguishes between at least two kinds of readers' pleasures: *plaisir* (pleasure) and *jouissance* (bliss/orgasm).[16] The latter is more concerned with disruption, with texts' gaping 'cleavages', while the former – *plaisir* – functions both as a category of linguistic excess and also sometimes as a catch-all for both types of pleasure.[17] Barthes states that he gains pleasure from skipping ahead in a text, looking up from it and returning to it to dip in: *la dérive*. He also takes pleasure from an excess of linguistic precision, of 'descriptive madness' (Barthes 1990: 26).[18] By contrast, *jouissance* is the experience of 'dissolve which seizes the subject in the midst of bliss' (1990: 6). It is experienced in reading when the 'body pursues its own ideas: for my body does not have the same ideas as I do' (1990: 17). This body is separate from self or subjectivity, and the cultural identity that language creates. As such, this body is neither conscious nor unconscious.

Barthes suggests that cinema sound offers the experience of *jouissance* in the sensory intimacy of closely miked speech:

> In fact, it suffices that the cinema capture the sound of speech *close up* (this is, in fact, the generalised definition of the 'grain' of writing) and make us hear in their materiality, their sensuality, the breath, the gutturals, the fleshiness of the lips, a whole presence of the human muzzle (that the voice, granular and vibrant as an animal's muzzle), to succeed in shifting the signified a great distance and in throwing, so to speak, the anonymous body of the actor into my ear: it granulates, it crackles, it caresses, it grates, it outs, it comes: that is bliss. (Barthes 1990: 67)

Following Barthes, I would argue that two kinds of aural pleasures may be experienced by the audience of contemporary Hollywood cinema: *plaisir*, in the verisimilitudinous presentation of the diegetic world in sound;[19] and *jouissance*, in Barthes' notion of sensual bodily response to sounding signifiers, sonic materials in themselves. Barthes locates *jouissance* with disruption of, or difference from, meaning or expression, and with the body's recognition of another body. The body here recognised is not human, however, and the meaning such moments disrupt is the recognition of sound sources as suggested by the image. The narrative requires only that a sound's source event is recognised and that it is synchronised with the image of the event. Moments of sonic, or aural, spectacle as generated by high definition (often spatialised) sound, on the other hand, may divert the audience from the onward trajectory of the narrative as their bodies respond to a 'set piece', a sonic spectacle. The detail and precision offered by a high definition recording (or generation) and playback of an explosion, for example, allows listeners to explore the interior of the sound – the many smaller sound events that make up the whole – and, in this way, withdraw from the sound's semantic meaning (the explosion) into the grain of the cinematic voice.

In the next section of this essay I suggest that while the surface of a Lynch soundtrack glistens with the same high production values that usually signify contemporary Hollywood production, it presents itself as something more musical due to Lynch's collaborative mode of production. Lynch writes sound into his films' scripts and his direction of them. As Chion points out, his cinema 'is transformed by the central role allotted to the ear, to the passage through the ear. Even if he made silent films, his films would still be auditory' (Chion 1995: 169).

From his very earliest films, Lynch has been both deeply interested, and directly involved, in the scope of sound on film. For example, on the 34-minute *The Grandmother* (1970), Lynch worked with specialist soundman Alan Splet for 63 days full-time creating and recording the soundtrack (Lynch in Rodley 1997: 45–6). Splet officially started work on the soundtrack to *Dune* 19 days before the start of principal photography, though discussions with Lynch had started several months before that (Splet in Gentry 1984: 63). Lynch also worked with engineers to produce the 'temp track' for an early screening of *Lost Highway*. 'Temp tracks' are used to accompany a film through the early stages of editing, usually before the composer has written the score, and before the sound designers have created and mixed the sound effects. Pre-recorded music and library sound effects are used to give the producers and other investors a rough idea of what the final cut will look and sound like. For the *Lost Highway* temp track, however, Lynch worked with engineers to create an approximation of what he actually wanted to use for the final cut: the temp track became an arena for experimentation (Lynch in Rodley 1997: 240–1). Indeed, Lynch has said that he sees the mix as the 'real focus' of the editing process, and prefers to have the opportunity to continue to experiment at that stage, though he admits that this is expensive and is thus something of a luxury.[20]

While most Hollywood blockbusters pride themselves on their sound design and effects, the quality of the music and dialogue recording, and perhaps also the name of the well-known film composer, in many cases there is little interaction or collaboration between the composer and the sound team.[21] By contrast, Lynch's films are planned in such a way that sound effects may be considered musical, both in their own terms and in their relationship to music and dialogue. Indeed, dialogue is also considered to be a sound effect on occasion (Lynch in Rodley 1997: 72). Dialogue, sound effects and music are all integrated in such a way as to create a musical whole, with relationships created between the signifiers of the different sonic objects.[22] In *Wild at Heart,* the most obvious examples that demonstrate the intricacy of sound, music and dialogue integration can be found in the music and sonic segues that overlap visual cuts.

Music Segues

Here the difference between two pieces of music that follow one another in quick succession is elided by a bridge which takes the form of a match in orchestration, pitch, rhythm, gesture or harmonic function. For example, the segue from an extract of Strauss's 'Im Abendrot' into a piece of bar-room pseudo-gypsy band music uses a match in orchestration and pitch (0.49.40). The Strauss accompanies a shot of Lula and Sailor non-diegetically as they stand next to their car at the roadside in open country. The camera pans steadily upward. As the lovers are lost from the frame, the horizon appears at the top, the sky red with the setting sun; literally *Abendrot.* As the camera stops, the shot is dissolved to that of a band playing on stage in a New Orleans restaurant. The Strauss excerpt is faded down just after the dissolve, at a point at which the upper strings have just risen to a higher pitch. The violinist on stage with the band, shot centre frame, plays several notes at this same pitch as the introduction to a new piece. As the supporting harmony of the Strauss excerpt disappears beneath this solo violin line, so the band begin to play. They play in a different key to that of the Strauss, but one which is consonant with the pitch played by the violinist and which acts as a bridge between the two pieces.[23]

Sonic Segues

Similarly to the music segues, the sonic segues involve movement from a sound in one shot to another in the next shot. More precisely, they usually involve the shift from a sound sourced by one object in one shot to a sound sourced by another in the next. The two sounds are usually physically similar, and it is this sonic isomorphism that forms the bridge between the two, masking the point of juncture. For example, the sound of a car running on tarmac, recorded close to source – a broad band of noise at mid-range frequencies – forms a bridge between a shot of Sailor and Lula's car and another of the lobby of the New Orleans hotel that Marietta and Johnnie are staying at, with a visual cue implying that the sound issues from a vacuum cleaner in the lobby (0.55.11).

Integration

There are also many examples of a high degree of integration between the film's sound and music, in which sound effects are used either in combination with, or as segues into or out of, music excerpts. For example, towards the end of the film

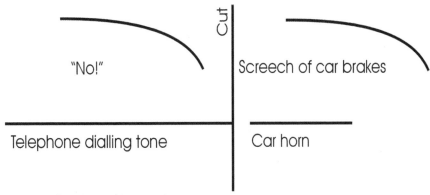

Integration: Sonic isomorphism around a cut

there is a shot in which Lula slams the telephone down on her mother for the last time.[24] This is followed by a loud sustained scream of 'No!' from Marietta, which is underscored by a combination of high dissonant pitches from synthetic strings, very low in the mix, and the dialling tone of the telephone in her hand (1.45.54). Immediately after Marietta herself slams down the phone, there is a cut to a shot of Lula driving, in which she narrowly avoids an accident. The loud interruption of the other car's horn matches the pitch of the phone's dialling tone in the previous shot. The screeching of car tyres offers a structural approximation of Marietta's scream at the same pitch. This creates a sonic isomorphism organised around the cut (see above).[25]

Contrast

In most of the sequences described above cuts are elided through the work of the soundtrack. During other sequences, cuts are emphasised by the soundtrack as a result of the contrast between successive sound levels. For example, in one scene we see an intimate shot of Sailor and Lula lying in bed. Lula says quietly, 'There's more 'an a few bad ideas running around loose out there...', at which point there is a cut to a four-second mid-close-up shot of Marietta smearing lipstick aggressively across her face. This cut is also synchronous with the first presentation of an extract from Krzysztof Penderecki's *Kosmogonia* at an extremely loud level (0.41.32). By contrast, the previous and subsequent shots are both very quiet: Sailor and Lula are seen in close-up, tucked up in bed whispering; a candle helps to set the intimate tone. Clearly, the intention in this shot sequence is to link Marietta with the 'bad ideas running around loose out there'.

Constellations

Just as Lynch's images flaunt their physicality, their 'sensory impact', in a way that images in Hollywood cinema tend not to (Nochimson 1997: 51), so Lynch's sonic constellations flaunt the sensory impact of their sounds, creating a rich, connective structure on a purely sonic level.[26] The physical similarity of certain sounds used in *Wild at Heart* – as demonstrated, at local level, by sonic segues – is used to create a network of thematic and sonorous relationships that run throughout the film and form constellations. The most prominent of these is centred around a short burst of broad band noise: it includes the auditory close-ups of flames, gusts of wind, cars passing Lula and Sailor as they drive, a sound that becomes associated with Santos, the cacophonous burst of orchestral 'noise' that occurs in the extracts from Penderecki's *Kosmogonia* and the excerpt of burning that we hear in the flashbacks to Clyde's murder.[27] This constellation is significant in its foregrounding of noisy sounds, that is, sounds with a high proportion of inharmonic spectral components. These sounds frequently interrupt scenes set in otherwise peaceful outdoor locations in broad daylight, or interiors lit with bright lights (the desert in the middle of a sunny day, or Marietta's garden or bathroom, for example). Such disruptive noises also make thematic reference to the scene of the crime at the heart of the film – the burning of Clyde by Santos at Marietta's instigation – which triggers the film's action: Marietta's attempts to murder Sailor.

The collaborative practices discussed in the sequences of *Wild at Heart* discussed above would ordinarily suggest the practice of a director working outside of Hollywood production. Lynch was not, however. Virtually all of his feature films produced during the 1980s were, at least in part, financed by Hollywood and retained its stars and sensual gloss.[28] Rather, I would argue that Lynch's production techniques actually locate the director (and his work) deep *within* Hollywood practice, though they offer a radical reconfiguration of the traditionally institutionalised, and highly specialised, modes of production that have prevailed in Hollywood since the advent of the studio system. Instead of reinforcing the institutionally conventional alienation of sound, music and image production, Lynch builds collaborative links between them, and materialises these links within the frame. In this way the potential for collaboration that was always a utopian possibility of the vertically-integrated studio system (though often unrealised) is an actuality of Lynch's work.

After the fight in the Hurricane, Sailor turns to the band and praises them: 'You fellas have a lot o' the same power E [Elvis] had. Y'all know this one?' The singer/lead guitarist throws Sailor the microphone. Sailor starts to sing immediately, and by the time he's finished the anacrustic introduction ('Treat me like a') the band are with him ('...fool'). Clearly they do know 'Love Me', and moreover, as in the tradition of every good film musical, they play it instantly in the same key that Sailor sings it, without a word of discussion. They also sing the backing parts, and in this way further establish that, in this film, music is music, whether it be speed-metal from the late 1980s or crooning songs from the 1950s. Rather than seeing this scene as a mere parodic reference to the Hollywood musical, however, I would suggest that it also both confirms Sailor's association with the band – his role as one of the musicians – and identifies him as a controlling figure around whom the music is played out.[29] This interpretation is further borne out by the fact that the only moments of direct (synchronised) correspondence between music and image appear in connection with Sailor. Furthermore, during the scene with the car radio, mentioned above, it is Sailor who takes control of the soundtrack: he can find music when Lula cannot.

At the very end of the film Sailor sings 'Love Me Tender' to Lula: the song he said that he would only sing to his wife. The song's title completes both the title of the earlier 'Love Me', and also his relationship with Lula, by acting as a proposal of marriage. During his performance of 'Love Me' in the Hurricane, Sailor takes control of the diegetic soundtrack, in the form of the band on stage. With 'Love Me Tender' he takes control of the non-diegetic soundtrack: he generates music out of thin air. No other characters in the film possess this ability. While, in some respects, Sailor appears to be a fugitive from a 1950s or 1960s Hollywood musical in which he plays the Elvis Presley character, he can also be considered to stand-in for Lynch himself. Sailor's control of *Wild at Heart*'s soundtrack, in combination with his collaborative association with the film's diegetic musicians, can be seen as standing for Lynch's own collaborative mode of Hollywood production. As Lynch makes clear, he considers himself to be a member of the sound team, rather than a film director.

Notes

1   'Up in Flames' is the title of a song with lyrics by Lynch and music by Angelo Badalamenti. It is sung by Koko Taylor in *Wild at Heart* (*David Lynch's Wild at Heart: original motion picture soundtrack*, London Records 845 128 2). The lyrics suggest that love is not always as powerful or constant as that shared by Sailor and Lula. In this song 'our love' has gone 'up in flames'. There is also a reference here to Marietta's past act of sending her husband 'up in flames'.

2   But see Martha Nochimson's chapter in this volume for a strongly contrasting reading.

3   Lynch was at the very least involved in the production of the sound for *Wild at Heart*'s credit sequence created by Pacific Titles. In a personal communication to the author by email on 26 November 1998, sound designer Randy Thom stated that the Strauss was Lynch's idea, while he (Thom) 'supplied the sounds of fire'.

4   It is implied that this presentation of the Strauss extract is diegetic, however. At the start of the shot, as the music begins to get louder, we see Lula turn up the volume control of a radio at the side of her bed. The radio is also a mount for an ornamental horse.

5   Formal analysis of this track falls short of explaining the kinds of meaning it generates in this film. The track opens with a short, slow theme in metrically regular common time, played in a (melodic) minor key, in unison, by multiple electric guitars with heavy chorus effects. The second bar is completed by emphatic snare hits on the second, third and fourth beats. The theme is then repeated with the metrically regular snare hits replaced by a (metrically unstable) quintuplet across the same three beats of the bar. The whole section

is then repeated a minor third higher. This forms the A section, which is then subsequently also repeated. The B section is based on the same thematic material, but develops its latent energy by articulating it in semiquavers and cutting the percussion breaks. A crescendo combined with a harsh vocal scream emphasises the move into the second section. I have not mentioned the song's vocal line because Lynch uses only the instrumental sections of the song in the film. Interestingly, heard in its entirety (and available on the film's soundtrack album), the song is introduced by a narrative of sorts, with the approaching sound of heavily reverberant footsteps and the unlocking and locking of prison cell doors. Similar sounds occur in *Wild at Heart* when Sailor is first locked up at the Pee Dee Correctional Facility.

6   Of course, these pieces of music also carry with them a whole host of fairly stable meanings that we have come to associate with musical works (as generic signifiers) through convention. For example, the Powermad track might be considered to represent youthful rebellion, perhaps also masculinity (or one version of masculinity). In this essay, however, I am focusing primarily on the meanings of these pieces as created through their association with the narrative and the extent to which the musical material can be considered to confirm my interpretation.

7   In fact, in the case of Sailor's fight with Bobby Ray Lemon, Randy Thom has stated that the sequence was choreographed to different music originally, with the 'Slaughterhouse' track grafted on top afterwards. Personal communication to the author by email, 26 November 1998.

8   See, for example, Daubney (2000), Gorbman (1987) and Kalinak (1992). Exceptions do exist, however, as Kalinak points out. On at least one occasion – John Ford's *The Informer* (1935) – composer Max Steiner was involved in collaborative discussion with the film's director about the music, and indeed composed some of the score, during (rather than after) film production (Kalinak 1992: 113–34).

9   Such a view was commonplace among composers and sound personnel who spoke at the School of Sound Symposium, London, UK, April 1998, though here too exceptions exist. They include the film editor, sound designer and editor, Walter Murch, who has worked with a number of directors living in the San Francisco Bay area, such as Philip Kaufman (*The Unbearable Lightness of Being*, 1987), George Lucas (*American Graffiti*, 1973) and Francis Ford Coppola (*Apocalypse Now*, 1979). Soundman Alan Splet, long-time collaborator with David Lynch, has suggested that there is a Bay-Area approach to sound, which encourages an imaginative use of sound rather than a reliance on library sounds. He has also stated that such directors spend longer in post-production than most in order to get the soundtrack that they want (Splet in Gentry 1984). See also Sergi (1998).

10 Of course, a film's producers usually have the final say, which can lead to the wholesale replacement of previously scored and recorded sequences with new (often pre-existent) tracks, frequently for economic reasons.

11 Lynch continues: 'You meet him, you tell him what you want, he sees the film, comes back with the score, and there's no more time: you're mixing. And if it doesn't work, you don't have time to fiddle and make it work. A lot of music just gets overlaid over sequences and it's the composer's sole interpretation of what you've done. And it may or may not marry. Sometimes it's painful to see what happens. It's better to pull it out. A scene might work better with no music' (Lynch in Rodley 1997: 127).

12 Of course, before the coming of sound, the presence of a large orchestra accompanying the exhibition of a film would similarly work to demonstrate high production values.

13 See Davison 2004 and Sergi 1998.

14 While magnetic sound preceded Dolby (optical) stereo in offering many of the same improvements, it was only with the Dolby system that they became more widely available and cost-effective (Belton 1992).

15 See, for example, Chion on the short promotional films which precede the feature film and which tell the audience that they are in a cinema with a particular kind of sound system (Chion 1994: 100).

16 However, it should be noted that this distinction is by no means a clear one. *Jouissance* appears at times to be distinct from *plaisir*, and on other occasions to be a subset of the latter category.

17 'Pleasure of the text, text of pleasure: these expressions are ambiguous because French has no word that simultaneously covers pleasure (contentment) and bliss (rapture). Therefore, "pleasure" here (and without our being able to anticipate) sometimes extends to bliss, sometimes is opposed to it' (Culler 1990: 19).

18 Barthes cites, in particular, the sentence: 'Cloths, sheets, napkins, were hanging vertically, attached by wooden clothespins to taut lines', from a Robbe-Grillet novel (Barthes 1990: 26). Indeed, while 'Pleasure [*plaisir*] can be expressed in words, bliss [*jouissance*] cannot' (1990: 21).

19 Both Rick Altman (1980) and Mary Ann Doane (1980; 1985) argue that since the coming of sound, the evolution of sound technology and the practices of sound editing and mixing have followed a course which moves ever closer to the representation of the real. Technological developments in the recording of early optical film sound in the 1930s and the sound editing practices developed during the same period, were all driven by the desire to hide the presence of the apparatus – and its work – from the soundtrack. Doane (1985) argues that more recent technological developments (such as Dolby noise reduction) are also grounded in the same ideology: in reducing the noise of the apparatus (and thus concealing its presence), the distance between the sound object and its representation is diminished. The history of innovation in sound technology is by no means straightforward, however: it is subject to the pressures of economics as well as ideology, as the development of stereo magnetic cinema sound in the early 1950s makes clear (see Belton 1992).

20 David Lynch, in a video-taped interview with Larry Sider, shown at the School of Sound, London, UK, April 1998, transcribed and published in Larry Sider

(ed.) *Soundscape: The School of Sound Lectures 1998–2001*. London: Wallflower Press, 49–53.

21 It is also clear that in practice, however, collaboration *can* occur. Such exceptions include discussions between sound designer Skip Lievsay, composer Carter Burwell, Joel Coen (director and co-writer) and Ethan Coen (co-writer) on *Barton Fink* (1991) (Brophy 1999: 24–7), and those between sound designer Randy Thom, composer Alan Silvestri, and director Robert Zemeckis on *Contact* (1997) (Shatkin 2000).

22 As mentioned above, this is not to say that no other Hollywood films exist in which sonic elements are integrated in this way. Indeed, Robynn Stilwell argues that just such moments occur in John McTiernan's *Die Hard* (1988); in particular, in Michael Kamen's reworking of the 'Ode to Joy' from Beethoven's *Ninth Symphony* as the underscore to a monologue by the film's villain, Hans (Stilwell 1997). Nonetheless, in the main, Hollywood cinema does not pay such consistent and careful attention to the integration of sonic elements for the duration of its films. Interestingly, Noël Burch (1986) argues that other world cinemas approach such integration more fully, in particular, Japanese cinema (in films by Kurosawa and Mizoguchi) and French cinemas (through the work of soundman and director Michel Fano). Burch also points out that the integration of all three sonic elements (dialogue, music, sound) is very rare, however, and 'would obviously require the total collaboration of film-maker and sound engineer [and composer?] throughout every stage of the conception and execution of a film' (Burch 1986: 206).

23 Other musical segues include the interchange from the pseudo-gypsy band music into the instrumental of Chris Isaak's 'Wicked Game' (0.51.55), and the move from the Strauss extract into 'Love Me Tender' (1.55.30).

24 The sound of the telephone being slammed down is combined with that of heavily reverberant shotgun fire (and possibly also a piano lid being banged shut harshly) (1.45.36). Lula then throws her drink at a photograph of her mother. The sound of this impact is also combined with that of shotgun fire, the implication being that Lula has finally destroyed her mother; effectively, by shooting her twice.

25 Another example of such integration occurs across the cut from a shot of Lula's feet pounding the bed in a hotel into another of her feet, now dancing to the music of Powermad in the Hurricane Club (0.16.56).

26 Despite the fact that *Wild at Heart* uses high definition sound quality throughout, the film's sonic spectacles are often created around its apparent opposite: noise (though high definition noise).

27 Chion also notes the prominence of these 'buffeting gusts' and suggests that they, 'express the way in which Sailor and Lula's present happiness and freedom [in the first half of the film] are doomed … because [the buffeting gusts] accentuate the fragility of their bodies and spirits, a fragility fatally determined by their life stories … These gusts may also be taken, inversely, as the chink in the door, opening on to a source of eternal fantastic power. What is at stake in the gusts is

a sense of ambiguity, and depending on the way these gusts are presented, they may express different things: a fresh charge or energy, a breath which weighs upon your fate and presses you down, or a hole which opens in despair beneath your feet' (Chion 1995: 140).

28 *The Elephant Man* (1980) was financed by Brooksfilms (Mel Brooks' production company) and Paramount; *Dune* (1984) and *Blue Velvet* (1986) were financed by the mini-major De Laurentiis Entertainment and Universal Pictures; *Wild at Heart* (1990) was financed by Propaganda Films for Polygram Filmed Entertainment.

29 It should also be noted that, throughout the film, there are allusions to one of the most well-known of Hollywood's film musicals: *The Wizard of Oz* (1939). For example, Glinda (the good witch) appears to Sailor at the end of the film; Lula clicks the heels of her red stilettos together after her ordeal at the hands of Bobby Peru; both Sailor and Lula make reference to the Yellow Brick Road, Kansas and the Wizard of Oz; and Lula has hallucinations in which her mother appears as a wicked witch, riding a broomstick and cackling.

CHAPTER TEN

Weird or Loopy? Specular Spaces, Feedback and Artifice in Lost Highway's Aesthetics of Sensation

Greg Hainge

References to David Lynch in the mainstream press almost without exception describe him as being somewhat less than normal. He has been dubbed 'Hollywood's reigning eccentric' (Woodward 1990), the 'Czar of Bizarre' (Corliss 1990), or just plain 'Weirdo' (Kermode 1997), whilst his films attract such critical responses as: 'on a weirdness scale of one to ten, Lynch's new movie, *Lost Highway*, scores about a 45' (Curtis 1997); 'It's a weird movie, in that spooky/sicko, deadpan way that Lynch's movies always are, and it's guaranteed to repel anyone who likes entertainment wrapped in tidy resolutions and optimistic fade-outs' (Guthmann 1997); or, alternatively, 'Glad to report that David Lynch is still circling planet earth in a spaceship with his mind located several galaxies beyond. This is delightfully bonkers' (Hemblade 1997: 46). That the films of David Lynch follow a logic of their own which shares little with that of the average product emanating from Hollywood would seem, then, incontrovertible. Indeed, Chris Rodley likens the sensation of watching a Lynch film to that sense of 'uncanniness' or '"unease" first experienced in the late eighteenth century', and writes, 'Conventional film narrative, with its demand for logic and legibility, is therefore of little interest to Lynch' (Rodley 1997: ix). Nonetheless, Slavoj Žižek sees in *Blue Velvet* (and, one can infer, the films of David Lynch in general) a certain conformity to a postmodern norm (if indeed there is such a thing).[1] Žižek writes:

A modernist work of art is by definition 'incomprehensible'; it functions as a shock, as the irruption of a trauma which undermines the complacency of our daily routine and resists being integrated into the symbolic universe of the prevailing ideology; thereupon, after this first encounter, interpretation enters the stage and enables us to integrate this shock.

What postmodernism does, however, is the very opposite: its objects *par excellence* are products with a distinctive mass appeal (films like *Blade Runner*, *Terminator* or *Blue Velvet*) – it is for the interpreter to detect in them an exemplification of the most esoteric theoretical finesses of Lacan, Derrida or Foucault. If, then, the pleasure of the modernist interpretation consists in the effect of recognition which 'gentrifies' the disquieting uncanniness of its object ... the aim of the postmodernist treatment is to estrange its very initial homeliness. (Žižek 1992: 1–2)

Few would disagree that the effect produced by the films of David Lynch is a disquieting one. Whether or not it is true that this effect comes from an estrangement of an initial homeliness, however, is not so certain. Although the opening sequences of *Blue Velvet* might indicate that this is the case, as they appear to present an idealised domestic idyll, a picture postcard, picket fence McCarthyised America, the subversion of this supposed everyday reality comes long before the discovery of a severed ear, even before the archetypal patriarch keels over from a heart attack. Indeed, the pseudo-idyllic images presented by Lynch from the outset of *Blue Velvet* never allow the viewer the initial sensation of homeliness, *das Heimliche*, that Žižek talks of. On the contrary, as Brian Jarvis notes, there is an inversion of the normal order between *heimlich* and *unheimlich*, since the surrealistic intensity of the colours and the slow-motion tracking in this scene serve to accentuate a dreamlike ambience, to present 'an image of the suburb as simulacrum, foregrounding geographical unreality through the use of colour filter and self-reflexive camera rhetoric' (Jarvis 1998: 177). As Rodley neatly surmises, 'Insecurity, estrangement and lack of orientation and balance are sometimes so acute in Lynchland that the question becomes one of whether it is possible ever to feel "at home"' (Rodley 1997: x).

This bypassing of the anaesthetic realm of the homely, this displacement directly into *das Unheimliche* is an effect achieved by the heightened artifice of the Lynchian universe. In the initial sequences of *Blue Velvet*, for instance, there can be no doubt that we are in an artificial realm. Fred Pfeil has noted that the initial sequences of *Blue Velvet* refuse to settle into assured conventionality and, indeed, break completely from it, and adds, 'simultaneously hyper-realising and de-centering narrative and cinematic convention ... is from the start what *Blue Velvet* is about, both its way of doing business and the business itself' (Pfeil 1992). Similarly, talking about the closing sequence of this film in which we observe an animatronic robin, Pfeil refers to 'the bird's obvious artificiality, the music's clichéd goopiness, and the hypercomposed flatness and stiffness of the *mise-en-scène*', noting that all of this as well as the characters are, therefore, 'constructions of sound and words and light, spaces where Lynch and Company's projections meet our own'. For Pfeil, in the final analysis *Blue Velvet* is thus

> a *gynesis* of both film and family that irresolves without overthrowing, that keeps home un-natural while forcing us to own up to the familiarity of all that is officially Other and strange, home-making and as dislocating, from blue-sky beginning (plenitude or emptiness? true blue to fake void?) to blue-sky end. (1992)

The space in which the films of David Lynch operate, then, might be said to be specular and not prismatic, their very content reflecting back on itself rather than refracting outwards and attempting to create a direct connection with the viewer – which is not to say that these films do not connect with their viewer. It is almost as though the image coming from the projector is absorbed by the screen rather than being reflected back to the audience, an impression intensified by Lynch's frequent use of extremely low lighting or absolute blackness. This is an impression that is often compounded by the soundscapes that accompany his images, the most obvious example being *Eraserhead* (1977), a film in which the almost constant background noise becomes the aural accompaniment not only of the world in which the protagonist Henry lives, but of that of the viewer, too. Its almost constant presence serves not only to submerge us in its own space. The noise permeating *Eraserhead* is an industrial drone which suggests that the viewer is inhabiting a machinic world, a world which is a production-line for sound.

The creation of a self-referential space is, of course, another common trait of the products of postmodernism, as Žižek rightly points out in his discussion of Hitchcock's films of the 1950s and early 1960s.[2] I will argue here that, in the films of David Lynch, it is precisely this self-referential, deliberately artificial aspect of the films that creates their original and enduring atmosphere of unhomeliness, and that, paradoxically, it is this very refusal to allow the spectator the sensation that s/he is on familiar territory, that allows the films to connect with their audience – for without a connection between product and consumer it is unlikely that Lynch would enjoy the 'mass appeal' that Žižek talks of. While I agree with Brian Jarvis when he writes that 'Lynch's postmodern intertextuality precisely relishes its adestinationality, its failure to go anywhere' (Jarvis 1998: 178), I will argue that it is precisely from within this failure that Lynch's aesthetic transmits itself to the viewer, and that his Baudrillardean road to nowhere does not therefore constitute 'a cinespace of affectless signs' (1998: 179). I will compare the manner in which the Lynchian aesthetic establishes a transversal relation from product to viewer through an intensification of self-reflexive processes to the way in which, according to Gilles Deleuze, the paintings of Francis Bacon do the same. Although it would arguably be possible to apply this reading to Lynch's work as a whole (including his paintings and photographs), the present discussion will limit itself primarily to *Lost Highway*, the film in which this similarity is most apparent.

Bacon's paintings have unquestionably had an important effect on Lynch. When asked by Chris Rodley (in an interview about his own paintings) which established artists had struck him, Lynch replied,

> – Francis Bacon is, to me, the main guy, the number one kinda hero painter. There's a lot of painters that I like. But for just the *thrill* of standing in front of a painting … I saw Bacon's show in the 1960s at the Marlborough Gallery and it was really one of the most powerful things I ever saw in my life.
> – *What excited you most about Bacon? The use of the paint, or the subject matter?*
> – Everything. The subject matter and the style were united, married, perfect. And the space, and the slow and the fast and, you know, the textures, everything. Normally I only like a couple of years of a painter's work, but I like everything of Bacon's. The guy, you know, had the stuff. (Lynch in Rodley 1997: 16–17)[3]

One might think that Bacon's influence would be more apparent in his paintings than in his films, but in fact the opposite appears to be the case. Lynch's paintings bear little resemblance to a Bacon canvas,[4] while his films use images that recur frequently in Bacon's paintings: the sectioned pig carcasses hanging outside a butcher's shop in *The Elephant Man*, blurred or deformed faces (John Merrick in *The Elephant Man*, Bob in *Twin Peaks: Fire Walk with Me*, Marietta Fortune in *Wild at Heart*, Fred Madison in *Lost Highway*), the omnipresent cigarettes.[5] This similarity has been noticed by critics sensitive to the visuality of the films: Chris Rodley notes, for instance, that the novelist J.G. Ballard said *Blue Velvet* was 'like *The Wizard of Oz* reshot with a script by Franz Kafka and décor by Francis Bacon' (Rodley 1997: 56), whilst *American Cinematographer*'s Stephen Pizzello has written of *Lost Highway*:

> For certain key scenes, super-minimal lighting schemes were employed to great effect. A particularly impressive example of this strategy is the film-maker's sepulchral rendering of the Madison home's main hallway, which has a foreboding quality reminiscent of the work of one of Lynch's favorite painters, Francis Bacon. Achieving this look required some deft interplay between the various crewmembers. (Pizzello 1997)

I will argue, however, that the similarities between Bacon and Lynch go far beyond a mere coincidence of visual elements, and that the aesthetic processes and affective intent of Lynch's films can be shown to be intimately linked to Bacon as analysed by Gilles Deleuze. In this respect, my analysis will go beyond that of Martha Nochimson at the same time as it differs radically from it. Nochimson's account of Bacon's influence is firmly centred on narrative, and accordingly, she gives great importance to Bacon's own pronouncements on that topic (Nochimson 1997: 11). The narrative she sees at the heart of the Baconian and Lynchian projects is that of what she and Lynch choose to refer to as the 'subconscious', a narrative that does not follow the linearity and logic of 'conventional' narrative and which, consequently, acts upon the viewer's nerves rather than his/her thoughts. Much as I agree with Nochimson's conclusions about the affective, not intellectual, intent of Lynch's and Bacon's aesthetic – especially in the light of Lynch's comment that in the four per cent of the audience who do not get his films 'the intellect has blocked the little area between nerves, the synapse. And the spark does not jump across' (Lynch in Kermode 1997) – where I differ is in the belief that this affect can be accessed from a structure to which the term 'narrative' can be applied.

Despite her insistence on Lynch's non-rational modes of communication, in her recourse to a psychoanalytic framework Nochimson inserts these aesthetic expressions into the formal strictures that she claims they evade. As lucid and convincing as her analyses are, the degree to which the individual viewer/reader accepts her analyses may depend, in the final analysis, on the extent to which s/he feels that the subconscious can be explained in psychoanalytic terms. The present study argues, on the contrary, that the bypassing of rationality in Lynch's films is a result, amongst other things, of a deliberate dissolution of narrative. In claiming this, I am not proposing a 'leftist, anarchic-obscurantist, anti-theoretical insistence that one should renounce all interpretive effort and let ourselves go to the full ambiguity and richness of the film's audio and visual texture' (Žižek 2000: 17), nor do I accept Žižek's proposition, somewhat similar to Nochimson's, that the 'circular form of narrative in *Lost Highway* directly renders the circularity of the psychoanalytic process' (ibid.). Rather, this circularity will be seen to be intimately linked to Figural processes in the film that bring these processes to their fruition and simultaneously fracture both narrative and its circle. Even though there is truth in Žižek's assertions that Lynch's films are like an imperceptible voice expressing to the viewer the *real-impossible*, a recognition of the inconsistent multitude of fantasies which we term 'reality',[6] this, I suggest, is their second, allegorical movement. In their first movement, they can ultimately be seen to question not 'reality' itself but rather the supposed realism of the cinematic medium and its capacity for coherent representation.

Meat

> – Bacon's paintings often imply a narrative, but it's unclear exactly what is going on. Does that interest you?
> – Exactly right. Fragments of narrative. If Bacon had made a movie, what would it have been and where would it have gone? And how would the cinema translate those textures and those spaces? (Lynch in Rodley 1997: 17)

In his work *Francis Bacon: logique de la sensation*, Gilles Deleuze proposes a reading of the work of Bacon as an art of sensation. In the paintings of Bacon, according to this analysis, every element conspires to isolate a primary Figure: the chromatic juxtapositions of the backgrounds, the lines of force inscribed on the canvas – Bacon's inimitable circles, arrows, parallelepipeds and evanescent cubes – and other elements all exert a centripetal force on this primary Figure. By doing this, Bacon isolates the Figure from the surroundings and thus breaks all notion of representation, narration or illustration (Deleuze 1981: 10). Estranged from the very context in which it is situated, the narrative of the Figure can no longer be determined by its context: the space it inhabits is no longer a narrative space, but merely the space of the painting in which the figure inhabiting that space becomes merely an Image or an Icon (1981: 9). Taking his inspiration from Lyotard, Deleuze terms the mechanism by which the Figure is thus isolated a figural process; having undergone this process, the Figure releases centrifugal forces as it attempts to escape itself through its very organs in a spasmodic movement so as to fade into the background, the very materiality of the painting (1981: 17). The effect of this, of course, is to further the narrative dissolution and thus intensify the pure immanence of the painting which is thus able to bypass the reflective mechanisms of mind and intellect to act directly on the spectator's emotive core on a plane of immediacy. As Mireille Buydens has put it,

> in painting the horror of a scene, the painter misses the cry, he spoils the pictural event. The very opposite of this sensational art (painting horror), Bacon seeks an art of sensation (painting the cry) which smacks us in the face, lifts us up from inside, like a force liberating other forces: each stroke must be a 'potential in action', a call to rebellion, a stick of dynamite inserted in our veins … It is no longer a case of *representing the world*, juxtaposing forms and weaving stories, but of *presenting the fluxes at work behind things* (the force of a cry), ripping open subjects and objects like wine skins so as to let out the wind or the wine of intensity… (Buydens 1990: 84–5, my translation (emphasis in original))

Few would deny that there is in *Lost Highway* a deliberate attempt to confound narrative linearity (indeed the October Films press release stated that Lynch and Gifford 'fashioned a script that actually subverts the rules of conventional filmmaking'[7]) and more generally, the viewer's understanding – when this latter term implies a hermeneutic reduction and not an intensive feeling. Rebecca and Samuel Umland even suggest that this might be particularly so for academic critical systems which they see as 'woefully inadequate to deal with Lynch's films' (Umland and Umland 1999: 2). Lynch is notoriously guarded about the 'meaning' of his film, as are his crew members and cast. Patricia Arquette appears to be the only one of the crew who is willing to proffer an explication of the apparent non-senses of the film (she suggests that, unable to cope with guilt at having killed his wife, Fred Madison psychically projects himself into Pete Dayton), but Lynch is quick to (kindly) dismiss her theory.[8] Even the press release seems to stress the unintelligibility of the film above every other aspect, warning against the temptation of making 'something linear and literal out of Lynch's Möbius strip', and stating, 'As post-modern *noir* detours into the realm of science fiction, it becomes apparent that in *Lost Highway*, the only certainty is uncertainty'. What is more, the release would appear to vindicate my claim not only that Lynch's filmic expression employs techniques normally reserved for painting, but that this very technique is used in order to break conventional narrative so as to bypass the intellect and reach the viewer on an affective, sensational level:

> Regardless of what label one tries to put on him, Lynch, like all modern artists – irrespective of their labels – brings a radically new attitude toward both the past and the present and, in his exploration of the film medium – a medium that has remained surprisingly realistic in its first century of existence – he reveals a modernism that has long been taken for granted in painting and music, but which is rarely exhibited on screen. 'In my mind,' he says, 'it's so much fun to have something that has clues and is mysterious – something that is understood intuitively rather than just being spoon-fed to you. That's the beauty of cinema, and it's hardly ever even tried. These days, most films are pretty easily understood, and so people's minds stop working.'

> Displaying an obvious affection for abstraction, Lynch's films have become increasingly non-narrative, fuelled less and less by what one might call 'story' and increasingly emphasizing mood, tone, feelings and a highly subjective vision of the world. (October Films 2000)

Lynch himself has voiced his preference for a subjective, aporetic narrative over a normalised linear narrative in numerous interviews. This deliberate avoidance of meaning at the diegetic level is what he refers to as 'mystery' or 'abstraction', and he not only accords these phenomena a privileged place in his own movies, he also constantly bemoans their disappearance in the filmic products of his contemporaries, stating in an interview in *Rolling Stone*, for instance, 'Every single element in a movie … now had to be understood – and understood at the lowest common denominator. It's a real shame, because there are so many places that people could go if they weren't corralled so tightly with those kinds of restraints' (Lynch in Gilmore 1997). The ways in which Lynch creates this sense of mystery, these abstractions, are manifold: the most obvious comes with the deliberate obfuscation and contravention of logic at the diegetic level; but at a stylistic level also, Lynch's aesthetic vision fractures narrative as do the canvases of Bacon. It will be argued here, however, that due to the greater perceptionality (and thus realist illusion) of cinema in comparison to painting, these two elements alone do not allow the aesthetic produced in and by the rupture of narrative to connect with the viewer as they do in Bacon's work.[9] In order to do this, Lynch employs a third mechanism, this being (paradoxically) a deliberate heightening of artifice and self-referentiality, elements which, in Metz's analysis, already constitute one side of the dual cinematic signifier (the other being its perceptionality) (Metz 1982: 45). It is to these three processes in *Lost Highway* that we will now turn our attention, concentrating firstly on the illogicalities of the diegesis, and then on the film's stylistics and artifice, elements which are, for Lynch, inseparable and which will, therefore, be treated together here.

Logic

> It's better not to know so much about what things mean or how they might
> be interpreted or you'll be too afraid to let things keep happening. Psychology
> destroys the mystery, this kind of magic quality. It can be reduced to certain
> neuroses or certain things, and since it is now named and defined, it's lost its
> mystery and the potential for a vast, infinite experience.
>
> – David Lynch[10]

If many critics not partisan to the Lynchian vision have vehemently criticised *Lost
Highway* for not making sense, then they have done so with good reason. The critic
Roger Ebert, for instance, has written that

> David Lynch's *Lost Highway* is like kissing a mirror: You like what you see,
> but it's not much fun, and kind of cold. It's a shaggy ghost story, an exercise
> in style, a film made with a certain breezy contempt for audiences. I've seen
> it twice, hoping to make sense of it. There is no sense to be made of it. To try
> is to miss the point. What you see is all you get. (Ebert 1997)

Although we may not share the sentiment expressed herein, the basic premise that
there is no rational explanation for the major diegetic events of the film holds true.
As Todd McCarthy has stated in *Variety*, 'the narrative strategies of Lynch and
co-screen writer Barry Gifford … combine with key casting decisions to create
intentional mysteries for which there are no answers' (McCarthy 1997: 44). In
Lost Highway there are no answers in spite of Lynch and Gifford's red herrings
concerning Möbius Strips, psychogenic fugues, teasing statements in the press
pack that imply certain scenes are telling the audience that Lynch has an answer
but that 'we, like Pete, will have to find it on our own' (October Films 2000), and
Lynch's wonderful exercises in self-contradiction in this same document: 'There are
explanations for a billion things in life that aren't so understandable, and yet inside
– somewhere – they are understandable.' It is interesting to note that it is in the press
release that we also find the following:

> Unfolding with the logic of a dream, which can be interpreted but never
> explained, *Lost Highway* is punctuated by a series of occurrences that simply
> can't have occurred: one man turns into another; a woman who may be
> dead seduces the man who might have killed her; a man phones himself
> and – inexplicably – is at the other end of the line to receive his own call!
> (October Films 2000)

The two main inexplicable events of the diegesis come half-way through the film and
then at the end. In the first, Fred Madison, locked up in his prison cell, is somehow
transformed into Pete Dayton. In order to see precisely how this happens, it is useful
to look at the screenplay (even if it is not identical to the final film version):

INT. PRISON. FRED'S CELL. NIGHT

Fred is still curled on the floor, but spasms begin to rock his body. He goes into convulsions, blood gushes from his nostrils. His head is badly swollen. Fred vomits repeatedly, and drags around in his mess. Fred turns, straining upwards as we've seen him do before. His face and head are hideously deformed.
Fred brings his shaking, tortured hand to his forehead. He pulls his hand down across his face, squeezing as it goes. As his hand passes over his face, Fred's features are removed, leaving a blank, white mass with eye sockets.
We move into the eye sockets and beyond.

CUT TO:
EXT. TWO-LANE HIGHWAY. NIGHT

We see a clean-moving POV illuminated by headlights. We are floating down an old two-lane highway through a desolate, desert landscape. This gliding, eerie POV continues until the headlights illuminate a figure standing at the side of the road. This figure is a man, Pete Dayton. Pete turns, unsettled; as he looks directly at us we move closer to him. The ghost image of a house appears behind Pete. There is a girl, Sheila, standing on the lawn in front of the house. She is afraid and is trying to communicate with Pete. Pete doesn't seem to hear her and continues to stare directly at us. Now Pete seems to move toward us as we move toward him. His head fills the screen.

DISSOLVE TO:
INT. PRISON. FRED'S CELL. NIGHT

Fred's blank face begins to contort and take on the appearance, feature by feature, of Pete Dayton.
Fred Madison is becoming Pete Drayton.

(Lynch and Gifford 1997: 48–9)

In this scene, the actual events taking place within the prison cell would seem to be a textbook rendition of the Figural processes of Bacon's paintings described above. Constrained by the centripetal forces of the prison cell – just as our viewpoint is unavoidably contained by the placement of this figure in a monochrome cube – Fred is isolated and able to transgress the fixed boundary of his identity. Precisely as in Deleuze's analysis of Bacon in which the body of the isolated figure attempts to escape itself via a spasm – be it a spasm of love, vomit or excrement (Deleuze 1981: 16–17) – in order to become a Figure, so here Fred vomits, his flesh appearing to peel away from him (the film version is less explicit in this regard, the viewer observing merely what one can only imagine is a close-up shot of raw – and extremely Baconesque – flesh), and he becomes, literally, an other. It is this very process that, for Deleuze, serves as a means for Bacon to 'break with representation, fracture narration, prohibit illustration, liberate the Figure' (1981: 10, my translation); little wonder, then, that when Lynch uses this same process the plot should stop making sense.

The second non-sense comes at the end of the film. Even if Lynch is careful in the opening sequence of *Lost Highway* to prefigure the car chase of the film's close by including a hint of police sirens on the soundtrack as an unknown (and unseen) interlocutor whispers 'Dick Laurent is dead' to Fred over an intercom, the apparent revelation at the end of the film that the interlocutor was Fred himself is anything but revelatory since it is a non-sense. The apparent return to a point of origin is not a return at all: not only does it contradict the exigencies of Euclidean time, it also contravenes the laws of physical reality (in the same way as does the Mystery Man's phone call earlier in the film). Whereas the return at the end of the film to the opening sequences, shot in the second instance from a different perspective, may give the impression that we are dealing with a Tarantinoesque discombobulated narrative structure, what is missing from Lynch's film is an analepsis that would allow this return to take place without the destruction of linearity, which is to say logic. Indeed, according to the internal structure of *Lost Highway*, the entire film (except for one incidental analepsis concerning the night when Pete disappeared from his parents' house) follows what appears to be a strict chronology, even if time is radically telescoped in certain sections (cf. Fred's conviction and incarceration). What happens in *Lost Highway*, therefore, is the establishment of a loop: just as Lynch employed a film loop in his early art experiments (a process by which the extremities of a length of film are stuck together so as to run continuously through a projector), so here one end of the linear timeline is appended to the other. As Marina Warner puts it, 'the plot of *Lost Highway* binds time's arrow into time's loop, forcing Euclidian space into Einsteinian curves where events lapse and pulse at different rates and everything might return eternally' (Warner 1997: 6).[11] However, the return to the initial sequence of the film does not, of course, itself constitute the end of the film for, having whispered into the intercom, Fred jumps into his car and flees the police. It would appear, therefore, that it is the establishment of this loop that actually allows that very loop to be exceeded and that consequently signals the complete dissolution of narrative (as the narrative closes here), logic and linear time (which is left as broken as the median strip of the road that frames the entire film). Finally, the establishment and subsequent surpassing of this loop also signals, as we shall see, the accomplishment of the film's Figural processes.

Style and Artifice

In *Lost Highway*, narrative convention is also broken by the cinematography. Filled with extreme close-up shots of matches lighting cigarettes, lips talking into telephones and skin in love scenes, the camera focuses our attention on specific areas of the frame, thereby partaking in the isolating mechanism of the Figural processes we have said to be at work in *Lost Highway*. This technique also contributes to the Figural dissolution of narrative, however, for the extreme close-up as employed by Lynch denies the viewer the full identification normally provided by the face shot and concentrates the viewer's attention on the specific acts of smoking, talking and love-making, not on the result of these acts as would be the case in a plot-driven narrative. Indeed, there is in these shots an intensification of the *jouissance* derived from the image itself to the point that the character is almost forgotten: we care little who is making love to whom in this film for we concentrate on the texture of the image, the interplay of two bodies; so sensuous are the lips it matters little what they are saying; and so what if smoking kills you? Lynch's smokers are anything but the *X-Files'* smoking man, whose habit has a purely diegetic, character-driven function. These are images of pure stylistic function in which diegetic elements become a part of the film's visuality, images in which matches and cigarettes emit the sole light and sound source of a shot, skin and lips become merely a reflective surface for light in a predominantly black shot, and (in the final love-making scene) car headlights provide the means to wash out the entire frame.

In much the same way, the lighting and décor of the filmic space also guide the viewer's gaze to specific areas of the frame, the most striking example of this perhaps being the sitting room of the Madison household where the only areas illuminated are those required for that section of the diegesis: the video player into which will be inserted the mysterious videotapes and the sofa on which Fred and Renée will sit to watch the tapes. Paradoxically, however, in focusing the viewer's attention on those areas of the frame of importance to the upcoming diegesis, Lynch's highly stylised *mise-en-scène* simultaneously collaborates with the film's processes of narrative dissolution, the stylistic isolation of diegetic elements being a transparent contrivance that lends an air of irreality/hyper-reality to the diegesis and disrupts, therefore, the transmission of narrative.

At the same time as stylistic elements are seen to augment the film's diegetic level so diegetic elements are absorbed into the film's very stylistics. There is in *Lost Highway* an inward specularity, a perpetual movement towards its own lost centre. Again, the image of the loop springs to mind, as well as that of an implosion, an image of crucial importance in *Lost Highway* and which recurs at key moments in the film in the form of the Mystery Man's (the 'mysterious' or 'weird' film-maker with a prosthetic camcorder-eye?) imploding shack. Always hyper-aware of its own style and artifice, Lynch's aesthetic can only ever seem unnatural, can only ever thrust the viewer directly into *das Unheimliche*. Even in his direction of his actors, Lynch appears intent on intensifying the very process of *acting*, as we can see clearly from some of Patricia Arquette's comments on Lynch's directorial manner:

> Bill and I were finally getting into it, getting excited about our roles, our relationship. When we did the first major scene together we thought, yeah, that was great! But David came in and said 'We're gonna go again'. And then we did it again and thought it was horrible and he would say 'Great! Take more time, take a lot longer, make it dreamier'. (Arquette in Todd 1997)

This comment perhaps explains the apparent awkwardness of many of Lynch's characters, the sense of uncanny, unease (or, depending on personal taste, annoyance) that they can inspire in the viewer. It also offers us an insight into Lynch's use of dialogue which often seems stilted and irrelevant or at best incidental. This, as well as Lynch's dislike for talking about his movies, has generally been interpreted as indicative of his mistrust towards language, but it is rather another means for the director to heighten the artifice of his work, to remove us from a realist mode in order to cast us further into his cinematic metaspaces. Every element of *Lost Highway* conspires in this inward specularity, this establishment of a loop, and it is precisely Lynch's attention to *every* detail that allows this film to extend beyond its own boundaries, to reach its audience, to bring the Figural processes and their attendant aesthetic of sensation to their fruition. Since both diegesis and style are perfectly in harmony and since they feedback into each other, the loop created exceeds itself as does a feedback loop in an electro-acoustic system. An electro-acoustic feedback loop is created as part of the amplified output signal is fed back into the input, which in turn again becomes output that feeds back into the input, etc. This loop will only be established if the output feeding back into the electro-acoustic system is identical to the original output; when this is the case and a feedback loop is established, the result does not resemble the original sound source at all but becomes, most often, a piercing shriek. In the same way, *Lost Highway* (every element being identical to itself, style and diegesis feeding back into each other in their mutual attempt to disrupt normalised narrative representation) exceeds its own loop and connects with the viewer, the final result being anything but the 'empty stylistic façade' that Roger Ebert sees (Ebert 1997: 2). This (of course) is achieved both stylistically and diegetically, for just as the final scene of the film is, in every respect, a massive crescendo towards an aesthetic of pure affect that tests the limits of our aural and visual senses (Michelle LeBlanc and Colin Odell comment on the film's remarkable contrasts of saturated colours and intense darkness and advise us to request that the projectionist 'turn up the volume to ear bleeding levels' (LeBlanc and Odell 2000: 72)), so at the diegetic level Fred escapes the loop established by the intercom scene and speeds off down a highway, the figural processes of his own body also reaching their apogee. This movement, then, is the very obverse of that taking place in the formation of a black hole, for whereas a supernova emits a blinding light before forming a black hole, a point of infinite density from which nothing can escape and at which all laws of physics collapse, in *Lost Highway* the massive inward density and darkness of the film leads to a massive release of energy in the film's climax. The final directions of the screenplay cannot possibly begin to render the effect of this final scene, but they do nonetheless give some indication of this process:

CLOSE-UP: *Fred's face – through the front windshield. The shot is wide enough to reveal the cop cars in hot pursuit.*
Fred's face begins to change again, grotesquely contorting as he races into the vortex. His tormented scream blends with the howling siren of the police car gaining on him. (Lynch and Gifford 1997: 144)

The tormented scream of Fred Madison (Bill Pullman)

The final scene of *Lost Highway* might enable us to apprehend precisely what an aesthetic of sensation entails for the viewer, what Deleuze means when he talks of an expression of pure immediacy that transmits itself to the spectator via a transversal relation.[12] Few films produce the kind of adrenaline rush experienced at the end of *Lost Highway* without recourse to the cheap stock-in-trade tricks of the average Hollywood horror or suspense movie. The final shot of Fred's contorting face with its undeniably Baconian overtones may also allow us to understand better what Bacon meant when he claimed he wanted to paint the cry, not the horror. Working in a medium in which it has for a long time been recognised that the very concept of realist representation is problematic, Bacon was able to break narrative merely by means of the dual movement of centripetality and centrifugality in his canvases' Figural processes and the narrative disjunction created by the space (physical and diegetic) between the apparent series of his triptychs. The increased perceptionality of the cinema, however, forces Lynch to add a further dimension to his aesthetic in order for it to have the same affect of sensation as the paintings of Bacon. The cinematic signifier, as Christian Metz has noted, has 'unaccustomed perceptual wealth' (Metz 1982: 45), as a result of which it is better equipped to immerse the viewer in its own spaces of realist illusion. Unlike Metz, however, we do not believe that the cinematic signifier is 'at the same time stamped with unreality to an unusual degree [drumming] up all perception, but to switch it immediately over into its own absence, which is nonetheless the only signifier present' (1982: 45). Lynch is aware of the fact that in the cinema the fracturing of narrative, the breaking of linearity that the shots of the median strip in *Lost Highway*'s opening and closing credit sequences indicate to be his goal, can only be achieved by the contrived heightening of artifice, by a deliberate avowal of film's phoney presence. This view is similar to that of Warner when she writes,

The conspicuous camerawork and flaring noise of *Lost Highway* don't enhance the story in a traditional thriller manner, but interrupt and disturb its flow, compelling the audience to see how film can take possession of your mind and estrange you from yourself, just as the characters in *Lost Highway* are estranged from themselves. (Warner 1997: 10)

Warner's comments illustrate well the way in which it is the very self-reflexive processes of *Lost Highway* that allow Lynch's aesthetic to affect the viewer. For, as we have seen, Lynch's aesthetic operates by fusing style and diegesis and by skewing cinema's realist modes so as to enter directly into the space of *das Unheimliche*, whilst at the same time creating a self-referential loop that is intensified until the Iconic Figure and the very aesthetic expression at the centre of that loop exceed both the loop and their own bounds. As Warner surmises, then, '*Lost Highway* is telling a story about the medium' (ibid.).

This tripartite aesthetic process could, arguably, be found in all of Lynch's films as well as in certain other aspects of his work. Most unusually, we can perhaps see a kind of summation of it in his comic strip, serialised in the *LA Reader*, *The Angriest Dog in the World*. Created by Lynch, this comic strip shows a dog straining at its leash in a backyard framed by a white picket fence and the side of a house. Purportedly about a 'dog who is so angry he cannot move' or eat or sleep, who is 'bound so tightly with tension and anger he approaches the state of rigor mortis', the reader's attention is focused not on the dog but on the speech bubbles coming from the house or, in the final frame which shows the exact same scene of the first three frames but at night, on the light coming from the window and which falls just short of the (black) dog.[13] Lynch therefore breaks narrative expectation by making the supposed focal point of his comic strip an almost incidental element, whilst intensifying the artifice of the medium by filling his speech bubbles with jokes so corny the laughter they elicit can only be knowingly ironic. Where *The Angriest Dog in the World* differs from Lynch's films, however, is in its failure to combine diegesis and style: the framing and narrative techniques of the strip do not exert a centrifugal force on the dog who remains, therefore, unable to break free from his leash, to engage in the Figural process that would enable him to escape the imposed limits of form. Considering David Lynch's entire career, what is perhaps most amazing about this director is not that he has continued to make films about characters who do succeed in exceeding their own boundaries, but that, tied to the fringes of major studios and production companies, he has been able to continue in his role as 'the anathema of the Hollywood system' (LeBlanc and Odell 2000: 7) and to make films that consistently exceed the limits of the Hollywood system.

Notes

1   This in spite of the following kind of critique: 'Is *Lost Highway* the condemned man's guilty fantasy? The dream of a man on the run? No answer is provided, and in the end I didn't much care. It would be generous to call this wilfully

baffling movie postmodern' (Rayner 1997).

2   According to Žižek, these films demonstrate aspects of '"postmodernism" formally epitomised by the accentuated allegorical dimension (the indexing, within the film's diegetic content, of its own process of enunciation and consumption: references to "voyeurism" from *Rear Window* to *Psycho*, etc.)' (Žižek 1992: 5).

3   It is important to stress that I am not implying any kind of imitation. As Lynch himself has said in an interview in which he significantly appears to conflate the practices of painting and film-making, 'One of my favorite painters is Francis Bacon – he's probably a favorite of lots of painters. I may be influenced by certain things in his painting, and someone else may be influenced by something else. It's so subjective. It's important to do your own work. There's a hundred years of cinema, so it's hard to do something that people can't compare to something that's come before it' (Lynch in *Psychology Today*, March–April 1997: 74).

4   Even if David Foster Wallace does thinks they are 'like stuff you could imagine Francis Bacon doing in junior high' (Wallace 1996).

5   Lynch has noted that a Bacon exhibition he saw at the Marlborough Gallery in New York in the 1960s was particularly influential on him, especially the 'images of meat and cigarettes'. He states that what struck him about these images was 'the beauty of the paint and the balance and contrast in the pictures. It was like perfection' (McKenna 1992).

6   Žižek 2000: 44, 41.

7   October Films. Online. Available at http://members.xoom.com/_XMCM/dugpa/lynch/lh/lhpress.html (15 June 2000).

8   In an interview with Bob Strauss, Lynch says, 'I'm sure it would be interesting to hear Patricia's take on it. But I guarantee you it'd be different from other people's takes' (Strauss n.d.). Žižek quotes Arquette's comments and proposes them as a precise reading of his Lacanian analysis, in which the status of the obstacle to desire is displaced from an inherent position to an externalised position in the form of Mr. Eddie (Žižek 2000: 16).

9   On the perceptional axes of cinema, see Metz 1982: 43.

10   Available at www.geocities.com/Hollywood/2093/quotecollection/psych. html (15 June 2000).

11   Rebecca and Samuel Umland also briefly mention the film's 'loopiness' and state that this trait of the film has already been remarked upon in *Wrapped in Plastic* 1, 28, 7.

12   In his study on Bacon, Deleuze talks of the immediacy of the Figure's affect on the nervous system and the co-existence of all of its various movements (Deleuze 1981: 27, 25). This notion of direct affect is expressed elsewhere in Deleuze's work by the concept of the transversal relation (see Deleuze 1996: 201–2) which deploys itself in a multilinear system (see especially Deleuze and Guattari 1987: 296–8).

13   Chris Rodley's series of interviews with the director contains a reproduction of four of these strips. See Rodley 1997: 122.

CHAPTER ELEVEN

Beyond Boundaries:
David Lynch's Lost Highway

Anne Jerslev

Boundlessness and Ambiguity

Many of David Lynch's films open by establishing a certain mode of spatial impossibility: ultra close-ups of something not easily recognisable at first sight, like the blue wavering curtain in *Blue Velvet* (1986); a painted surface that turns out to be a painted ceiling in *Wild at Heart* (1990); flickering dots in *Twin Peaks: Fire Walk with Me* (1992); or the yellow texture of wavering corn fields in *The Straight Story* (1999). These ultra close-ups create a kind of perceptual disorientation, but at the same time they constitute an almost physical sense of tactile presence or intimacy, of fabrics and surfaces. It is also common to these openings that after a while the camera tracks back, more or less rapidly, in order to reveal an identifiable *mise-en-scène*, and thus to create the missing in-between, a cinematic space.

These initial destabilisations are immediate and poignant references to the kind of cinematic space that Lynch's oeuvre constructs again and again. Space in Lynch's films is fluctuating and profoundly ambiguous. Characters' locations are never firmly identified. In *Lost Highway* (1997), especially in the first half of the film, images of this diffuse topicality abound. Although placed in the same room, Renée and Fred communicate as if they were situated in different times and spaces. Likewise, their house constructs a disturbing transparency. Fred walks through doors that are not

The Lost Highway Hotel

there and is engulfed by dark corridors that seem endless. Lynch's earlier choice of directing *Dune* (1984), a science fiction film, is explicable in these terms, as is also the fact that he has made two road movies, *Wild at Heart* and *The Straight Story*, since this is a genre where characters float through spaces that are hardly constructed as places but rather as locations, non-places. Time becomes spatial or space turns into time spans in these road movies, in pointing, in *Wild at Heart*, to the inability to construct a proper home, in *The Straight Story* to the painful arrival of life reaching its end. A rare example of a well-defined place is the point in *Lost Highway* when Fred and Renée watch shots of their house on video. Renée's immediate reaction is that the tape must be from a real estate agent, but her remark functions as a joke in the filmic discourse, implying that an image so unimaginative and so empty as to be of an easily recognisable object can only have a sales purpose. The opposite, joyful idea of boundless space is visualised in the image of the starry sky in *The Straight Story*. In the closing zoom into the stars, after the two brothers have been reunited and reoccupied their positions of contemplative childhood, the boundless universe paradoxically through the ultra slow change of perspective, transforms into a proper space that the two men can enter and occupy with their souls.

Space, whether it be the entire sky or just the Milky Way is an important *topos* in Lynch's work. This goes back to *Eraserhead* (1977), which opens with an image of Henry's head floating weightlessly in front of what appears to be a planet. The sky is the ultimate idea of boundlessness as both utopian and dystopian figuration with Lynch. In *The Straight Story* and in *Dune* it functions as the poetical reflection of the personal past and future; it is connected to both origins and death. In *Lost Highway* it represents both the impenetrability of darkness and the danger of dissolution. In the following I shall address the ambiguous and paradoxical testing, blurring and transgression of the formal limits of space in *Lost Highway*. I shall begin, however, with David Lynch's *general* interest in *texture* – a subject he actually discusses again and again, although never in very specific ways. Thus I shall start by discussing the construction of a certain perceptual field in his work *in general*. Then I move on to discuss time and space in *Lost Highway* as a specific chronotope, a specific interrelationship between time and space. Mikhail Bakhtin's notion of the (literary) chronotope seems especially adequate to *Lost Highway*,[1] since discussions of time and space pervade the whole film as a 'formative constitutive category' (Bakhtin 1981: 85), and since, as Bakhtin likewise puts it, the chronotope also forms the 'image of man' (1981: 84). I also address a concern related to the issue of boundlessness, that is, the film's obsession with woman as unsolvable mystery. Finally I return to vision in *Lost Highway* by discussing the uncanny Mystery Man. It seems to me that ways of seeing have always been a focal point in Lynch's *oeuvre*, most obviously so in *Lost Highway*, since vision is explicitly thematised in the film. In a certain respect *Lost Highway* is about video tapes; about an uncanny pervasive video gaze; and about a mysterious character with a video camera attached to his eye like the *vision prosthesis* or *vision machine* of French philosopher and architect Paul Virilio.

Texture

In interviews, David Lynch often talks about his fascination with *texture*, the materiality and tactile surface of objects. For example, in a television programme from 1989, in a discussion about the director's interest in dead bodies that are not 'really frightening', Lynch says to interviewer John Powers:

> They have their own sort of texture. I always say that as soon as you take the name off something and you see that this is an abstract texture, a lot of things that you wouldn't normally think of as being beautiful are very beautiful. Those are interesting textures and so they got their own beauty to them. As soon as you realise what they are they're sort of terrifying.[2]

This statement illustrates an ongoing aesthetic endeavour in Lynch, one that surfaces now and then across his whole work: the attempt to produce in close-ups a sensuous feeling of the physical materiality of the surfaces of the depicted objects and thus to deprive the objects of their precise referentiality and their codification in the world of objects. What is signified is still there but transformed into a 'something', a beautiful, uncanny, almost obscene *thing,* and at the same time as a disturbing imprint of a sensation of 'the real thing'.

Michel Chion refers to these images of texture as 'micro-reliefs' (Chion 1995: 196) and claims that they 'appear whenever one erases words' (ibid.). According to him, they are 'a close-up on the dress of nature' (ibid.). If I understand Chion correctly, he is trying to conceptualise the same transgressive gestures in Lynch's work as I am: to understand and to describe these images as both inside and outside representation at one and the same time. Using Slavoj Žižek's Lacanian terminology, we might say that Lynch's images are placed within the symbolic and at the same time they are also disturbingly pointing to the real (Žižek 2000a).

Thus, the 'micro-relief' at once demands and creates a short-sighted perception which involves both visual and tactile senses: visual objects are synaesthetically transformed into pure aesthetic artefacts. As a textual element, texture might thus correspond to the fragment – that which is only minimally signifying. This kind of tactile visual field seems to represent to Lynch an ideal mode of vision. Texture produces a visual field of uncertainty and ambiguity, and it is this that he seeks to produce.

Texture is the blue dots in the opening shot of *Twin Peaks: Fire Walk with Me*. They form slowly into flickering lines and finally, as the camera tracks back, are given meaning. At this very moment, a violent act takes place and a scream is heard. This may indicate that it is the very act of being deprived of this tactile vision that is terrifying; but it indicates, too, that texture is a transient mode of visuality. In the same film, texture is the ultra close-up of Teresa Banks' nail lifted from the tip of her finger. In a final example, texture is the short film made with the Lumière Cinematograph for the film *Lumière et Compagnie* in 1995.[3] The very materiality of the film stock, the uneven exposure of the image and the manually produced speed of motion form a kind of perceptible tactile filter across the represented space. It places the spectator in an intimate, tactile relation to the screen and points to the fundamental non-transparency of the film medium.

American art historian Craig Owens has described photography and film as *transparent media*, 'based as they are on a single point perspective' (Owens 1992: 111). But this is precisely not the case with Lynch's films, which seem to switch easily and without further warning between two different constructions of vision – on one hand, this intimate and tactile occupation with surfaces, on the other a more traditional cinematic vision of space. In ultra close-ups but also in the pan close to the rugged surface of the planet at the beginning of *Eraserhead*, it seems as if Lynch wants in an almost physical manner to emphasise the two-dimensional film surface, but at the same time also to transform the represented texture into a sort of three-dimensional relief, just as he had done in his first film experiment in 1967, *Six Men Getting Sick* – 'more of a moving painting than a film', as he recalls in Toby Keeler's documentary *Pretty as a Picture: The Art of David Lynch* from 1997.[4] It seems as if Lynch wanted to wrest from the represented objects their absent physicality or to provide, in the camera, a visual apparatus with the kind of bodily, tactile quality which characterises the hand that carries the painter's brush. As if he wanted to attach vision to the body again or to provide it with a poignant materiality.

In *Pretty as a Picture*, Lynch's former wife Peggy Reeves argues that what made him turn from painting to film was that

> he wanted his paintings to move. It's really what it came out of. He wanted his paintings to move. He wanted them to do more. He wanted them to make sounds. He wanted them to move.

In *Lost Highway* too, it seems as if he aims at arresting the moving images as a coherent flow; as if he wants to transform each frame into a painting and thus to obstruct a basic ontological principle of film language.[5] David Lynch creates in a very literal way paintings that move – or perhaps paintings that aspire toward other genres such as the sculpture or the relief.[6] In his paintings, too, texture has a prominent place, or perhaps they merely *are* texture, composed or modelled out of rough brush strokes of oil paint, with small pieces of printed letters pasted on, wads of cotton, pieces of cardboard, feathers, tiny pieces of bone from the skeletons of birds.[7] In a very literal manner one of his paintings, called *Rat Meets Bird*, is a 'moving image', or more correctly an installation. In the middle of an oil-painted canvas a piece of raw meat is alive with dozens of small ants.[8]

Time and Space in Lost Highway

Lost Highway is a claustrophobic intertextual journey into Lynch's *oeuvre*, here recycled as a floating audio-visual iconicity. But even though *Lost Highway* tries in every conceivable way to present itself as fragmentary and incoherent, it seems to me only possible to understand this film, as well as his other films, within the context of classical Hollywood cinema as a narrative form. Classical Hollywood narration is the invisibly present textual order – or other – that Lynch's films to a greater or lesser degree address and subvert. Classical Hollywood narration is always there, and yet not – as if the films were continually testing how much the classical narrative could be expanded and extended towards other narrative and non-narrative forms without collapsing completely, without escaping narration altogether. This search, this struggle, or this wrestling forms the overall intensity and aesthetic tension in Lynch's films. It informs the horror and the beauty of his work.

More than *Twin Peaks: Fire Walk with Me*, *Lost Highway* takes the form of a radical departure from classical principles of coherence, unity and closure. The film has no beginning, no middle and no ending, and it closes exactly the way it started. In the credit sequence and in the end – after Fred has vanished again – we have the ultra-fast superimposed shots of a 'lost highway' seen from the windscreen of a fast-moving car. This highway comes from nowhere and leads nowhere – thus, lost. *Lost Highway* can be understood then as both a visual construction and uncanny result of boundlessness as an aesthetic strategy. Where *The Straight Story*, as a kind of structuring absence to *Lost Highway*, forms the poetic beauty of the transgression of boundaries, *Lost Highway* represents the dark side of this endeavour.

Despite this lack of coherence it seems paradoxically almost unavoidable to identify a key line – or perhaps a line that is a key – to *Lost Highway*. It is advanced by Alice towards the end of the film, in the desert, when she and Pete make love under the whitish light of the car. 'I want you', Pete breathes several times during the act. But Alice replies coldly and brutally, in an air of *coitus interruptus*: 'You'll never have me.' Her remark refers not only to the fact that she will never be Pete's, but also that he will never be able to solve her riddle. Just as her appearance has strangely vanished from the picture in Andy's house, she will remain a mystery. If the film has an explicit meaning it is a story about jealousy; a man is tortured with jealousy because he thinks his wife betrays him. But on a more implicit level the film might be regarded as a kind of imaginary journey into the very essence of jealousy, from the point of view of a male character. Thus, *Lost Highway* may be understood as an ecstatic nightmarish vision about woman as fatal mystery and uncontrollable desire. But finally, Alice's remark can be understood as a sort of meta-commentary which refers to the film itself but also addresses the spectator. We should not expect to be able to make sense of this film and thus to create the sense of (narrative) certainty that the film itself so insistently denies.

There is a profound vision of culture and modernity in this departure from a motivationally organised, chronological story. The film seems to imply that reality is not that simple, no matter how much we wish. Yet the director constantly excites narrative desire. He arouses our wish for solutions and closure by constantly referring to the classical crime plot, by cueing us to pose questions that seek answers. Even characters pose questions all the time in order to obtain solutions. 'Who are you?' Fred asks Mystery Man at Andy's party. But the only answer he gets is a laugh. 'What happened to me?' Pete asks his parents. But they never tell what they saw on the evening when Pete probably ended up in Fred's cell, perhaps through some kind of interference on the part of Mystery Man. And finally Pete asks Alice 'Why me? Why choose me?' when they arrive at the mysterious cabin in the desert in order to wait for – only Alice knows who. Pete, too, gets no answer.

This deconstruction of the classical narrative form, whilst keeping it as a founding formal principle – this giving and taking – is not unique in the director's work. Think also of *Twin Peaks: Fire Walk with Me* with its insistence on telling a crime mystery whose solution was already well-known from the television series *Twin Peaks*.[9] *Lost Highway* is a more radical wrestling with the spectator's effort to construct a story. Much of the film's uncanniness comes from the fact that there seems to be no story, and thus no exit from its delirious imagery.

Elsewhere (in Jerslev 1991) I have discussed the giant's enigmatic statement in *Twin Peaks* that 'the owls are not what they seem'. I interpreted the phrase as a metaphor for Lynch's continuous aesthetic and thematic insistence that nothing is the way it seems. Both the films and *Twin Peaks* are centred around revelations of the hidden perverse 'underneath' of family and small town life. Lynch's Americana of violence and uncanniness is constructed in terms of a false idyllic appearance that hides an essential truth underneath. But simultaneously the films obviously negate this simple binarism. They show that these two levels both in culture and in the human consciousness are always mutually interdependent. Normality always carries the traces of perversion – think of the uncannily repeated closing shots of the photograph of Laura Palmer in *Twin Peaks* – even more Stella Nova than Stella Nova. Or the white fence in the opening scene in *Blue Velvet* which is exactly that: perversely white.

Lost Highway differs from the earlier films in that it lets go of even the slightest glimpse of cultural order. There is no surface to dive below, as there is at the beginning of *Blue Velvet* where the camera penetrates the grass and ends up in a frenzy of bugs. In *Lost Highway* we are below the surface from the start. And what is more, the film constructs no alternative place to this claustrophobic below. To a certain extent Lynch has returned to the suffocating, labyrinthine form of *Eraserhead*. Like the surrealistic dream imagery in the earlier film, and the impossible convolutions of *Mulholland Drive* (2001), *Lost Highway* is like a nest of Chinese boxes. The film is thus analogously structured to the unconscious which, according to Freud, contains an amorphous, associatively organised mass of immediate sense impressions with-out spatial or temporal extent and, thus, without narrative structure. Using an intertextual analogy, I might suggest that in *Lost Highway* we have finally entered The Black Lodge, the fiendish, perverse non-place outside time that finally captured Dale Cooper in the closing episode of *Twin Peaks*. Certainly the red curtain in Fred and Renée's house reminds us of the labyrinthine structure in The Black Lodge.

Since there is no linear logic in *Lost Highway* and no ordering dichotomies, is it then possible to identify any structuring principle in the film? Lynch has himself in several interviews referred to the Möbius strip and this figure seems to me a sufficient metaphor for the structuring absence in *Lost Highway*.[10] The Möbius strip is a twisted and thus paradoxical topological figure. On one hand there is always a point on the front that corresponds to a point on the back of the spring. On the other hand, if one follows the outer edge of the spring all the way round one is suddenly on the inner edge without having crossed the surface. Thus, the Möbius strip is a figure where 'front' and 'back' form a coherent uninterrupted surface.[11] The metaphor underlines the lack of exit and narrative closure. Fred cannot wake up from a nightmare in which he has the lead. Likewise, the film may continue *ad infinitum* without really getting anywhere. But the metaphor also points to the film's refusal of any unifying interpretative effort whatsoever. It allows for no unambiguous correspondences between visual signifiers and culturally determined signifieds, no easy connotative anchorings. One image, one apparent meaning, is easily transformed or metamorphosised into another – the Renée/Alice character is just one obvious example of this principle. Even though Renée is dressed all in black when she picks up the first videotape from the stairs and even though Alice is all in white when she sees Pete the first time, the 'two' women are not constructed as diametrically opposite aspects of the same woman. Neither does an overabundance of the colour white simply position Alice as the reverse of innocence, a noirish *femme fatale*. And they both seem to wear masks without ever being unmasked; at least they both look as if they wear a wig. Ultimately, Renée/Alice might be nothing but intertextual icons that point to 1940s *film noir* – and to *Twin Peaks*.

The film only pretends to present itself as a frame narrative. Usually frame narratives function to create both a spatial distance and a temporal distance in relation to the narrative middle. But there is no such difference in *Lost Highway*. The opening and closing images of the yellow lines on the road taken from a fast speeding car seemingly out of control through a 'nuit sans fin' (Rouyer 1997: 6–7) designates no difference in temporality. Rather than a question of temporal order the framing sequences point to the end of time and to space without extension.

The speed of motion that seems to distort any distinct shape and erase any distinct difference as well as the shots of a road leading nowhere recalls Jean Baudrillard's notion of speed in his study *America*. Here he says that

> speed creates a consecrated space, that may contain death. The only rule is that all traces are erased. The victory of oblivion over memory, a raw memory impaired intoxication (Baudrillard 1987: 14, my translation).

Having Baudrillard in the back of the mind might prompt us to understand the opening images as a kind of warning – what shall come will be accompanied by death. But contrary to Baudrillard, who seems to find a kind of ecstasy in speed as a stand-in for a visual and mental collapse, the closing images in *Lost Highway* refer to agony and the disintegration of subjectivity and the body. Or at least they point to a bodily discord with speed.

Cars turn into props and driving is an overdetermined trope in Lynch. Thus, to drive a car is never just a formal solution to the question of how to take characters from one place to another. In *America,* Baudrillard also advances the idea that driving is a 'dramatic form of amnesia. Everything comes into sight, everything disappears … Experiencing the desert from a moving car comes very close to the eternity of the film reel' (1987: 9, my translation). Correspondingly, the camera and the car coalesce in Lynch's frame. Windscreen transforms into cinema screen and the desert implodes into speed and night. Time seems to crystallise into space and the black nocturnal space is infinite and shrunk at the same time.

The desert is as symbolically condensed in Lynch's film as it is in Baudrillard's book. It seems to be the place of all beginning and all end. As a visual symbolisation of a diffuse no-place *the desert* seems to me what *the ocean* was to Robert Aldrich's *Kiss Me Deadly* (1955). *Lost Highway* possibly refers to this strange and hysterical *noir* masterpiece several times. The two films start in much the same manner – fast moving shots of a highway at night – and in the final atomic inferno in *Kiss Me Deadly* a cabin by the sea catches fire explosively in exactly the same manner as the cabin in the desert in *Lost Highway*.[12]

Finally, the framing shots of the highway contribute one more example of the film's chronotope, namely the Nietzschean *eternal return*, a principle of cyclical time or synchronicity that means that the past returns and the future has already been. Thus it is meaningless to distinguish between past and future, because past and future are both present in every moment. It seems to me that *Lost Highway* displays exactly this notion of time. Besides the uncanny repetition of the opening images at the level of narration, the cyclical notion of time is diegetically related to Fred who advances this notion of time when he states that 'I like to remember things my own way. Not necessarily the way they happened.' Time repeats itself and the past turns into present when Fred returns to his home in the end. What happens in the present ('Dick Laurent is dead,' says Fred) changes both past events and their place in time ('Dick Laurent is dead,' he has already heard before). Thus, the film is also a very literal illustration of Freud's notion of *Nachträglichkeit*, the mechanism of belatedness. In the very same moment Fred repeats to himself in the buzzer that 'Dick Laurent is dead', he turns present to past, to an occurrence that has already been. But whereas this principle of eternal return has been regarded as a Dionysian hymn to life, eternal return is also 'spooky'.[13]

Jealousy and Masculine Desire

After Fred's 'resurrection' in the desert he asks Mystery Man for Alice. But Mystery Man answers that 'if she told you her name is Alice she is lying'. This remark too, could be regarded in light of the Möbius logic; thus we will never know whether Mystery Man is the real liar. But the statement points to Alice as *femme fatale* and thus to a hidden motive for her infatuation with the young mechanic. Alice is straight out of 1940s *film noir*: she seduces Pete to get him to do her dirty work. This often paranoid and melancholic Hollywood 'genre' has strong textual resonances in *Lost Highway* and it deals, to a certain extent, with the same fantasies: male desire and 'masculinity in crisis'.

The *femme fatale* is often the protagonist in *film noir*. She is the one who ruins – or accomplishes the (self)destruction of – the male main character by seducing him, for example, into helping her to kill her husband. *Film noir* is visually obsessed with this spider woman at the same time as its narrative is preoccupied with punishing her.[14] Most often she dies or is arrested, and thus is in the end degraded and demystified. However, there is an important difference between the Alice/Pete part of *Lost Highway* and 1940s *noir*. Whereas the dangerous desire has to be eliminated in classical *noir* in order that masculinity may rise powerfully in the end, what ultimately remains by the end of *Lost Highway* is Alice's prophetic statement that 'you'll never have me'. In *Lost Highway*, woman remains an unsolved mystery, an otherness. The film constructs no powerful masculine principle – even Mr. Eddy/Dick Laurent dies pathetically. The jealous husband falls victim to his own desire. Pete gets, as one of the surveilling officers says, 'more pussy than a toilet seat'. But he doesn't get the woman. Throughout the film she is thus constructed as radically other.

David Lynch has shown an interest in *film noir* before. In *Twin Peaks*, motorcycle boy James finally left Twin Peaks only to drive directly into the arms of cool rich Evelyn March who pretends to be a weak maltreated wife, but is more likely her chauffeur's lover and needs James to kill her husband. The question seems to be why Lynch is so fascinated with this dark, style-conscious Hollywood 'genre'. One explanation – besides the genre's general mood – might be that *film noir*'s tensions, just like Lynch's films, in large part stem from the *mise-en-scène* of fantasies about sexuality as a dangerous threat. Different stagings of the same fantasy run through Lynch's *oeuvre*, from the nightmare about the foetus in *Eraserhead*, apparently the result of Harry's intercourse with Mary, to myth about John Merrick (*The Elephant Man*, 1980) allegedly the result of John's mother's impregnation by elephants, to the many scenarios of violent sexuality in *Blue Velvet*, *Wild at Heart* and, especially, *Twin Peaks: Fire Walk with Me*. One very poignant example of this thorough linking of death with sexuality is that the strange and hymnic music that accompanies a short part of Fred's and Renée's unsuccessful sex in the beginning of *Lost Highway* is similar to the non-diegetic chorus music that accompanies Leland Palmer's murder of his daughter in *Twin Peaks: Fire Walk with Me*.[15]

But *film noir* is more broadly an obvious film historical intertext for visualisations of the riddle of femininity: woman as the very materialisation of boundlessness. Lynch has stated again and again in interviews that he is fascinated with mysteries and the idea of entering other worlds. Woman represents this mystery, the other-worldly, in his work. She is at once fascinating and disturbing. She is what his male characters desire to possess and what they cannot get. The more or less obvious pornographic elements in *Twin Peaks: Fire Walk with Me* and *Lost Highway* are interesting in this context. Pornography works to objectify the woman and to demystify gender – thus Linda Williams claims that porno is characterised by 'maximum visibility' (Williams 1989: 48). Therefore, it would be tempting to claim that – at least in *Lost Highway* – hard core pornographic images work to create the visual mastering of the riddle of femininity that Lynch's *oeuvre* cannot otherwise establish. But what seems to me to be really interesting is that hard core pornography is never really able to create this demystifying certainty. On the contrary, the pornographic sequences in *Lost Highway,* especially the silent projection on the large screen seen when Pete enters Andy's home, can be seen as yet another staging of the impossible masculine desire to master the female. According to Linda Willliams, one of the main incentives and pleasures of watching hard core pornography is the wish to be assured that what one is witnessing is not a show but the involuntary confession of female pleasure (Williams 1989: 50). But the truth is rather that the truth of the female orgasm cannot be captured in images. So therefore, one can never really be sure:

> The woman's ability to fake the orgasm that the man can never fake (at least according to certain standards of evidence) seems to be at the root of all the genre's attempts to solicit what it can never be sure of: the out-of-control confession of pleasure, a hard core 'frenzy of the visible'. (ibid.)

In *Lost Highway*'s porno film-within-the-film it is equally difficult to actually read the close-ups of Alice's face as she is being taken from behind. Her expression seems almost invisibly to change back and forth between pain and lust. Thus when it comes to it, the porn sequence is just one more example of the principle of the Möbius strip.

The ambiguity inherent in pornography is underlined by having Andy's porn film projected without sound, without 'the sounds of pleasure' as Williams puts it (1989: 121). Sound in hard core pornography is not, and is not meant to be, perceived as diegetic sound, so the spatial relation of sound to image mimes, but is not equal to, classical narrative cinema. Instead, the sounds coming from the woman's mouth ('a dubbed-over "disembodied" female voice' (1989: 122) function as aural stand-ins or substitutions for the orgasm whose reality cannot be confirmed visually, 'aural fetishes of the female pleasures we cannot see' (1989: 123)). Therefore, in *Lost Highway*'s mute projection, female desire is not even controlled by this simulated aural assurance.

The embedded pornographic scenes and the erotic *noir* scenes between Alice and Pete are thus, finally, expressions of one and the same thing: an insatiable and impossible desire to control female desire. Mystery Man makes it equally clear to porn king Mr Eddy/Dick Laurent in his moment of death that even though he regards Alice as his property, it is merely an illusion. Earlier in the film we have seen how Dick Laurent's powerful voyeuristic gaze almost literally undressed Alice. Here in the nightly desert Mystery Man turns his video camera against Mr. Eddy like a Peeping Tom and demonstrates how easy it is for him to transform Mr. Eddy's gaze into a disempowered look. What Mystery Man's video camera shows to Mr. Eddy is not only himself and Alice watching snuff movies. But, more important, that they were surveilled by yet another, disembodied, camera. What Mr. Eddy sees when he dies is that someone else was watching him watching. An invisible camera eye relegates his own gaze to an inferior position.

Visual Prosthesis and Vision Machine

Lost Highway's visual imagery might be discussed from one more point of view: as an uncanny fantasy about entrapment in the maelstrom of visual culture; the nightmare that, after all, and beyond postmodern euphoria, images constitute the sole reality, a kind of obscene boundless non-referentiality. Following from this, Mystery Man, who carries this uncanny, indeterminably androgyne and ageless face, and who seems to represent an obscene position beyond desire and beyond gender, can be understood as the one who has produced all the video images of death and sexuality. He may be the one who uses the camera for the purpose of voyeuristic surveillance; he is the one who is able to make the video camera penetrate time in order to record things that might not have happened yet. He may, finally, also corporealise some unmotivated shots, for example extreme birds' eye points of view when Fred is in his cell or when the police officers leave Fred's and Renée's house.

Thus, Mystery Man may be understood as a personified perverse visual principle, one that seems to be the opposite of the tactile, intimate field of vision created in ultra close-ups. Mystery Man is staged as a *vision machine,* a body with a *visual prosthesis* attached to one eye, the video camera, that transforms the eye into a televisual receiver able to project itself into and penetrate space.[16] The eye is thus provided with the ability to telescope near and far. Through Mystery Man's video camera eye we watch Fred escape into the desert night in Andy's car, and the flickering video screen twice fills the whole frame. These shots may be understood as subjective point of view shots, as if the video camera, or technology itself had become part of Mystery Man's body – corresponding with Paul Virilio's argument that vision machines are making their way into the bodies of man.

Mystery Man's vision machine distorts space, dimensions and perspective in a kind of *instantaneous ubiquity of the audio-visual mix* (Virilio 1994: 6). Fred and Renée sit in their living room and look at a tiny representation of the very same living room on their television screen. Likewise, Mr. Eddy looks at Fred and Mystery Man on the miniature screen that Mystery Man hands him at the same time as they are in reality standing just a few metres away from him. The camera presents and represents at the same time. It is used for surveillance (telescoping) and representation (television). Thus it represents the *principle of telescoping*, which is the concept Paul Virilio uses to name the perceptual field of the *vision machine* (1994: 4). These vision machines invalidate the 'natural' perceptual capacity to judge distance and dimension and replace it with the ability visually to penetrate perceptually unknown territory, what Virilio calls the *aesthetics of disappearance* (Virilio 1991). Let me add that this line of argument could also be extended to include *Twin Peaks: Fire Walk with Me*. I am thinking in particular about the ending of the first part of the film, where Dale Cooper places himself in front of the surveillance camera in the corridor and then quickly hurries into the control room in order to find out whether the camera has left traces of his appearance. It is as if Cooper is trying to figure out whether it is possible to negate the camera's means of presenting and surveying reality and to refigure it as a device to re-present reality – a *vision machine* that is able to re-present more than the merely visible reality.

Mystery Man is a demoniac Mélièsque magician but he lacks Méliès' childish playfulness. He is a visual manipulator, to whom nothing is secret and nothing sacred. Ultimately, he embodies the uncanny ability to rewind the film (the flashes of the burning cabin, which seems uncannily to swallow up its own flames). And Mystery Man might be the cause of the many very Lynchian flashes in the film, as if they were flashes from a camera, and the finished film was in a paradoxical way still in the very process of being shot. As if the film-maker was doubled *inside* the diegesis,[17] Lynch in this way calls attention to the very instability of meaning by denying the authorial gaze as a place of truth. Fred asks him, 'Who are you?' But he receives no answer. The answer is perhaps that Mystery Man is everything and nothing. He is not 'Who'? But 'What?' He is an obscene visual principle outside the law and outside desire. This is why Mystery Man is less than human and placed above gender.

Maybe it is a car without driver that runs away in the final shots from the highway. Maybe it is the reel itself, circling infinitely in the twisting of the Möbius strip. The ending is almost like a quotation from Baudrillard. On the first page of *America* Baudrillard states that 'experiencing the desert from a moving car comes very close to the eternity of the film reel' (Baudrillard 1987: 9, my translation). In the boundlessness of the desert reality disappears and might as well be experienced as a film. To Baudrillard, the desert is the quintessence of America, the condensation of America as the scene of simulation. Just like driving a car and speed itself, the desert forms the ecstasy and agony of the dissolution of meaning. The desert in Lynch's film functions to condense death, perdition and resurrection into the ultimate magical symbolisation of the eternal recurrence. It is thus in itself the narrative form of *Lost Highway*.

Notes

1 See also Sobchack 1998 and Stam 1989.

2 The programme was called *Don't Look at Me*. It was shot in December 1989 and released as a co-production between Channel 4 and Sept Art/Art Production, directed by Guy Girard.

3 The project was initiated by Musée du Cinema in Lyon. It is a European co-production supported by Eurimage and le Conseil de l'Europe. Forty film directors speak briefly about their work and they each make a 52-second film with Lumière's original Cinematograph.

4 See also Keeler in Miller 1997.

5 Barry Gifford called the film 'a moving portrait' in Rodley 1997: 215.

6 For a related argument, see Erica Sheen's reading in this volume of Lynch's work across media as a process of 'remediation'.

7 For example shown at an exhibition of Lynch's paintings and photos in Valencia in 1992. During an interview printed in the catalogue, writer Kristine McKenna asks: 'I also notice that the surface of your paintings are becoming increasingly modeled and sculptural; was it a conscious decision to take the work in this direction? Lynch answers: 'Yes – I'd like to build them out even more. The idea of paint on a flat surface doesn't excite me so much right now. I like the idea of a field where someone's dumped some garbage – the garbage puffs up higher than the surface on the field, and I like that.'

8 Lynch talks about this 'picture' in *Pretty as a Picture* and emphasises that 'I like the organic textures of it'. In an interview in *American Cinematographer* he says that he is working on another, similar piece (cf. Pizzello 1997).

9 Martha Nochimson has a very convincing argument in defence of *Twin Peaks: Fire Walk with Me* as a narrative construction. She says of Laura Palmer that 'In *Twin Peaks*, Laura teaches Cooper how to solve the mystery of her death and plays a major role in his boundary crossing: in *Fire*, through a mysterious negotiation of time and an involvement in her transformation, we see what she had to become before she could be what she is to Cooper in *Twin Peaks*' (Nochimson 1997: 174).

10 For a discussion of the Möbius strip see Rhodes 1998.

11 Svein Haugsgjerd's *Jacques Lacan og psykoanalysen: En presentasjon av Lacans liv og verk* (Oslo: Gyldendal norsk forlag, 1986: 63, my translation).

12 For an account of the relation between the two films see Lucas 1998.

13 See, for example, Eriksen 1989. For a discussion of this difficult concept in Nietzsche, see Nehamas 1985.

14 See, for example, Place 1998.

15 Annette Davison tells me that the music used for the impotence scene in *Lost Highway* is a cover version of Tim Buckley's 'Song to the Siren', performed by This Mortal Coil. Apparently, Lynch had originally wanted to use this track on *Blue Velvet* but 'they were asking a lot of money for the track, and we didn't have any money' (Lynch in Rodley: 132). By *Lost Highway*, Lynch was able to afford

the rights to use it. In fact the music occurs on three occasions: in one of the prison cell scenes; before Fred 'turns into' Pete; and, as I discuss here, in the sex scene between Pete and Alice in the desert, where it is followed by Alice's own siren song 'you'll never have me', and Fred's return.

16 For the 'vision machine' see Virilio 1994.

17 For this argument see the opening of Annette Davison's chapter in this volume.

CHAPTER TWELVE

'All I Need is the Girl': The Life and Death of Creativity in Mulholland Drive

Martha P. Nochimson

From his first feature-length film, *Eraserhead* (1977), David Lynch has manifested an intense interest in the female performer. Though she is often shadowed by dubious associations, in film after film Lynch's performing women send fresh, erotic energy to his male protagonists, annihilating inhibiting patterns of death and decay. The liberational Lady in the Radiator (Laurel Near) who invites Henry Spencer to escape a cramped, oppressive existence – and simultaneously destroys spermlike blobs of matter – is a dancing and singing actress in a stage setting, as is Dorothy Vallens (Isabella Rossellini), whose tormented penchant for sexual violence drives Jeffrey Beaumont beyond the constraints of the role of the good, small-town boy in *Blue Velvet* (1986). In *The Elephant Man* (1980), the actress Mrs Kendal (Anne Bancroft) is the erotic focus for John Merrick (John Hurt) inspiring him with confidence and opening doors to the glittering cultural life of London in a way that both expands his horizons and leads him toward suicide. Just as complex are Lynch's evocations of female performance in everyday life: the confused and fatal exhibitionism of Laura Palmer (Sheryl Lee) in *Twin Peaks* (1990) and the bewildered Monroe-esque flamboyance of Lula Fortune (Laura Dern) in *Wild at Heart* (1989) are the hallmarks of yearning and courageous struggle in the face of terrible oppressions, but they are also intimately connected with the attractions of violence. This electrifying female has crucial implications for the survival of the creative moment, a theme of abiding importance to Lynch.

However, in these and other previous films, female performance effects imaginative transformations of lives rooted in mundane reality: hardware stores, hospitals, domestic settings, gas stations. In *Mulholland Drive* (2001) the figure of the performing woman is situated within a narrative about the official site of fantasy and female performance, the Hollywood film, and it is here that she reaches a pitch of dark intensity never before achieved in Lynch's work. If the performing woman has previously been the axle of fortunate metamorphosis, here she is the axle of disintegration.[1] In *Mulholland Drive*, the fate of 'the girl' – the female star – is the fate of the industry itself. At first sight, this attribution of importance to 'the girl' may seem excessive, since women in Hollywood are radically disempowered. But consider the hordes of very young women who come and go as flavour of the month, objects of desire on whom hundreds of inconsequential, money-making films depend, and we must acknowledge how much hinges on the exploitation of this disposable figure whose energy briefly attracts and enchants. In focusing his tale of the stagnation of creative promise on 'the girl' in all her power and insignificance, Lynch manifests his characteristic imaginative acuity about what drives the human community.

Mulholland Drive presents the spectator with three roughly simultaneous events that combine to kill the 'the girl's' capacity to effect the happy imaginative transformations of his earlier films. The result is the sapping of the creative energies of a film in the early stages of production, and the death of a number of the people involved with it. One of the catalytic events is the attempt on the life of the darkly beautiful actress (Laura Elena Harring) who was originally cast as the heroine of the film-within-the-film; she is saved at the last moment by a car crash that causes her to lose her memory and wander off into the night, while the search for her begins. Another is the arrival in Hollywood from a small town in Canada of blonde, hopeful Betty Elms (Naomi Watts), dreaming of stardom. Betty ultimately will be evoked by the film as the best creative option for a re-cast of the part, but she is not the choice of a sinister death-dealing power structure that looms over the world of *Mulholland Drive*. Finally, there is the attempt by this power structure to intimidate the director of the film Adam Kesher (Justin Theroux). Initially, the connections between these events are only glancingly hinted, their crucial, fatal relationship only emerging well into the film, conveying the absurd, almost imperceptible way the power structure of Hollywood – because it is concerned with power rather than creativity – erodes hopes and dreams.

However, what is starkly evident almost from the beginning is that, despite abundant confusion about the function and identity of various different girls, '*the* girl' is of enormous importance. This becomes clear as we watch how the destinies of Betty, the dark girl, and Adam are shaped by the insistence of a sinister, invisible power-broker called Mr. Roque (Michael J. Anderson), who stipulates that Adam's film will be made only on the condition that Adam yield to him the choice of female star. Indeed the fragile reality of *Mulholland Drive* itself hangs in the balance of that mandated choice. Before Adam pronounces the words he is instructed to use – 'this is the girl' – the situation is fluid, hopeful, positive. After the fateful words are spoken, a series of eerie reversals occur that initiate for the characters not only new names and/or personalities, but also a downward spiral of decay and disintegration.

But, even before Roque puts Adam's feet to the fire, 'the girl' looms large. She appears in the surreal images of the film's opening sequence, superimposed over a crowd of lively, bright dancing couples, each of whose forms are doubled and tripled, creating a *doppelgänger* effect that prefigures the film's later development. 'The girl', a young blonde, smiling hopefully, is accompanied by an older couple who look like grandparents. These images defy conventional exposition, creating a dreamy, unreal space. The young blonde and the older couple burst over the dancing figures in a white cloud illuminated by a blaze of brilliant white light, two images for which Lynch has historically shown a partiality. Juxtaposed to these evocations of light and life is a scene of enervation and fear in a bedroom in which we hear laboured, anxious breathing; a brief scene that terminates in a dissolve into a pillow that matches sheets the colour of dried blood. This dissolve signals the spectator's move into a dreamlike realm.[2] In this dream-like terrain, it is not the the girl's presence but her absence that is emphasised as the film opens. We see her smiling face in superimposition, but we do not see her either among the crush of dancers or in the bed, where no body is actually seen. She is linked to both scenes, but her figure is evoked in negative space.

But the blonde is not the only girl. Immediately, there appears another and with her another intimation of absence. This second girl is a dark, sullen beauty, whose glamorous attire and languid posture in the back of the chauffeur-driven limousine slowly negotiating Mulholland Drive mark her as a person of wealth and importance heading for an evening of festivity. Yet the low vibration of non-diegetic music presages something sinister, which erupts in the attempt of the chauffeur and his unidentified companion to kill the glamorous woman. Her situation changes when a couple of cars filled with teenagers, wildly screaming around the curves of Mulholland Drive crash into the limousine, killing themselves and the would-be assassins. The girl alone survives. Now an amnesiac, she wanders down into a residential street in a daze, terrified that she is being hunted. When the police arrive at the accident scene, she is already gone, but she has left behind a trace, a pearl earring. Another evocation of a girl who is not there.

At this point the film follows neither the bright girl nor the dark girl, but moves instead to an entirely different setting and two completely new characters, a dark young man (Herb Fishler) and a fair older man (Michael Cooke) in a bright, sun-filled fast food restaurant called Winkies. Again the combination of dark and light emerges: as the dark young man recounts a terrible dream he has had about this restaurant, a dream in which he realises that there is a man 'in back of this place. He's the one who's doing it.' The two then go to the back of Winkies for a reality check, where in full daylight, a dark, Bigfoot-like figure (Bonnie Aarons), identified in the credits as a bum, emerges from behind a wall and causes the dreamer to collapse. Since these two figures do not become involved in the central events of the film, and only the dreamer appears again, in a flash-cut at the end of the film, they may seem to derail the delicate process of exposition, but in fact they cast light on the web of machinations surrounding the girls. Here's how. Immediately following the Winkies scene, there is a flash-cut of the dark amnesiac which yields to the image of a bizarre, static figure in a wheelchair, his head small, his body huge, in a large, sterile, vacuum-like room, who initiates a series of phone calls about a 'missing girl'. The juxtaposition of cuts suggests that the amnesiac girl asleep in her refuge is the absent person being discussed. Here too there is a 'man behind' who is 'doing it': Mr. Roque. Thus the dreaming mind of the fast-food scene has been evoked to tell us about terrible, overwhelming forces that lie beyond material perception. But it cannot tell us what these forces are doing. We can only assume that Roque is doing something to the dark girl, probably that he is the one trying to have her killed. To go further than that, we will have to watch the events that follow.

What has been outlined so far is a non-linear pattern of association and juxta-position. It is at this point that we return to the blonde girl and the older couple from the opening montage, this time in a realistic setting and what seems to be an ordinary story. Now identified as Betty, the girl has just de-planed in Los Angeles along with the older couple, who turn out to be cheerful strangers and wish Betty well in the career in film she has come to pursue. Betty then proceeds to her Aunt Ruth's apartment, where she will live while she tries her luck in the movies. But just as we sigh with relief at the prospect of having gotten beyond the 'strange stuff' to a conventional 'making it in Hollywood' narrative, we find ourselves careening faster than before along the twists and turns of a fun-house slide, where reversals are the order of the day.[3] The key reversal so far unnoticed by all previous critical literature on this film, upends our assumptions about Mr Roque's relationship to the missing girl, that element that the dreaming mind cannot reveal, and about which only the unfolding of events can tell us. And it is on this reversal that the entire film turns. The attempted murder is not what it seems, but we are not yet ready to make this crucial leap of imagination.

'Her name is Camilla Rhodes. The director doesn't want her.'

The two girls now meet at Aunt Ruth's, where the dark girl has furtively taken shelter. Betty finds this stranger in the shower, and her assumption that she a friend of Aunt Ruth's initiates a train of misunderstandings that cluster around the amnesiac dark girl's identification of herself as 'Rita', a name she glimpses, in a mirror, on a poster of *Gilda* (1946) hanging in the apartment.[4] Betty's sweet concern when Rita tells her she's been in a car accident, her chatter about her ambitions, and her euphoria about being in Aunt Ruth's beautiful apartment – 'this dream place' – clash tonally with the earlier images of attempted murder. But Betty has no idea what she's getting into. This scene is immediately juxtaposed to global, aerial images of Los Angeles, which again suggest the unknown powers that lurk behind appearances and absences. The girls' meeting is part of an eerie larger picture.

The unsettling sense of lurking unknown powers now blooms into anxiety, as we watch Roque's emissaries, two thuggish, sinister 'suits', the Castigiliane brothers (Dan Hedaya and Angelo Badalamenti) as they introduce us to the third defining

'Rita' (Laura Elena Harring) in *Mulholland Drive*: 'a name she glimpses in a mirror…'

event in the film: their invasion of Adam Kesher's pre-production meeting. The mysterious, almost silent Castiglianes turn the meeting upside down when they laconically inform the befuddled director, 'This is the girl,' as they proffer a head shot of a standard, blonde starlet-type identified on the photo as Camilla Rhodes (Melissa George). If we do not know when we first see them that the absurd Castiglianes are associated with Roque, their monosyllabic intransigence reminds us of the 'man behind' and his vacuum-like room, and their connection with him is endorsed as we suddenly see Mr. Roque in a flash-cut, listening to the meeting from his seclusion. Although Adam does not understand, as we do, that he is at the mercy of a lurking power, he soon finds out that he is in trouble. 'There is no way that girl is in my movie; that girl is not in my film', he yells. 'It's no longer your film', one of the brothers (Dan Hedaya) tells him.

Adam does not accept the sentence pronounced on his tenure as director, but his resistance to intimidation takes the form of a puerile attack with a golf club on the Castiglianes' limousine. What chance does such a person have against the stealthy, omnipresent Roque and his thugs?[5] And indeed, his meagre struggle yields to amazed capitulation when within the space of 24 hours he is mysteriously stripped of all his financial resources, as well as his film. He also loses his wife Lorraine (Lori Heuring), whom, in a hilariously manic scene, he discovers in bed with the pool man when he returns home from the meeting with the Castiglianes. Lorraine inadvertently becomes Roque's accomplice when she excoriates Adam for arriving home too early for her to cover up her extramarital fling. Adam again takes immediate infantile revenge on her, as he pours pink paint into her jewellery box. Clearly, his life is built on sand, both professionally and emotionally. Ultimately, he cannot withstand the pressure. As he gives in and casts 'the girl' chosen by Mr Roque, he unwittingly initiates a train of mortal events.

This mortality issues from Mr Roque's office. Flash-cuts of this airless domain and its robotic inhabitant pervade the first hour of the film: an image of evil as enforced stasis and inorganic disconnection. How disconnected he is from the damage he does is evident in an unsettling conversation he has with a studio executive who comes to report that Adam is not co-operating: 'Her name is Camilla Rhodes. The director doesn't want her. Do you want him replaced?' Evidently Roque does not even know the name of the girl on whom the fate of Adam's film depends, let alone whether she is the right girl, and this defines the nature of this terrible, lifeless, absurd exercise of power that gradually squeezes the life out of Adam, Betty and Rita without any one of the three ever coming in contact with him. Lynch does not proffer the usual indictment of the exploitative, callous womaniser in Tinseltown. Rather, he plays with the aspect of commercial film-making that depletes reality of its material fullness and leaves only ghosts, traces of organic life. With Mr Roque in control, the hopes with which Betty and Adam enter the film are already dashed, even though they do not yet know it, and Rita's identity, once revealed, will prove to be the name of their despair. But we are still not ready to deal with that.

Lynch thus signals us early and often through tone and mood that life and death, defeat and hope are fused in his tale of Hollywood. Only later, as the film is almost over, will we learn the cut and dried narrative events that this tone and mood refer to: Betty Elms won a dance contest that brought her to Hollywood, and her experiences with Rita and missed connections with Adam led to her later suicide. This belatedness of explicit narrative meanings, the foregrounding of tonal/ emotional depictions of unspoken narrative events is primary to an understanding of Lynch's work, which urges us to contemplate events with the larger faculty of imagination before the reductive words are spoken, for it is only the larger faculty that can apprehend what is really going on, a truth too absurd for ordinary logic and reason. A part of this approach to the spectator is the main title's conflation of death and life that will characterise *Mulholland Drive* as it did the beginning of another magisterial film about Hollywood, Billy Wilder's *Sunset Boulevard* (1950) – though Lynch works with much greater freedom and audacity than the speaking corpse of Joe Gillis (William Holden). *Mulholland Drive* is Lynch's own *Sunset Boulevard*, though it is neither a remake nor an imitation of Wilder's remarkable saga of the dark side of the movies – if not Lynch's favourite film, at least one of the classical masterpieces he holds in highest esteem. *Mulholland Drive* is a *re-vision* of what also held Wilder's attention: the transition from human hope to putrefaction.[6] But there I leave Wilder. Pushing the analogies and allusions to *Sunset Boulevard* – the Sunset Boulevard street sign at the beginning of *Mulholland Drive*, Lynch's shots of Betty's courtyard evoking shots of the courtyard of Norma Desmond's house – would not be a productive strategy. Rather the relationship of the two films measures the distance between their interpretations of the tradition of reflexive Hollywood movies and the immensity of the creative leap Lynch has taken from the springboard of the best of his forerunners.

Lynch takes precisely those risks that are not taken by Adam Kesher as he tells the story of the putrefaction of the creative process as a siege in which those who are defeated never have the chance to fight back, or even to know the adversary. Betty arrives in Hollywood with everything that it takes to 'make it': the perky blonde charm, the talent and the connections. And, yes, even all these assets cannot win her the brass ring in an industry of voids and black holes created by power for the sake of power. Adam is similarly mystified by the sudden erosion of the earth beneath his feet. Roque, behind the scenes and 'doing it' in sterile near-silence, defeats the protagonists indirectly, a situation that defies the Hollywood convention that films reach a climax in hand-to-hand combat.

The Hollywood cautionary tale as Lynch envisions it thus prohibits the use of a cause-and-effect plot, which relies on the kind of confrontation Roque does not allow. Instead, *Mulholland Drive* propels the audience through a set of disorienting transformations in order to follow the life of creative integrity to its demise, an issue of life and death importance to David Lynch. Such an extinction is not, according to this film, a single event, but the devastation of the web of interconnection that supports a secure reality; an onslaught against the very stability on which time and space depends.[7] The absurdly laconic Castiglianes, foreclosing any dialogue or debate, are only the first onslaught from the oxygen-deprived world of Mr Roque. The decisive foot soldier is the Cowboy (Lafayette Montgomery) whom Adam is compelled to meet with when he is at the nadir of his life, stripped of his wealth and hounded out even of the inner city flophouse in which he has tried to hide.

The scene between Adam and the Cowboy defines the way Roque engineers the destruction of creativity. His minion, the Cowboy, creates a situation which Adam recognises as absurd, a western scenario straight out of a bad movie, with no roots in the reality of the ordinary life of Los Angeles, as Adam is directed to meet the mysterious Cowboy at a corral, complete with the skeleton of the head of a steer and the signature flickering light of the Lynch film. The situation moves further into the ludicrous when the Cowboy arrives, a pale slug of a man, dressed up in the ersatz rugged western garb associated with ruddy outdoor men. The Cowboy is a more intense and coercive version of the thuggish Castiglianes. Where the Castiglianes act as immovable obstructions in Adam's way, the Cowboy is an irresistible force as he plays out the western motif by aggressively framing his questions like lassos, compelling Adam to think only within the context he creates. This form of intimidation dramatises the aggressive disregard of reality that renders Camilla Rhodes the *only* choice Adam can have for no discernible reason, not even the box office or the usual casting couch. How crucial is their relentless desire to dominate Adam's project? The Roque/Castigliane/Cowboy axis is deadly even though it is only a single aspect of Adam's production that they insist on controlling: any obstacle to the creative process kills its organicity. Roque's deployment of the Brothers and the Cowboy puts Adam between a Roque and a hard place. He is the death of popular culture as a vital cultural force.

That death is portrayed in terms of the absence that has been building as the film progresses. The mysteries of the interconnections within the stories of Betty,

Rita and Adam permit a meeting between Betty and Rita, and later Adam and Rita; ironically, the most important link among them is the connection that is pointedly *not* made, that between Adam and Betty. An Adam/Betty meeting becomes possible after an audition prearranged for Betty by her Aunt. But the meeting pointedly does not take place. It begins to seem inevitable, but sadly, even horribly, what we watch is not the encounter itself, but its failure to materialise.

The missed meeting is prepared for by the extraordinary high comedy of the audition scene in which Betty shows her acting stuff for a sweet-natured producer named Wally (James Karen), in a reading with a has-been matinée idol, Woody Katz (Chad Everett). Her reading portrays the magic and wonder of artistic creativity when she creates something – a dangerously erotic mood – out of absolutely nothing. The audition script Betty is given is utterly clichéd, the directions she receives from the director, Bob Brooker (Wayne Grace) are droolingly incomprehensible, and her scene partner is made up of equal parts snake oil and suntan. Betty's creation is a distillation of the magic of mass market movies, a chemistry that appears out of the blue without either warning or significance. (A previous scene in which Rita helped Betty rehearse seems to be pointless until we realise that the dark girl's emotionally stupid reading shows that this woman, who ultimately will be forced on Adam by Roque's cartel, has no talent, an important detail in a film about the death of creativity.) As a result of Betty's brilliance, casting director Linney James (Rita Taggert) is inspired to steal her from Wally for Adam's movie, and brings her to Adam's set. The mixture of larceny and Betty's innocent freshness is unsettling, and while the audience at this point hopes against hope that it is after all possible to get clean water from a polluted well, we are soon brought back to a darker reality.

In the gloom of Adam's set where he morosely awaits the mandated appearance of Camilla Rhodes, Betty breaks through the darkness momentarily, literally shining. No one is lit as she is in this scene, as if there were a soft radiance emanating from within. Her appearance is a sophisticated, visionary re-reading of the extremely familiar plot point when a director is struck immediately by an unknown girl whom he catapults to stardom, and indeed, although we did not know it until this moment, Adam is working on a musical. We have laughed at that cliché, defined indelibly in the musical movie *42ⁿᵈ Street* (Lloyd Bacon, 1933), but we have not forgotten it. In giving us a story in which that moment of inspiration does not take place Lynch reveals why. What has long been thought of as a tired old cliché is revealed here as an expression of a very meaningful part of the entertainment industry: the necessary moment of creation which is unexpected, unplanned, and makes possible the vitality of mass culture. Betty represents that unexpected moment for Adam but he is too stuck in the grip of The Powers That Be to seize the fresh energy she brings with her.

Instead of meeting, Betty and Adam only graze each other's narrative trajectories, intersecting momentarily in a mutual gaze when Adam turns to see Betty for the first time. A sequence unlike any other in *Mulholland Drive*, this interlocking gaze stimulated by 'the girl' is a part of a long history of similar gazes in the films of David Lynch that goes all the way back to *Eraserhead*. It is the shock of authentic contact, the Lynchian site of what is most precious in human life, and one of the few interactions in his filmic universes endowed with the power to pierce hollow social forms. For most of Lynch's career, he has celebrated the power of this gaze, particularly in how a fruitful feminine energy is communicated through the eyes, and here in *Mulholland Drive* it is the one rush of authentic energy in a world of dry husks and violent manipulation. But in *Lost Highway*, Lynch began to explore a situation in which its abundance of meaning is overwhelmed by the power of solipsistic emptiness.[8] In *Mulholland Drive*, he continues travelling in that new direction, showing us very clearly the precise moment of spiritual atrophy. When Betty leaves the set, when Adam does not call her back, the great sorrow that each of them radiates marks their profound, unspoken, unacknowledged foreboding that, although her suicide does not take place until much later, this is the end of Betty's life. It is also the moment when Adam's already tenuous hold on emotional life is destroyed, although it will not be until much later that he reaches full putrefaction. The sublime gaze was the portal, now closed, to the finer reaches of the imagination, and the wrong girl is the sign of the usurpation of Adam's higher, imaginative, creative vision.

'Someone is in trouble; something bad is happening.'

The multiple ramifications of Adam's capitulation surprise the film with the kind of connections predicted by chaos theory, which explores the way the beating of a butterfly's wings in Hong Kong can affect the weather halfway around the world. Because Adam falls, and is prevented from meeting her, Betty's cheerful expectations, both about her career and about her ability to help Rita, fall into a black hole, never to be seen again. But that does not mean that her original, sweetly flaky euphoria is not real. Rather, the film makes us understand that her initial overconfidence is a part of her obliviousness to the unseen power of Mr Roque, whom no one in the film understands, none of the main characters ever see, and over whom no one has control. In fact, Mr Roque is only visible to the spectator at the beginning of the film when he has lost control through the disappearance of 'the girl'. Once Adam capitulates, Roque disappears from the film, and all that is left are the traces of his awful power. Betty never knows what has hit her. By the time it has happened, she is not Betty any more but a new entity spawned by the destruction of her dreams: Diane Selwyn.

It is no accident that when Betty turns away from Adam she joins Rita instead to search for her identity in a trip to the house of a woman called Diane Selwyn (Lyssie Powell). The discovery Betty makes is a part of her journey down the *wrong* road taken, and when she finds Diane Selwyn's corpse, she is beginning her discovery of her own identity, not Rita's, a sign that the dead zone Roque inhabits behind known events means that nothing is as it seems. Ultimately we will discover that Rita was never the real victim. She is Hollywood's deadly, powerful, but utterly insignificant exploited girl: lethal, but always a pawn. From her position as shell-shocked survivor of the accident, she is always, if involuntarily, drawing Betty toward the discovery of her own despair. Moreover, Betty is not totally innocent in the events leading to her destruction. Her generosity toward Rita is, perhaps, not quite as altruistic as it might seem; she is also in love with the control she seems to have over her. Thus, when Betty runs off Adam's sound stage, he is not the only one who is captive to forces that negate the sublime possibilities of their gaze. In the Lynchian world, it is always an over-fondness for the will to control that leads to ruin.[9] Betty's dire transformation, moving through a space of darkness rather than cause and effect, is a form of typical Lynchian dream logic. At the deepest level of our beings, we know that this transformation has taken place for all of us in subconscious darkness, more and less desperately, varying with our circumstances. In life we maintain continuous signs of identity, like our names. But our young, inexperienced dreams routinely undergo such transformations as they collide with forces unleashed by power establishments and our own internal obsessions that a new name and identity would be entirely in keeping with the profound alterations in us, especially the commutation of early assumptions about our possibilities. Betty's sea change is catastrophic, and it is not only about her. Beginning in someone else's life, it hits just when all her dreams seem magically on the brink of fulfilment.

That this terrible metamorphosis is already in progress just at the moment that Betty is assured, to all appearances, of the blonde ingenue's stereotypical happy ending and that the downward turn is connected with her generous attempt to help Rita, is prefigured in the sybilline visit of Louise Bonner (Lee Grant) to Betty's apartment. Just before Betty's audition, Louise, a previously unknown character, a resident of the complex in which Aunt Ruth's apartment is located, is suddenly thrust into view. Louise appears in the dark at Betty's door, her face old and mysterious, wearing a hooded cloak and murmuring prophetically that there is trouble in Betty's domain. Clearly she expects to find Betty's Aunt Ruth, and when she asks who Betty is, the girl tells her, 'My name is Betty.' Louise's enigmatic reply is, 'No, no it's not. That's not what she said. Someone is in trouble. Something bad is happening.' Here is another hint from beyond ordinary rationality, and it speaks of Betty's identity.

The narrative turn toward sterile solipsism has started at the top with Mr. Roque but has worked its way down into the mockery of Betty's hopeful attempt to help Rita. With the terrifying discovery of Selwyn's putrifying corpse, Betty's dead hopes stare her in the face. To drive home the imaginative level on which these events are taking place, and their impact on the instability of identity once creativity is thwarted, things are already beginning to reverse themselves. As they run horrified from the site of Selwyn's death, the first stages of the metamorphoses to come occur when Betty and Rita fan out into multiple images of themselves, as if layers of their personhood were being shaken apart. And they are. Back at Betty's apartment, the layers are reconfigured as Rita takes on Betty's appearance by covering her luxuriant, dark hair with a short, blonde wig. The narrative excuse for this is that Rita is fearful that the murder of Selwyn means that the thugs chasing her are getting closer. But the tonal weight of this image is the move of Rita into Betty's place as the dominant personality, which she becomes when Betty invites her to share the bed rather than sleeping on the couch and Rita initiates sex.

The sex, seemingly sweet and innocent, like Betty's first meeting with Rita, is pretty poison, another part of Betty's drift into despair and death that continues when Rita maintains her new leadership position in their mutating friendship and convinces Betty to go with her to an after-hours place called the Club Silencio. The moment that Rita awakens from post-coital sleep, in the early morning hours, we see that she is undergoing a transformation which is coming from a place beyond her control. She opens her eyes compulsively muttering in Spanish of absence and nothingness: 'There is no band.' The dark girl takes charge at the very moment that Roque has conquered Kesher. As the consequences of Roque's victory play out, she will become a dominant, sinister figure herself, a parallelism that calls into question a universal critical assumption about the early scenes in *Mulholland Drive*. Here at last, we are ready to encounter the pivotal reversal in the film.

The attempted murder at the beginning of the film cannot have been initiated by Roque, as all previously published commentary on this film has assumed, and as all the information that we first receive in the film seems to prompt us to suppose. Yes, in our earliest view of Roque he says on the phone, 'The girl is still missing.' But those words, wrongly assumed to be part of an initiative to finish the job interrupted by the car crash, are pronounced by someone who is looking to recover her. When the dark girl is ultimately revealed as Camilla Rhodes, Roque's designated girl, this reversal calls for a re-evaluation of everything we originally believed about Roque's terse words just after the accident that saves Rita's life. Looking back over the initial scenes, we must now take into account that indeed none of Mr Roque's other crude, stupid thugs look remotely like the smooth, polished assassins of the opening scene. The spectator has misread the clues just as Betty did when she first encountered the lost girl. Rita is not Roque's victim. Betty is, and she becomes his victim *because* she helps Rita find her identity. Betty's charity, with which the spectator is likely to sympathise, leads us away from any inkling that the elimination of Rita/Camilla at the beginning of the film would have cleared the way for the genuinely creative moment. However, subsequent events strongly suggest that the best part of Rita is her aspect when she is lost and submissive, not when she is found and dominant. A dominant Rita turns out to be the found Camilla, and Camilla is the triumph of the Roquean state of nothingness and un-being.[10]

This reading makes sense of an otherwise incomprehensible scene also in the first part of the film, in which a careless but vicious gangster shoots his 'friend' to take possession of a phone book. Once it becomes apparent that the dark girl is Camilla Rhodes, Roque's power lever, we can now see what we did not see before: that there must be two sets of shady men in the film, those who challenge Roque's power by attempting to kill his designated girl, and those who seek to restore her to her place. (At the very least there are conflicted factions within Roque's regime.) The conversation between Joe (Mark Pellegrino), the shooter, and Ed (Vincent Castellanos), custodian of the phone book, becomes meaningful only if there are two factions. When Ed speaks of the accident, it is clear that *he* sees it as the interruption of a job that was supposed to be completed. When Joe shoots Ed to get the phone book, it suggests that he is working for someone who did not want the job completed. This explains why Joe is linked by visual juxtaposition to Mr Roque, while Ed and the initial assassins are not.

Roque's near invisibility as a prime mover makes his allegiances difficult to tease out. The even more submerged identity of whatever group is working against him is even more problematic, though typical of Lynch, as a sign of opposing forces that are always present to balance the energies in his filmic worlds. But there is enough information. Rita is the object of simultaneous initiatives to destroy and restore her; she is trouble for Betty, victory for Roque. Even Coco (Ann Miller), the common sense, anything but visionary, concierge of Aunt Ruth's apartment complex, adds her down-to-earth voice to the chorus of rejected warnings to Betty: 'Louise Bonner said there's trouble in there. Remember last night? Well, sometimes she's wrong. But if there is trouble, get rid of it.' Betty's goodness and warmth, and alas, her all too human frailty inclining her toward the thrill of being the one in charge, deafen her to counsel about her own best interests. Horribly, everything works for Roque.

This is a mind-bending reversal, and it defies conventional film practice. Instead of setting up the situation for the audience to follow, the opening scenes have misled us, or more correctly they have led us to re-vision them completely. With the reversal, the opening scene takes on new meaning: Rita's survival, not her near death, becomes the catastrophe. Like Betty, the audience has been hoping to protect the agent of death and imaginative impoverishment, a form of seduction that is all too material in its consequences. This becomes manifest when Rita drags Betty out of bed in the small hours to Club Silencio. Too little has been made of Rita/Camilla's announcement that she has something to show Betty before leading her to the Silencio, where Betty is broken irreparably. What is the sudden urgency? As it turns out what happens at the club is that Betty and Rita are confronted with a revelation of the void, the closest anyone in this film will come to seeing the otherwise invisible vacuum from within which Roque operates. Though Rita/Camilla is only an instrument, not the deliberate malefactor, she is driven by powerful forces of disintegration. Though she too is also distraught by what she sees, the revelation is the beginning of her ascendancy and Betty's decline. The knowledge that she forces upon Betty, perhaps because it is only partial and continues to shield Roque from direct identification as the source of evil, is the prologue to Betty's extreme disempowerment.

The show at Club Silencio, the most original and stunning sequence in an original and stunning film, directs attention to its insubstantiality and the empty condition of absence that is the nature of Roque's power and the opposite of Betty's and Adam's creative reaching into the unknown. We hear a band, but there is no band; everything is tape recorded. Nor are the apparently present bodies really there. They disappear and appear abruptly, illusions of sight and sound in a reality of silence. The most powerful of these silences is obliquely rendered by Rebekah Del Rio, singing a Spanish translation of Roy Orbison's 'Crying'. Del Rio, a seemingly sensual, full-bodied presence, at one point collapses like a hollow doll, while her rich voice continues to intone. The issue here may seem to be about life and death, but it is actually about fullness and the void, as is the entire film. It explains why later on the initial photographic image of Camilla Rhodes as a blonde yields to Rita's sudden appearance with that name. Why may a blonde image not suddenly materialise as a brunette? Dark-haired Rita has already appeared as a blonde through the magic of wigs. Roque has no material, visceral, organic interest in the film. Anyone with the designated label pinned on her fulfils his purposes. Later, when the world of the three protagonists has become a lifeless mockery of their early desires, the complicity of the two images is tragi-comically portrayed at an awful engagement party for Adam and Camilla, when blonde Camilla suddenly and briefly appears and kisses dark Camilla on the lips resulting in both a zany print of dark Camilla's lipstick on the blonde's mouth and an energy force field that definitively exiles Diane/Betty outside the circle of success. At Club Silencio, Betty is filled with a premonition of the terrible way the image will play itself out, and it sends her into heaving convulsions. She is quite literally coming apart. Her discovery of the eerie blue box in her purse at Club Silencio is the sign that Betty is approaching a transformation, and, sure enough, when the two return to the apartment, she disappears. A puzzled Rita then retrieves the key to the blue box from its hiding place in *her* purse and uses it to open the box.

The blue box, empty, does not represent anything, as an audience trained to think in terms of allegory and symbols will assume. It *is* the darkness that has been waiting since the beginning of the film, foreshadowed by a mysterious blue key initially discovered in Rita's purse, which she cannot identify, ostensibly because of her amnesia. Yes, Rita has held the key from the beginning. It will be helpful to mention here that Lynch does not see darkness as a morally negative space, but as a space of the unknown of the subconscious from which anything, both the marvellous and the terrible, can emerge. In this case, however, from the moment when Adam and Betty do not meet, what emerges from the darkness is destined to be terrible because the betrayal of Adam's creative choices has rendered the unknown toxic. Rita now disappears and the audience moves into the space of the unknown through a dissolve into the seemingly endless darkness of the box.

This is a mesmerising representation of the condition of film production, which by nature mandates illusion rather than substance. It would be possible (and reasonable) to argue that on this basis the potentially fruitful meeting of Adam and Betty can never take place. And yet the breathtaking, indeterminate presentation of that moment – there is a tremulous instant when we are not sure whether or not Adam will turn toward Betty – suggests, as have Lynch's previous films, that popular culture can provide a fullness of meaning even though, or perhaps *because*, it is an imaginary signifier. There was a moment in this process when fullness might have been married to its images: the question for Lynch is always whether the imaginary connects with something beyond itself or languishes in the void of solipsism. Popular culture maintains its integrity in its vision and its coherence. Adam had that possibility but was defeated by the solipsistic world of the Roque group. What might have grown from the fertile, richly filled silence of the glance between him and Betty remains a possibility in this film. It is the circumstantial defeat of the integrity of that possibility that renders the subconscious toxic: bodies that mask emptiness with their seeming heft, but which slide into decomposition in the absence of a healthy imaginative force that might have sustained them as creations.

Diane Selwyn, the detritus that remains after Betty's immersion in the Roquean darkness of depleted imaginative vision, inhabits a room desaturated of colour: we have found the trembling figure of the main title and know it to be the defeat of Betty's initial possibilities. It is of note that Mr Roque does not appear in the last half of the film, and his emissaries, one of the Castiglianes (Angelo Badalamenti) and the Cowboy, appear only in brief sightings at Adam and Camilla's engagement party, and in the Cowboy's brief appearance in Selwyn's bedroom. Roque's victory is implicit in his invisibility and in the Cowboy's function as a stage manager for Diane. 'Time to wake up, pretty girl', he tells her, peeking into her room just before she rises to a day depleted of all the hopes with which the film began: a double mockery, since she is not even all that pretty any more. Though Betty/Diane never sees him or his accomplice there, Roque is now in control. The Cowboy's heavy knock at her door is a wake-up call to tell her she has been robbed of her dreams.

In Diane's desaturated room there is but one object rich in colour, a blue key, the same colour as the mysterious triangular key and the blue box it opens, but here in the shape of an ordinary latchkey, a key only to the most reduced level of reality, not the possibilities of the darkness within the blue box. Narratively, this is established as the sign that the contract killer has killed Rita/Camilla for Betty/Diane, but it is conveyed to the spectator in a non-linear fashion way before Diane makes the contract with a killer. Time and space have come unglued, along with the identities of the three leading characters. Betty/Diane and Rita/Camilla now share a sadistic/vampiric relationship, and Adam and Rita/Camilla share a travesty of romance. Camilla enters Diane's room as a hyper-vital force. Her make-up is exaggeratedly rich in colour, her skin glowing while Diane's is almost grey. In her metamorphosis, she is placidly sated, as if with her victim's blood. Energised by Diane's thwarted passion, she incites her sexually, then rejects her; and, at a fateful party on Mulholland Drive, enjoys watching Diane squirm at Adam's announcement of what appears to be their engagement. But things are not as Rita/Camilla believes. The announcement aborts, as Adam, with a malign laugh, leaves off the word '…married' from his initial 'we are going to be…' prefiguring the fact that they are not going to *be* anything at all. Through Adam's fatal capitulation, being has been supplanted by nothingness; 'the girl' has become a vehicle of death. Betty will kill both Rita and herself, and Adam and his film are already dead.

Silencio

Thus in *Mulholland Drive*, the performing girl follows a destiny quite different from Lynch's previously life-giving versions of the figure. Or perhaps it would be more accurate to say that the destructive elements previously subordinated to creativity have been foregrounded and energised by the pervasive cultural repressiveness emanating from Roque. Herein, in this account of the failure of Adam's musical, Lynch has located his events in the very Hollywood domain in which the girl's body is traditionally the visible sign of the industry's creative potency, as in the Busby Berkeley musical, the Astaire/Rogers vehicle, the Gene Kelly musical. In *Mulholland Drive*, creative energy is blocked, and 'the girl's' body is ultimately the sign of the industry's putrefaction, the corpse of Diane Selwyn a horrible, disfigured, rotted *memento mori* for pop culture.

A grim view of mass entertainment, and of life in general? Well, perhaps a grim angle of perception. The narrative structure, dependent on the neutral, Lynchian darkness of the blue box, creates its last reversal when it relativises the events that have unfolded. Given Lynch's faith in darkness as the loam of both creativity and destruction, what aspects of the unseen that emerge from the box are most fruitfully read as contingent on the integrity of the sensibility that enters the darkness. Had Adam not capitulated … But even though he could not resist Roque at that point in his life, destruction is never final in the Lynchian universe. Lynch has told me that there is always hope. According to him, Fred Madison's seeming doom at the end of *Lost Highway* would have been mitigated had there been more time to pursue his story. In my five years of interviews with Lynch, I have gleaned the importance to him of an optimism that most critics overlook. In each Lynch film there is, regardless of the troubles that beset the protagonists, a strong intimation of a force for good that occurs when the human will is relaxed or even abdicated, and for most of his career Lynch has celebrated the power of this force. From *Eraserhead* to *Twin Peaks: Fire Walk with Me* (1992), Lynch's protagonists have in some *involuntary* manner had their chance for a modicum of victory over whatever threatens to oppress them.[11] *Mulholland Drive* represents a new direction for Lynch, however, one that he began in *Lost Highway*, a new concern with protagonists who miss their moment. Yet even his tales of missed opportunities conserve hope. Had *Mulholland Drive* been the continuing story on television for which Lynch had originally planned, the detective audience would have moved fluidly between the emptiness and fullness of the dark unknown from which all manner of things are born – surely also Lynch's thwarted plan for *Twin Peaks*. Perhaps the Internet, Lynch's newest passion, with *its* capacity for continuing narrative will serve his turn as the Mr Roques of network television have not.[12]

As it is, at the closure of *Mulholland Drive* Lynch seeds the darkness with hope when he haunts the screen with radiant, clouds illuminated by brilliant light through which Betty and Rita reappear in the darkness suddenly, as they once were. Despite the narrative triumph of Hollywood's criminal solipsism, traces of better possibilities remain in the film: the once hopeful aspects of both girls do not die simply because the narrative has run its course. In the final frames, Lynch returns to Club Silencio, the place of revelation. It is empty now save for a heavily made-up woman, dressed with extravagant elegance (Cori Glazer), seated in a box overlooking the stage. We have seen her before, this apparition whose blue hair, the colour of the mysterious box that holds the darkness of the unknown, tops a face haughty and secretive. Before, there was no reason to think of her as any more important than any of the other fantastic details of the scene. Yet here she is in the important final frames of the film, murmuring 'Silencio'. Club Silencio now belongs to the audience, its empty space alive with questions. Is the blue-haired woman there, or is she only a hollow appearance, like Rebekah Del Rio? Why do the important closing frames focus on this previously minor figure? This is a closure sparkling with complex resonances. Considering the dark face of the entertainment media revealed in *Mulholland Drive*, it is perhaps no wonder that Disney/ABC pulled away from their earlier commitment to the film.[13] But, if that was the case, the network is guilty of both cowardice *and* myopia. Lynch has not unequivocally impugned the popular media. Certainly the Blue Haired Woman is only a photographic image, but at the same time she has not disappeared with all the empty traces. A woman in a dreamlike space, excessively artificial in her appearance, emphatically *not* a 'girl', like *Mulholland Drive* itself she is full of the signs both of empty illusion and the fullness of possibility. This closure opens onto an as yet undetermined future for popular culture: not for Betty, Rita or Adam, but for us.

Notes

1　Strictly speaking, we have already seen Lynch experimenting with an alternate function for the performing woman as a potential catalyst for disaster in *Lost Highway* (1997), in which Patricia Arquette plays the double role of Alice (blonde) and Renée (dark), who may or may not be one person. Alice is a porn actress whose desires lead the equally split male protagonist Fred Madison (Bill Pullman)/Pete Dayton (Balthazar Getty) down a very lost highway indeed.

2　Almost all critics agree that the film is dreamlike. However, there is a widespread misunderstanding that the film divides into dream and reality, the first half of the film being Betty's euphoric dream and the second her dismal reality. For examples of this approach see Wyman, Garrone and Klein 2001. You know a film review is in trouble when one of the final subheadings is 'What the *fuck* is going on in this movie?' Phillip Lopate takes a similar approach (Lopate 2001).

3　The multi-plot narrative has driven many critics to focus predominantly on plot developments, trying to translate them into a more linear, therefore conventional, less challenging form. Needless to say, this kind of criticism works against Lynch's artistry. See, for example, Travers 2001.

4　Charles Vidor's *Gilda* starred Rita Hayworth and Glenn Ford.

5　Theroux has much of interest to say about this scene and about the thug-like representation of Hollywood producers in the film: see his interview in *Wrapped in Plastic* (Thorne and Miller 2001b). He belongs to a new generation of actors, familiar with Lynch's early work, who have a great deal more insight into what Lynch his trying to achieve than the actors in Lynch's previous films. Interviews I was privileged to have with Catherine Coulson and Jack Nance suggested that they and the other actors they worked with were able to give Lynch what he asked for, and enjoyed the process, but remained rather puzzled about what was going on.

6　Lynch used the term 'putrefaction' several times during his press conference at the New York Film Festival 2001.

7　Stephen Holden is extremely perceptive about the relationship *Mulholland Drive* has to Hollywood and to the dream: 'For *Mulholland Drive* finally has little to do with any single character's love life or professional ambition. The movie is an ever-deepening reflection on the allure of Hollywood and on the multiple role-playing and self-invention that the movie-going experience promises. That same promise of identity loss extends to the star-making process, in which the star can disappear into other lives and become other people's fantasies' (Holden 2001).

8 For the importance of the gaze, see my commentary on *Wild at Heart* (Nochimson 1997: 68). I initially developed this theme relative to *Mulholland Drive* in Nochimson 2002.

9 Naomi Watts, who is as perceptive about her work with Lynch as Justin Theroux, has also developed this theme: see her interview in *Wrapped in Plastic* (Thorne and Miller 2001c: 6). Germane to this point is Theroux's comment in his own interview (see n. 5 above) about Diane Selwyn's masturbation scene and her tearful inability to reach a climax, which also reflects the troublesome nature of the relationship between Betty/Diane and Rita/Camilla: 'She's in love with what this girl has, which is celebrity. She's in love with this girl's life, which is money and a relationship with a director. And she's masturbating to *all* that' [emphases in original]. The combination of Betty's wilful need to take charge and Diane's self-destructive (con)fusion of sexuality and the desire for success and fame is suggestive of the way Mr Roque's control of Hollywood is emblematic of similar problems in all the characters, even sweet Betty. Even in Lynch's previous work it is obvious that the worst oppressors cannot win if the protagonists refuse to internalise the villain's evil: for example, for all the savagery of BOB's power in *Twin Peaks*, it is only when Dale Cooper internalises him that he is really in trouble.

10 There is an odd, probably accidental, but still interesting confluence between the confusion, fear and disorientation experienced by Rita Hayworth and that of her namesake in *Mulholland Drive*. A childhood victim of incest, Hayworth was acutely shy and struggled through battles over divorce and child custody. At the age of 42, she suffered from a very early onset of Alzheimer's disease, which remained undiagnosed for 20 years until 1980. She fought against its effect on her abilities, but it limited and ultimately destroyed her career. See Leaming 1989.

11 See Nochimson 1997: 1–15 and 16–45. The conversations I was privileged to have with David Lynch repeatedly returned to the theme of the necessity of giving over the will to control, the need for receptivity in the creative process. This theme runs through his work, from his earliest student films to *Mulholland Drive*, as all the ills of his fictional universes stem from the unrestrained, marauding will and all the blessings from the insights that permit characters to move away from that kind of obsession.

12 For a complementary perspective on the relation between Lynch's interest in continuing narrative and the idea of possibility in his films, see Erica Sheen's chapter in this volume.

13 For a full account of the production history of *Mulholland Drive* see Hughes 2001: 236–42 and Thorne and Miller 2001 a, b and c.

FILMOGRAPHY

d: director; w: writer; ph: principal photographer; p: producer; c: cast

Six Men Getting Sick
US 1967 1 min. (animation loop)
w & ph: David Lynch
p: Pennsylvania Academy of Fine Arts

The Alphabet
US 1968 4 mins. (part animation)
d, w & ph: David Lynch
p: Pennsylvania Academy of Fine Arts, H. Barton Wasserman
c: Peggy Lynch

The Grandmother
1970 34 mins. (part animation)
d, w & ph: David Lynch
p: American Film Institute, David Lynch
c: Richard White, Dorothy McGinnis, Virginia Maitland, Robert Chadwick

The Amputee
1974 5 mins.
d & w: David Lynch
ph: Herb Cardwell, Frederick Elmes
p: American Film Institute, David Lynch
c: Catherine E. Coulson, David Lynch

Eraserhead
1977 89 mins. American Film Institute for Advanced Studies
d & w: David Lynch
ph: Frederick Elmes
p: David Lynch
c: John [Jack] Nance, Charlotte Stewart, Jeanne Bates, Allen Joseph, Judith Anna Roberts, Jack Fisk, Laurel Near

The Elephant Man
1980 124 mins. Brooksfilms
d: David Lynch
w: Eric Bergren, Christopher DeVore, and David Lynch (based on the book *The Elephant Man and Other Reminiscences* by Sir Frederick Treves and *The Elephant Man: A Study in Human Dignity* by Ashley Montagu)
ph: Freddie Francis
p: Jonathan Sanger
c: Anthony Hopkins, John Hurt, Anne Bancroft, Sir John Gielgud, Wendy Hiller, Freddie Jones, Michael Elphick, Hannah Gordon

Dune
1984 137 mins. Dino De Laurentiis/Universal
d: David Lynch
w: David Lynch from Frank Herbert's novel
ph: Freddie Francis
p: Raffaella De Laurentiis
c: Francesca Annis, Kyle MacLachlan, Sting, Dean Stockwell, Sian Phillips, Max Von Sydow, Jurgen Prochnow, José Ferrer, Brad Dourif, Freddie Jones, Linda Hunt, Sean Young, Kenneth McMillan, Everett McGill

Arena: Ruth Roses and Revolver
UK 1987 40 mins. (Television documentary)
First UK transmission 20 February 1987 on BBC2.
d: Helen Gallagher
w: David Lynch

Blue Velvet
1986 120 mins. De Laurentiis Entertainment Group

d & w: David Lynch
ph: Frederick Elmes
p: Fred Caruso
c: Kyle MacLachlan, Laura Dern, Dennis Hopper, Isabella Rossellini, Hope Lange, Dean Stockwell, George Dickerson

The Cowboy and the Frenchman
France 1988 22 mins. Erato Films, Socpress, Figaro
d & w: David Lynch
ph: Frederick Elmes
p: Daniel Toscan du Plantier
c: Harry Dean Stanton, Frederic Golchan, Tracey Walter, Jack Nance, Michael Horse

Twin Peaks
1989 Television Serial (pilot and 29 episodes) Lynch-Frost Productions, Propaganda Films, Spelling Entertainment, Worldvision Enterprises
First transmission (pilot, 120m): 8 April 1990 at 21:00 on ABC (UK: 23 October 1990 at 21:00 on BBC2); Episode 1: Transmitted 30 September 1990 at 21:00 on ABC.
d: David Lynch (pilot and episodes 2, 8, 9, 14, and 29)
w: David Lynch, Mark Frost (plus co-writers)
ph: Ron Garcia (pilot), Frank Byers
p: Monty Montgomery, Gregg Fienberg, Harley Peyton
c: Kyle MacLachlan, Sheryl Lee, Michael Ontkean, Mädchen Amick, Dana Ashbrook, Richard Beymer, Lara Flynn Boyle, Joan Chen, Sherilyn Fenn, Piper Laurie, Peggy Lipton, James Marshall, Everett McGill, Jack Nance, Ray Wise, Grace Zabriskie

Twin Peaks
1990 Pilot of television series with scenes from other episodes, released as feature 112 mins.
Lynch-Frost Productions in association with Propaganda Films and Spelling Entertainment
d: David Lynch
w: David Lynch, Mark Frost
ph: Ron Garcia
p: David J. Latt
c: as above

Wild at Heart
1990 124 mins. Propaganda Films for Polygram
d: David Lynch
w: David Lynch, from a novel by Barry Gifford
ph: Frederick Elmes
p: Monty Montgomery, Steve Golin, Siguron Sighvatsson
c: Nicolas Cage, Laura Dern, Diane Ladd, Willem Dafoe, Isabella Rossellini, Harry Dean Stanton, J. E. Freeman

Industrial Symphony No. 1
1990 49 mins.
d & w: David Lynch
ph: John Schwartzmann
p: Steve Golin, Monty Montgomery, Siguron Sighvatsson
c: Laura Dern, Nicolas Cage, Julee Cruise

American Chronicles
1990–91 Television documentary series Lynch-Frost Productions.
UK transmission 21 June 1992 at 17.00 on Channel 4 Television
d: Lynch and Frost (one contribution): Champions

On The Air
1991-92 Television serial (7 episodes) Lynch-Frost Productions, Twin Peaks Productions (episode 1 only), for ABC Worldvision Entertainments
First transmitted : 20 June 1992 at 21:30 on ABC (UK: 25 July 1993 at 01:55 on BBC2)
d: David Lynch (episode 1)
w: Mark Frost and David Lynch (episode 1)
ph: Ron Garcia (episode 1)
p: Gregg Fienberg (episode 1) and Deepak Nayar (episodes 2–7)
c: Ian Buchanan, Nancye Ferguson, Miguel Ferrer, Gary Grossman, Mel Johnson Jr, Marvin Kaplan, David Lander, Kim McGuire, Maria Jeanette Rubinoff, Tracey Walter

Hotel Room
1992 90 mins. Television anthology (3 episodes) Asymmetrical Productions and Propaganda Films for HBO
First US transmission: 8 January 1993 at 23:00 on HBO.
d: David Lynch: 'Tricks' and 'Blackout'; James Signorelli: 'Getting Rid of Robert'
w: Barry Gifford: 'Tricks' and 'Blackout'; Jay McInerney: 'Getting Rid of Robert'
p: Deepak Nayar
ph: Peter Deming
c: 'Tricks': Glenne Headly, Freddie Jones, Harry Dean Stanton
'Getting Rid of Robert': Griffin Dunne, Deborah Unger, Mariska Hargitay, Chelsea Field
'Blackout': Crispin Glover, Alicia Witt, Clark Heathcliffe Brolly, Camilla Overbye Roos, John Solari, Carl Sundstrom

Twin Peaks: Fire Walk with Me
1992 134 mins. Twin Peaks Productions
d: David Lynch
w: David Lynch, Robert Engels
ph: Ron Garcia
p: Greg Fienberg
c: Kyle MacLachlan, Sheryl Lee, Mädchen Amick, Dana Ashbrook, Catherine E. Coulson, Eric DaRe, Chris Isaak, Moira Kelly, Peggy Lipton, David Lynch, James Marshall, Frank Silva, Ray Wise

Lumière et Compagnie

co-production: Cinétévé, Igeldo Komunikazioa, La Sept-Arte, Le Studio Canal+, Søren
Stærmose AB

France 1995 52 secs. (segment of film)

d & w: David Lynch

p: Neal Edelstein

ph: Peter Deming

c: Jeff Alperi, Mark Wood, Stan Lothridge, Russ Pearlman, Pam Pierrocish, Clyde Small, Joan
Rurelstein, Michele Carlyle, Kathleen Raymond, Dawn Salcedo

Lost Highway

1997 135 mins. CIBY-2000, Asymmetrical Productions

d: David Lynch

w: David Lynch and Barry Gifford

ph: Peter Deming

p: Deepak Nayar, Tom Sternberg, Mary Sweeney

c: Bill Pullman, Patricia Arquette, Balthazar Getty, Robert Blake, Natasha Gregson Wagner,
Richard Pryor, Michael Massee, Jack Nance, Lucy Butler, Gary Busey, Robert Loggia

The Straight Story

USA/France/UK 1999 112 mins. Walt Disney Pictures in association with Alain Sarde and Le
Studio Canal+, with the participation of Film Four and Picture Factory Productions.

d: David Lynch

w: John Roach, Mary Sweeney

ph: Freddie Francis

p: Mary Sweeney, Neal Edelstein

c: Richard Farnsworth, Sissy Spacek, Harry Dean Stanton

Mulholland Drive

France/USA 2001 146 mins. Asymmetrical Productions, Le Studio Canal+, Les Films Alain
Sarde

d & w: David Lynch

ph: Peter Deming

p: Neal Edelstein, Tony Krantz, Michael Polaire, Alain Sarde, Mary Sweeney

c: Laura Elena Harring, Naomi Watts, Justin Theroux, Ann Miller, Dan Hedaya, Mark
Pellegrino, Michael J. Anderson

BIBLIOGRAPHY

Acker, K. (1990) 'Dead Doll Humility', *Postmodern Culture*, 1, 1. Online. Available at www.muse.jhu.edu/journals/postmodern_culture/v001/1.1acker.html (15 June 2000).

_____ (1994) 'The Dead Doll Prophecy', in C. Becker, *The Subversive Imagination: Artists, Society and Social Responsibility*. London and New York: Routledge, 20–34.

Alexander, J. (1993) *The Films of David Lynch*. London: Charles Letts.

Allen, R. (1999) 'Psychoanalytic Film Theory', in T. Miller and R. Stam (eds) *A Companion to Film Theory*. Malden, MA and Oxford: Blackwell Publishers, 131–2.

Alliez, É. (1991) *Les Temps Capitaux, Tome 1, Récits de la conquête du temps*. Paris: Les Éditions du Cerf.

_____ (1996) *Capital Times*. Trans. G. Van Den Abbeele. Minneapolis: University of Minnesota Press.

Altman, R. (1980) 'The Evolution of Sound Technology', *Yale French Studies*, 60, 67–79.

Annandale, D. E. (1998) 'Beast with a Million Eyes: Unleashing Horror through Deleuze and Guattari', unpublished PhD thesis, University of Alberta.

Arnheim, R. (1956) *Art and Visual Perception: A Psychology of the Creative Eye*. London: Faber and Faber.

Atkinson, M. (1997) *Blue Velvet*. London: BFI.

Attanasio, P. (1986) 'Blue Velvet', *Washington Post*, 19 September.

Aumont, J. (1992) *Du Visage au Cinéma*. Paris: Éditions de l'Étoile.

Bakhtin, M. M. (1981) 'Forms of Time and of the Chronotope in the Novel', in M. Holquist (ed.) *The Dialogic Imagination: Four Essays by M. M Bakhtin*. Austin: University of Texas Press, 84–259.

Balázs, B. (1972) *Theory of the Film: Character and Growth of a New Art*. New York: Arno.

Balio, T. (1999) '"A major presence in all of the world's important markets": the globalization of Hollywood in the 1990s', in S. Neale and M. Smith (eds) *Contemporary Hollywood Cinema*. London: Routledge, 58–73.

Barthes, R. (1977a) *Image, Music, Text*. Trans. S. Heath. New York: Hill and Wang.

____ (1977b) 'The Grain of the Voice', in *Image, Music, Text*. Trans. S. Heath. New York: Hill and Wang, 179–89.

____ (1972) 'The Face of Garbo', in *Mythologies*. London: Paladin, 62–4.

____ (1990) *The Pleasure of the Text*. Trans. R. Miller. Oxford: Blackwell.

Baudrillard, J. (1987) *Amerika*. København: Akademisk forlag.

____ (1994) *In the Shadow of the Silent Majorities*. New York: Semiotext[e].

Belton, J. (1992) *Widescreen Cinema*. Cambridge, MA and London: Harvard University Press.

Benjamin, W. (1977a) 'Allegory and Trauerspiel', in *The Origin of German Tragic Drama*. Trans. J. Osborne. London: New Left Books, 159–235.

____ (1977b) 'The Work of Art in the Age of Mechanical Reproduction', in W. Benjamin *Illuminations*. Ed. H. Arendt. Trans. H. Zohn. London: Fontana, 211–44.

____ (1999a) *The Arcades Project*. Trans. H. Elland and K. McLaughlin. Cambridge, MA: Belknap Press of Harvard University Press.

____ (1999b) *Selected Writings, Volume 2, 1927–1934*. Trans. R. Livingstone *et al.* Cambridge, MA: Belknap Press of Harvard University Press.

Berry, B. (1988) 'Forever, in My Dreams: Generic Conventions and the Subversive Imagination in *Blue Velvet*', *Literature–Film Quarterly*, 16, 2, 82–90.

Bersani, L. (1995) 'Foucault, Freud, Fantasy, and Power', *GLQ: A Journal of Lesbian and Gay Studies*, 2, 11–33.

Bogue, R. (1989) *Deleuze and Guattari*. London and New York: Routledge.

____ (1996) 'Gilles Deleuze: The Aesthetics of Force', in P. Patton (ed.) *Deleuze: A Critical Reader*. Cambridge, MA: Blackwell Publishers, 257–69.

Bolter, J. D. and R. Grusin (1999) *Remediation: Understanding New Media*. Cambridge, MA: MIT

Bordwell, D. (1985) *Narration in the Fiction Film*. London: Methuen.

____ (1989) *Making Meaning: Inference and Rhetoric in the Interpretation of Cinema*. Cambridge, MA: Harvard University Press.

Bornstein, K. (1993) *Gender Outlaw: Men, Women and the Rest of Us*. London and New York: Routledge.

Boundas, C. V. and D. Olkowski (eds) (1994) *Gilles Deleuze and the Theater of Philosophy*. London and New York: Routledge.

Bouzereau, L. (1987) '*Blue Velvet*: An Interview with David Lynch', *Cineaste*, 15, 3, 39.

Braidotti, R. (1994a) *Nomadic Subjects: Embodiment and Sexual Difference in Contemporary Feminist Theory*. New York: Columbia University Press.

____ (1994b) 'Toward a New Nomadism: Feminist Deleuzian Tracks; or, Metaphysics and Metabolism', in C. V. Boundas and D. Olkowski (eds) *Deleuze and the Theater of Philosophy*. London and New York: Routledge, 157–86.

____ (1994c) 'Introduction: By Way of Nomadism', in R. Braidotti, *Nomadic Subjects: Embodiment and Sexual Difference in Contemporary Feminist Theory*. New York: Columbia University Press, 1–40.

Braziel, J. E. (1998) '"Becoming–Woman–dog–goldfish–flower–molecular" and the "non–becoming–Québécois": Dissolution and Other Deleuzian Traversals in Flora Balzano's *Soigne ta chute*', *Tessera: Feminist Interventions in Writing and Culture*, Summer, 125–34.

____ (2001) 'Sex and Fat Chics? Deterritorialising the Fat Female Body', in J. E. Braziel and K. LeBesco (eds) *Bodies Out of Bounds: Fatness and Transgression*. Berkeley: University of California Press, 231–56.

Braziel, J. E. and K. LeBesco (eds) (2001) *Bodies Out of Bounds: Fatness and Transgression*. Berkeley: University of California Press.

Breskin, I. (1990) 'Interview with David Lynch', *Rolling Stone*, 6 September.

Brophy, P. (ed.) (1999) 'Music for the Films of Joel and Ethan Coen: Carter Burwell in Conversation', in *Cinesonic: the world of sound in films*. Sydney: AFTRS, 15–39.

Brown, L. (1998) 'The American Networks', in A. Smith and R. Paterson (eds) *Television: An International History* (second edn.). Oxford: Oxford University Press, 147–61.

Brown, R. (1994) *Overtones and Undertones: Reading Film Music*. Berkeley: University of California Press.

Brunette P. and D. Wills (1989) 'Black and Blue', in *Screen/Play: Derrida and Film Theory*. Princeton: Princeton University Press, 139–71.

Brusseau, J. (1998) *Isolated Experiences: Gilles Deleuze and the Solitudes of Reversed Platonism*. Albany: State University of New York Press.

Buci–Glucksmann, C. (1994) *Baroque Reason: The Aesthetics of Modernity*. Trans. P. Camiller. London and Thousand Oaks, CA: SAGE Publications.

Buckland, W. (2003) '"A Sad, Bad Traffic Accident": The Televisual Pre-History of David Lynch's Film *Mulholland Drive*', *New Review of Film and Television Studies* 1, 1, 131–47.

Bundtzen, L. K. (1988) '"Don't look at me!" Woman's Body, Woman's Voice in *Blue Velvet*', *Western Humanities Review*, 42, 3, 187–203.

Burch, Noël (1986) 'On the Structural Use of Sound', in E. Weis and J. Belton (eds) *Film Sound: Theory and Practice*. New York: Columbia University Press, 200–9.

Butler, J. (1990) 'Subjects of Sex/Gender/Desire', in J. Butler *Gender Trouble: Feminism and the Subversion of Identity*. London and New York: Routledge, 1–34.

____ (1993) *Bodies that Matter*. London and New York: Routledge.

____ (1994) 'Bodies that Matter', in C. Burke, N. Schor and M. Whitford (eds) *Engaging with Irigaray*. New York: Columbia University Press, 141–73.

Buydens, M. (1990) *Sahara: l'esthétique de Gilles Deleuze*. Paris: J. Vrin.

Carroll, N. (1990) *The Philosophy of Horror; or, Paradoxes of the Heart*. New York: Routledge.

____ (1996) 'Toward a Theory of Point-of-View Editing: Communication, Emotion and the Movies', in N. Carroll, *Theorizing the Moving Image*. Cambridge: Cambridge University Press, 125–38.

Chauvin, S. (1996) 'Le Miroir aux rouges-gorges ou d'incertains *happy ends*: Remarques eparses autour de *Blue Velvet*', *La Licorne*, 36, 205–12.

Chion, M. (1982) *La Voix au Cinéma*. Paris: Editions de l'Etoile/Cahiers du Cinéma.

____ (1992) *David Lynch*. Paris: Cahiers du Cinema.

____ (1994) *Audio–Vision: Sound on Screen*. Trans. C. Gorbman. New York and Chichester: Columbia University Press.

____ (1995) *David Lynch*. Trans. R. Julian. London: BFI.

____ (1999) *The Voice in Cinema*. Trans. C. Gorbman. New York: Columbia University Press.

____ (2001) *Kubrick's Cinema Odyssey*. Trans. C. Gorbman. London: BFI.

Chisholm, K. A. (1993) 'Toward a Rhetorical Hermeneutic for Film: *Blue Velvet* as Cinematic Text', unpublished PhD thesis, University of Minnesota.

Cobb, S. (1999) 'Writing the New Film *Noir*', in A. Silver and J. Ursini (eds) *Film Noir Reader 2*. New York: Limelight Editions, 207–13.

Collins, J. (1992) 'Television and Postmodernism', in R. Allen (ed.) *Channels of Discourse, Reassembled: Television and Contemporary Criticism* (second edn.). Chapel Hill: University of North Carolina Press, 342–5.

Corliss, Richard (1990) 'Czar of Bizarre', *The Times*, 1 October. Online. Available at www.geocities.com/Hollywood/2093/ (15 June 2000).

Cowie, E. (1984) 'Fantasia', *M/F*, 9, 71–104.

Crutchfield, S. (1999) 'Touching Scenes and Finishing Touches: Blindness in the Slasher Film', in C. Sharrett (ed.) *Mythologies of Violence in Postmodern Media*. Detroit: Wayne State University Press, 275–99.

Crutchfield, S. and M. Epstein (eds) (2000) *Points of Contact: Disability, Art and Culture*. Ann Arbor: University of Michigan Press.

Cubitt, S. (1998) 'Introduction: Le réel s'est impossible – the sublime time of special effects', *Screen*, 40, 2, 123–30.

Culler, J. (1990) *Roland Barthes*. London: Fontana.

Curtis, Q. (1997) 'Driven to the Edge of the Mind: A Bizarre Fantasy from David Lynch', *Daily Telegraph*, 22 August. Online. Available at www.geocities.com/Hollywood/2093/lost highway/lhtelegraph.html (15 June 2000).

Darke, P. A. (1994) '*The Elephant Man* (David Lynch, EMI Films, 1980): An Analysis from a Disabled Perspective', *Disability and Society*, 9, 3, 327–42.

Daubney, K. (2000) *Max Steiner's Now Voyager: A Film Score Guide*. Westport, Connecticut and London: Greenwood Press.

Davison, A. (2004) *Hollywood Theory, Non–Hollywood Practice: cinema soundtracks in the 1980s and 1990s*. Aldershot: Ashgate.

Dayan, J. (1995) *Haiti, History and the Gods*. Berkeley: University of California Press.

De Lauretis, T. (1993) 'Sexual Indifference and Lesbian Representation', in H. Abelove, M. A. Barale and D. M. Halperin (eds) *The Lesbian and Gay Studies Reader*. London and New York: Routledge, 141–58.

Deleuze, G. (1968) *Spinoza et le problème de l'expression*. Paris: Les Éditions de Minuit.

_____ (1970) *Spinoza: Philosophie pratique*. Paris: Presses Universitaires de France.

_____ (1981) *Francis Bacon: Logique de la sensation*. 2 Vols. Paris: Éditions de la Différence.

_____ (1988a) *Le Pli: Leibniz et le baroque*. Paris: Les Éditions de Minuit.

_____ (1988b) *Spinoza: Practical Philosophy*. Trans. R. Hurley. San Francisco: City Lights.

_____ (1993) *The Fold: Leibniz and the Baroque*. Trans. T. Conley. Minneapolis and London: University of Minnesota Press.

_____ (1996) *Proust et les signes*. Paris: Quadridge/Presses Universitaires de France.

Deleuze, G. and C. Parnet (1977) *Dialogues*. Paris: Flammarion.

_____ (1987a) *Dialogues*. Trans. H. Tomlinson and B. Habberjam. New York: Columbia University Press.

_____ (1987b) 'Dead Psychoanalysis: Analyse' in G. Deleuze and C. Parnet *Dialogues*. Trans. H. Tomlinson and B. Habberjam. New York: Columbia University Press, 77–123.

Deleuze, G. and F. Guattari (1969) *L'Anti–Œdipe: capitalisme et schizophrénie*. Paris: Éditions de Minuit.

_____ (1975) *Kafka: Pour une littérature mineure*. Paris: Éditions de Minuit.

_____ (1980) *Mille plateaux: capitalisme et schizophrénie II*. Paris: Éditions de Minuit.

_____ (1983a) *Anti–Oedipus. Capitalism and Schizophrenia*. Trans. R. Hurley, H. R. Lane and M. Seem. Minneapolis and London: University of Minnesota Press.

_____ (1983b) 'What Is a Minor Literature?' *Mississippi Review*, 11, 3, 13–33.

_____ (1986) *Kafka: Toward a Minor Literature*. Trans. D. Polan. Minneapolis and London: University of Minnesota Press.

_____ (1987) *A Thousand Plateaus: Capitalism and Schizophrenia 2*. Trans. B. Massumi. Minneapolis and London: University of Minnesota Press.

Deleuze, G. and M. Foucault (1972) 'Les Intellectuels et Le Pouvoir' (entretien), *L'Arc*, 3–10.

Doane, M. A. (1980) 'The Voice in the Cinema: The Articulation of Body and Space', *Yale French Studies*, 60, 33–50.

_____ (1985) 'Ideology and the Practice of Sound Editing and Mixing', in E. Weis and J. Belton (eds) *Film Sound: Theory and Practice*. New York: Columbia University Press, 47–56.

_____ (1991) *Femmes Fatales: Feminism, Film Theory, Psychoanalysis*. London and New York: Routledge.

Dolan, M. (1995) 'The Peaks and Valleys of Serial Creativity: What Happened to/on *Twin Peaks*', in D. Lavery (ed.) *Full of Secrets: Critical Approaches to Twin Peaks*. Detroit: Wayne State University Press, 30–50.

Dunne, M. (1995) '*Wild at Heart* Three Ways: Lynch, Gifford, Bakhtin', *Literature-Film Quarterly*, 23, 1, 6–13.

Dwyer, M. (1999) 'Straight from the Heart', *Irish Times*, 27 November.

Dyer, R. (1978) 'Resistance through Charisma: Rita Hayworth and *Gilda*', in E. A. Kaplan (ed.) *Women in Film Noir*. London: BFI, 91–9.

_____ (1991) 'A Star is Born and the Construction of Authenticity', in C. Gledhill (ed.) *Stardom: Industry of Desire*. London: Routledge, 132–40.

Ebert, R. (1986) 'Blue Velvet', *Chicago Sun–Times*, 2, 28 September.

_____ (1990) 'Wild at Heart', *Chicago Sun–Times*, 2, 17 August.

_____ (1997) 'Review of *Lost Highway*', *Chicago Sun–Times*, February. Online. Available at www.geocities.com/Hollywood/2093/losthighway/lhebert.html (15 June 2000).

Eisenstein, S. M. (1988) 'The Montage of Film Attractions', in R. Taylor (ed.) *Selected Works, 1922–34*. London: BFI, 39–58.

Elsaesser, T. (1972) 'Tales of Sound and Fury: Observations on the Family Melodrama', *Monogram*, 4, 10–35.

Eriksen, T. B. (1989) *Nietzsche og det moderne*. Oslo: Universitetsforlaget.

Feinberg, L. (1992) *Transgender Liberation: A Movement Whose Time Has Come*. New York: World View Forum.

_____ (1996) *Transgender Warriors*. Boston: Beacon Press.

Freeland, C. (2000) *The Naked and the Undead: Evil and the Appeal of Horror*. Boulder, CO.: Westview Press.

Freud, S. (1915) 'A Case of Paranoia Running Counter to the Psychoanalytical Theory of the Disease', *Standard Edition*, 14, 261–73.

_____ (1918) 'From The History of an Infantile Neurosis', *Standard Edition*, 17, 7–122.

_____ (1919) 'A Child is Being Beaten', *Standard Edition*, 17, 177–204.

_____ (1938) 'Constructions in Analysis', *Standard Edition*, 23, 257–69.

_____ (1953–74) *The Standard Edition of the Complete Psychological Works of Sigmund Freud*. Trans. and ed. J. Strachey. 24 Vols. London: Hogarth Press.

—— (1958) 'The "Uncanny" (1919)' in *On Creativity and the Unconscious: Papers on the Psychology of Art, Literature, Love, Religion*. New York: Harper & Row.

Fuchs, C. J. (1989) '"I Looked for You in My Closet Tonight": Voyeurs and Victims in *Blue Velvet*', *Spring: A Journal of Archetype & Culture*, 49, 85–98.

Gaggi, S. (1997) *From Text to Hypertext: Decentering the Subject in Fiction, Film, the Visual Arts and Electronic Media*. Philadelphia: University of Pennsylvania Press.

Garber, M. (1992) *Vested Interests: Cross-Dressing and Cultural Anxiety*. London and New York: Routledge.

Gatens, M. (1988) 'Towards a feminist philosophy of the body', in B. Caine, E. A. Grosz, and M. de Lepervanche (eds) *Crossing Boundaries: Feminisms and the Critique of Knowledges*. Sydney: Allen & Unwin, 59–70.

_____ (1996) 'Through a Spinozist Lens: Ethnology, Difference, Power', in P. Patton (ed.) *Deleuze: A Critical Reader*. Cambridge, MA: Blackwell Publishers, 162–87.

Gentry, R. (1984) 'Alan Splet and the Sound Effects for *Dune*', *American Cinematographer*, 65, 12, 62–72.

George, D. H. (1995) 'Lynching Women: A Feminist Reading of *Twin Peaks*', in D. Lavery (ed.) *Full of Secrets: Critical Approaches to Twin Peaks*. Detroit: Wayne State University Press, 109–19.

Giddens, A. (1981) *A Contemporary Critique of Historical Materialism, Vol. 1: Power, Property and the State*. London: Macmillan.

_____ (1991) *Modernity and Self-Identity: Self and Society in the Late Modern Age*. Stanford, CA: Stanford University Press.

Gilmore, M. (1997) '*Lost Highway*: Lynch Interview', *Rolling Stone*, 6 March. Online. Available at www.geocities.com/Hollywood/2093/losthighway/intlhstone.html (15 June 2000).

Givens, R. (2000) 'Composer Badalamenti Explains the Love Theme — and Lunch', in *Entertainment Weekly Online*. Available at www.ew.com (10 August 2000).

Gledhill, C. (1978) '*Klute* 1: a contemporary film noir and feminist criticism', in E. A. Kaplan (ed.) *Women in Film Noir*. London: BFI, 6–21.

Godwin, K. G. (1984) '*Eraserhead*: The story behind the strangest film ever made, and the cinematic genius who directed it', *Cinefantastique*, 14, 4–5, 41–72.

Gomery, Douglas (1992) *Shared Pleasures: A History of Movie Presentation in the US*. London: BFI.

_____ (1999) 'Hollywood corporate business practice and periodising contemporary film history', in S. Neale and M. Smith (eds) *Contemporary Hollywood Cinema*. London: Routledge, 47–57.

Gorbman, C. (1987) *Unheard Melodies: Narrative Film Music*. Bloomington and London: Indiana University Press with the BFI.

Graham, P. W. and F. H. Oehlschlaeger (1992) *Articulating the Elephant Man: Joseph Merrick and his Interpreters*. London: Johns Hopkins University Press.

Grosz, E. (1989) *Sexual Subversions: Three French Feminists*. Sydney: Unwin & Allen.

_____ (1994) 'A Thousand Tiny Sexes: Feminism and Rhizomatics', in C. V. Boundas and D. Olkowski (eds) *Deleuze and the Theater of Philosophy*. London and New York: Routledge, 187–210.

_____ (1995) *Volatile Bodies: Toward a Corporeal Feminism*. Indianapolis and Bloomington: Indiana University Press.

_____ (1996) *Space, Time and Perversion*. London and New York: Routledge.

Gunning, T. (1997) 'In Your Face: Physiognomy, Photography and the Gnostic Mission of Early Film', *MODERNISM/modernity*, 4, 1–29.

Guthmann, E. (1997) '*Lost Highway* Travels a Weird Route: David Lynch film is captivatingly bizarre', *San Francisco Chronicle*, 28 February. Online. Available at www.geocities.com/ Hollywood/2093/losthighway/lhsfcc.html (15 June 2000).

Halberstam, J. (1999) *Female Masculinity*. Durham and London: Duke University Press.

Halberstam, J. with D. LaGrace Volcano (photographer) (1999) *The Drag King Book*. New York: Serpent's Tail.

Hampton, H. (1993) 'David Lynch's Secret History of the United States', *Film Comment*, 29, 3, 38–49.

Hardie, M. J. (1995) '"I Embrace the Difference": Elizabeth Taylor and the Closet', in E. Grosz and E. Probyn (eds) *Sexy Bodies: the strange carnalities of feminism*. London and New York: Routledge, 155–71.

Hardt, M. (1993) *Gilles Deleuze: An Apprenticeship in Philosophy*. Minneapolis and London: University of Minnesota Press.

Haugsgjerd, S. (1986) *Jacques Lacan og psykoanalysen. En presentasjon av Lacans liv og verk*. Oslo: Gyldendal norsk forlag.

Hayden, P. (1998) *Multiplicity and Becoming: The Pluralist Empiricism of Gilles Deleuze*. New York: Peter Lang.

Hemblade, C. (1997) '*Lost Highway*', *Empire*, 99 (September), 46.

Hendershot, C. (1995) 'Postmodern Allegory and David Lynch's *Wild at Heart*', *Critical Arts*, 9, 1, 5–20.

Henry, M. (1999) 'Un Déplacement de 180 degrés', *Positif*, 465, 17–21.

Hertz, N. (1997) '"The Scene Came Alive": Autobiography and Anger', *Differences: A Journal of Feminist Cultural Studies*, 9, 1, 36–48.

Herzogenrath, B. (1999) 'On the *Lost Highway*: Lynch and Lacan, Cinema and Cultural Pathology', *Other Voices*, 1, 3. Online. Available at www.othervoices.org/1.3/bh/ highway.html (10 May 2002).

Hickenlooper, G. (1991) 'Interview with David Lynch', in G. Hickenlooper (ed.) *Reel Conversations: Candid Interviews with Film's Foremost Directors and Critics*. New York:

Citadel, 90–104.

Hoberman, J. and J. Rosenbaum (1983) *Midnight Movies*. New York: Da Capo.

Holden, S. (2001) 'Hollywood: A Funhouse of Fantasy', *The New York Times*, 6 October, A13. Also online. Available at www.nytimes.com (20 April 2003).

Holladay, W. E. and S. Watt (1989) 'Viewing the Elephant Man', *Proceedings of the Modern Language Association*, 104, 5, 868–81.

Holland, E. (1999) *Anti-Oedipus: An Introduction to Capitalism and Schizophrenia*. London and New York: Routledge.

Holmstrom, J. (ed.) (1996) *Punk: The Original*. New York: Trans-High Publishing.

Horn, M. (1990) 'TV's Leap into the Unknown', in *US News and World Report*, 23 April, 56.

Hughes, D. (2001) 'Mulholland Drive', in *The Complete Lynch*. London: Virgin, 236–42.

Hutcheon, L. (1985) *A Theory of Parody: The Teachings of Twentieth-Century Art Forms*. London: Routledge.

____ (1989) *The Politics of Postmodernism*. London: Routledge.

Huyssen, A. (1986) *After the Great Divide: Modernism, Mass Culture, Postmodernism*. Bloomington: Indiana University Press.

Ingstad, B. and S. Reynolds Whyte (eds) (1995) *Disability and Culture*. Berkeley and London: University of California Press.

Irigaray, L. (1974) *Speculum. De l'autre femme*. Paris: Éditions de Minuit.

____ (1985) *Speculum of the Other Woman*. Trans. by G. C. Gill. Ithaca, New York: Cornell University Press.

Jackson, K. (1999) 'Review of *The Straight Story*', *Sight and Sound*, 9, 12, 57–8.

Jameson, F. (1983) 'Postmodernism and Consumer Society', in H. Foster (ed.) *Postmodern Culture*. London: Pluto Press, 111–25.

____ (1989) 'Nostalgia for the Present', *South Atlantic Quarterly*, 88, 2, 517–37.

____ (1991) *Postmodernism or, The Cultural Logic of Late Capitalism*. Durham: Duke University Press.

____ (1996) 'Postmodernism and Consumer Society', in J. Belton (ed.) *Movies and Mass Culture*. New Brunswick: Rutgers University Press, 185–202.

Jardine, A. (1984) 'Deleuze and his Br(others)', *Sub–Stance*, 13, 3–4, 46–60.

____ (1985) 'Becoming a Body without Organs: Gilles Deleuze and his Br(others)', in A. Jardine *Gynesis: Configurations of Woman and Modernity*. New York: Cornell University Press, 208–23.

Jarvis, B. (1998) *Postmodern Cartographies: The Geographical Imagination in Contemporary American Culture*. London: Pluto Press.

Jeffords, S. (1994) *Hard Bodies: Hollywood Masculinity in the Reagan Era*. New Brunswick: Rutgers University Press.

Jenkins, H. (1995) '"Do You Enjoy Making the Rest of Us Feel Stupid": alt.tv.twinpeaks, the Trickster Author and Viewer Mastery', in D. Lavery (ed.) *Full of Secrets: Critical Approaches to Twin Peaks*. Detroit: Wayne State University Press, 51–69.

Jerome, J. (1990) 'Bio', *People*, 3 September, 34, 82.

Jerslev, A. (1991) *David Lynch i vore øjne*. København: Frydenlund.

Kaleta, K. C. (1993) *David Lynch*. New York and Don Mills: Twayne Publishers and Maxwell Macmillan Canada.

Kalinak, K. (1992) *Settling the Score: Music and the Classical Hollywood Film*. London and Madison, Wisconsin: University of Wisconsin Press.

____ (1995) '"Disturbing the Guests with This Racket": Music and *Twin Peaks*', in D. Lavery (ed.) *Full of Secrets: Critical Approaches to Twin Peaks*. Detroit: Wayne State University Press, 82–92.

Kämmerling, C. (1990) 'Kafka gives me a good mood: Interview with David Lynch', *Süddeutsche Zeitung* [supplement], 21 September. Also online. Available at www.geocities.com/Hollywood/2093/intsz.html [trans. by M. Hartmann] (September 2000).

Kaplan, E. A. (1978) 'Introduction', in E. A. Kaplan (ed.) *Women in Film Noir*. London: BFI, 1–5.

_____ (1983) 'Is the Gaze Male?', in A. Snitow, C. Stansell and S. Thompson (eds) *Powers of Desire: The Politics of Sexuality*. New York: Monthly Review Press, 309–27.

Kaufman, E. and K. J. Heller (eds) (1998) *Deleuze & Guattari. New Mappings in Politics, Philosophy, and Culture*. Minneapolis and London: University of Minnesota Press.

Keller, J. R. (1995) '"Like to a Chaos": Deformity and Depravity in Contemporary Film', *Journal of Popular Film & Television*, 23, 1, 8–14.

Kember, Joe (2001) 'Face-to-Face: The Facial Expressions Genre in Early Film', in A. Burton and L. Porter (eds) *Showmen, Spectacle and the Two Minute Silence: Performing British Cinema Before 1930*. Trowbridge: Flicks Books, 28–39.

Kermode, Mark (1997) 'Weirdo', *Q Magazine*, September. Online. Available at www.geocities.com/Hollywood/2093/losthighway/intlhqmag.html (15 June 2000).

Kipnis, L. (1996) 'Life in the Fat Lane', in L. Kipnis *Bound and Gagged: Pornography and the Politics of Fantasy in America*. New York: Grove Press, 93–121.

Kristeva, J. (1980a) *Desire in Language: A Semiotic Approach to Literature and Art*. Ed. L. S. Roudiez. Trans. T. Gora, A. Jardine and L. Roudiez. New York: Columbia University Press.

_____ (1980b) *Pouvoirs de l'horreur: Essai sur l'abjection*. Paris : Éditions du Seuil.

Kuzniar, A. (1989) '"Ears Looking at You": E. T. A. Hoffmann's *The Sandman* and David Lynch's *Blue Velvet*', *South Atlantic Review*, 54, 2, 7–21.

_____ (1995) 'Double Talk in *Twin Peaks*', in D. Lavery (ed.) *Full of Secrets: Critical Approaches to Twin Peaks*. Detroit: Wayne State University Press, 120–9.

Lack, R. (1997) *Twenty Four Frames Under: A Buried History of Film Music*. London: Quartet Books.

Lantos, Jeffrey (1999) 'The ABC of going from the big screen to the small', *Movieline*, 11, 70.

Laplanche, J. (1989) 'Foundations: Towards a General Theory of Seduction', in *New Foundations for Psychoanalysis*. Trans. D. Macey. Oxford: Basic Blackwell, 89–151.

Laplanche, J. and J.–B. Pontalis (1973) *The Language of Psycho–Analysis*. Trans. D. Nicholson–Smith. New York and London: W.W. Norton.

_____ (1986) 'Fantasy and the Origin of Sexuality', in V. Burgin, J. Donald and C. Kaplan (eds) *Formations of Fantasy*. New York: Methuen, 5–34.

Latham, R. (1988) 'There's No Place Like Home: Simulating Postmodern America in *The Wizard of Oz* and *Blue Velvet*', *Journal of the Fantastic in the Arts*, 1, 4, 49–58.

Lavery, D. (ed.) (1995) *Full of Secrets: Critical Approaches to* Twin Peaks. Detroit: Wayne State University Press.

Layton, L. (1994) '*Blue Velvet*: Parable of Male Development', *Screen*, 35, 4, 374–93.

Leaming, B. (1989) *A Biography of Rita Hayworth: If This Was Happiness*. New York: Viking.

Le Blanc, M. and C. Odell (2000) *The Pocket Essential David Lynch*. Harpenden: Pocket Essentials.

Levy, E. (1999) *Cinema of Outsiders: The Rise of American Independent Film*. New York: New York University Press.

Lindroth, J. (1990) 'Down the Yellow Brick Road: Two Dorothys and the Journey of Initiation in Dream and Nightmare', *Literature-Film Quarterly*, 18, 3, 160–6.

Lopate, P. (2001) 'Welcome to LA: Hollywood Outsider David Lynch Plunges into Tinseltown's Dark Psyche', *Film Comment*, September/October, 44–50.

Lucas, T. (1998) 'Kiss Me Doubly: Notes on David Lynch's *Lost Highway*', *Video Watchdog*, 43, 28–35.

Luckhurst, R. (1990) 'Shut(ting) the Fuck Up: Narrating *Blue Velvet* in the Postmodernist Frame', *Bête Noire*, 8–9, 170–82.

Lynch, D. (1994) *Images* (Photography and paintings). New York: Hyperion.

Lynch, D. and B. Gifford (1997) *Lost Highway*. New York and London: Faber and Faber.

Maltby, R. (1981) 'The Political Economy of Hollywood: The Studio System', in P. Davies and B. Neve (eds) *Cinema, Politics and Society in America*. Manchester: Manchester University Press, 42–58.

Marcus, G. (1993) *In the Fascist Bathroom: Punk in Pop Music, 1977–1992*. Cambridge, MA: Harvard University Press.

Marks, L. (1994) 'Deterritorialised Filmmaking: A Deleuzian Politics of Hybrid Cinema', *Screen*, 35, 3, 244–64.

Marx, K. (1967) *Capital: A Critique of Political Economy, Volume I*. Trans. S. Moore and E. Aveling. New York: International Publishers Co., Inc.

Marzec, M. S. (1994) '*Blue Velvet* as Psychomania', *Journal of Evolutionary Psychology*, 15, 1–2, 87–92.

Massumi, B. (1992) *A User's Guide to Capitalism and Schizophrenia: Deviations from Deleuze and Guattari*. Cambridge and London: MIT Press.

Mayne, J. (1993) *Cinema and Spectatorship*. London: Routledge.

McCartney, T. (1997) '*Lost Highway*', *Variety*, 20–26 January, 44, 48.

McClary, S. (1991) *Feminine Endings*. Minneapolis and London: University of Minnesota Press.

McGowan, T. (2000) 'Finding Ourselves on a *Lost Highway*: David Lynch's Lesson in Fantasy', *Cinema Journal*, 39, 2, 51–73.

McKenna, K. (1992) 'An Interview with David Lynch', in *Colección Imagen: David Lynch*. Valencia: Edicions Alfons el Magnànim, Institució Valenciana D'Estudis, I investigació, 21–33. Excerpts online. Available at www.geocities.com/Hollywood/2093/ (15 June 2000).

McKinney, D. (1991–2) '*Wild at Heart*', *Film Quarterly*, 45, 2, 41–6.

McLean, A. L. (1993) '"It's Only That I Do What I Love and Love What I Do": Film Noir and the Musical Woman', *Cinema Journal*, 33, 1, 3–16.

McLemore, E. (1995) 'From Revelation to Dream: Allegory in David Lynch's *Blue Velvet*', in J. W. Martin and C. E. Ostwalt, Jr. (eds) *Screening the Sacred: Religion, Myth, and Ideology in Popular American Film*. Boulder, CO: Westview Press, 134–41.

Mendik, X. and S. J. Schneider (eds) (2002) *Underground USA: Filmmaking Beyond the Hollywood Canon*. London: Wallflower Press.

Metz, C. (1982) *The Imaginary Signifier: Psychoanalysis and the Cinema*. Trans. C. Britton, A Williams, B. Brewster and A Guzzetti. Bloomington: Indiana University Press.

Meyer, M. (ed.) (1994) *The Politics and Poetics of Camp*. London and New York: Routledge.

Miller, C. (1997) 'Toby Keeler interview', *Wrapped in Plastic*, 1, 32 (December), 9–13.

Moon, M. (1991) 'A Small Boy and Others: Sexual Disorientation in Henry James, Kenneth Anger and David Lynch', in H. J. Spillers (ed.) *Comparative American Identities: Race, Sex and Nationality in the Modern Text*. London and New York: Routledge, 151–6.

Morain, J.-B. (2002) 'Le Mirage Américain', *Les Inrockuptibles: Hors–série David Lynch*, 17–21.

Mulvey, L. (1975) 'Visual Pleasure and Narrative Cinema', *Screen*, 16, 3, 6–18.

_____ (1996a) 'Netherworlds and the Unconscious: Oedipus and *Blue Velvet*', in *Fetishism and Curiosity*. Bloomington: Indiana University Press, 137–54.

—— (1996b) 'The Pre–Oedipal Father: The Gothicism of *Blue Velvet*', in V. Sage and A. L. Smith (eds) *Modern Gothic: A Reader*. Manchester University Press, 38–57.

Murphy, T. S. (1996) 'Bibliography of the Works of Gilles Deleuze', in P. Patton (ed.) *Deleuze: A Critical Reader*. Cambridge, MA: Blackwell Publishers, 270–98.

Nehamas, A. (1985) *Nietzsche: Life as Literature*. Cambridge, MA and London: Harvard University Press.

Neale, S. and M. Smith (eds) (1999) *Contemporary Hollywood Cinema*. London: Routledge.

Neill, A. (1996) 'Empathy and (Film) Fiction', in D. Bordwell and N. Carroll (eds) *Post-Theory: Reconstructing Film Studies*. Madison: University of Wisconsin Press, 175–94.

Newman, K. (1997) 'Review of *Lost Highway*', *Sight and Sound*, 7, 9, 48–9.

Newton, E. (1970) *Mother Camp: Female Impersonators in America*. Chicago: University of Chicago Press.

Nochimson, M. (1995) 'Desire Under the Douglas Firs: Entering the Body of Reality', in D. Lavery (ed.) *Full of Secrets: Critical Approaches to Twin Peaks*. Detroit: Wayne State University Press, 144–59.

____ (1997) *The Passion of David Lynch: Wild at Heart in Hollywood*. Austin: University of Texas Press.

____ (2002) '*Mulholland Drive*', *Film Quarterly*, 56, 1, 37–45.

Norman, T. ([n.d.]) *Memoirs of Tom Norman: The Silver King*, unpublished MS, National Fairground Archive, University of Sheffield.

____ (1985) *The Penny Showman: Memoirs of Tom Norman 'Silver King'*. London: privately printed.

O'Connor, F. (1978) *The Habit of Being: The Letters of Flannery O'Connor*. S. Fitzgerald (ed.). New York: Farrar, Straus, Giroux.

Olalquiaga, C. (1992) *Megalopolis: Contemporary Cultural Sensibilities*. Minneapolis: University of Minnesota Press.

Owens, C. (1992) *Beyond Recognition: Representation, Power and Culture*. Berkeley, Los Angeles and London: University of California Press.

Patton, P. (ed.) (1996) *Deleuze: A Critical Reader*. Cambridge, MA: Blackwell Publishers.

Pearson, K. A (ed.) (1997) *Deleuze and Philosophy: the difference engineer*. London and New York: Routledge.

Peary, D. (1988) '*Blue Velvet*', in *Cult Movies 3*. New York: Simon and Schuster, 38–42.

Pellow, C. K. (1990) '*Blue Velvet* Once More', *Literature-Film Quarterly*, 18, 3, 173–8.

Pfeil, F. (1992) 'Revolting Yet Conserved: Family Noir in *Blue Velvet* and *Terminator 2*', *Postmodern Culture: an Electronic Journal of Interdisciplinary Criticism*, 2, 3: 49 paragraphs. Online. Available at http://muse/jhu.edu/journals/postmodern_culture/v002/2.3pfeil.html (15 June 2000).

____ (1993) 'Home Fires Burning: Family Noir in *Blue Velvet* and *Terminator 2*', in J. Copjec (ed.) *Shades of Noir: A Reader*. London: Verso, 227–59.

Pizzello, S. (1997) 'Highway to Hell', *American Cinematographer*, 78, 3, 34–42. Online. Available at www.geocities.com/Hollywood/2093/losthighway/intlhdeming2.html (15 June 2000).

Place, J. (1978) 'Women in film noir', in E. A. Kaplan (ed.) *Women in Film Noir*. London: BFI, 35–67; Revised edition (1998), 47–68.

Plantinga, C. (1993) 'Affect, Cognition and the Power of Movies', *Postscript*, 13, 1, 10–29.

____ (1999) 'The Scene of Empathy and the Human Face on Film', in C. Plantinga and G. M. Smith (eds) *Passionate Views: Film, Cognition and Emotion*. London: Johns Hopkins University Press, 239–55.

Poe, E. A. (1980) 'The Tell–Tale Heart (1843)', in J. Symons (ed.) *Selected Tales*. Oxford: Oxford University Press, 186–90.

Porfirio, R. G. (1999) 'Dark Jazz: Music in the Film Noir', in A. Silver and J. Ursini (eds) *Film Noir Reader 2*. New York: Limelight Editions, 176–87.

Prendergast, R. M. (1991) *Film Music: A Neglected Art*. New York and London: W. W. Norton.

Preston, J. L. (1990) 'Dantean Imagery in *Blue Velvet*', *Literature-Film Quarterly*, 18, 3, 167–72.

Quart, L. and A. Auster (1992) *American Film and Society Since 1945*. New York: Praeger.

Ray, R. (1985) *A Certain Tendency in the Hollywood Cinema, 1930–1980*. Princeton: Princeton University Press.

Rayner, R.(1997) 'Review of *Lost Highway*', *Harper's Bazaar*, 1 February. Online. Available at www.geocities.com/Hollywood/2093/losthighway/lhharper.html (15 June 2000).

Reagan, R. (1982) 'The Evil Empire'. Online. Avalaible at http://reaganlegacy.org/speeches/reagan.evil.empire.7.8.82.html (10 May 2002).

_____ (1990) 'Speech at the Westminster College Cold War Memorial'. Online. Available at http://reaganlegacy.org/speeches/reagan.westminster.1990 (10 May 2002).

Rees, A. L. (1999) *A History of Experimental Film and Video: From the Canonical Avant–Garde to Contemporary British Practice.* London: BFI.

Rhodes, E. B. (1998) '*Lost Highway*', *Film Quarterly*, 51, 3, 57–61.

Richardson, J. (1998) '"Black and White" Music: Dialogue, Dysphoric Coding and the Death Drive in the Music of Bernard Herrmann, The Beatles, Stevie Wonder and Coolio', in Y. Heinonen, T. Eerola, J. Koskimäki, T. Nurmesjärvi and J. Richardson (eds) *Beatlestudies 1: Songwriting, Recording, and Style Change.* Jyväskylä, Finland: University Press of Jyväskylä, 161–82.

_____ (1999) *Singing Archaeology: Philip Glass's Akhnaten.* Hanover, NH: Wesleyan University Press.

Rickels, L. A. (1988) *Aberrations of Mourning: Writing on German Crypts.* Detroit: Wayne State University Press.

Roberts, J. (1999) 'Philosophising the Everyday: The Philosophy of Praxis and the Fate of Cultural Studies', *Radical Philosophy*, 98, 16–29.

Rodley, C. (ed.) (1996) 'David Lynch: Mr. Contradiction', *Sight and Sound*, 6, 7, 6–10.

_____ (1997) *Lynch on Lynch.* New York and London: Faber and Faber.

Rodowick, D. N. (1991) *The Difficulty of Difference: Psychoanalysis, Sexual Difference and Film Theory.* New York and London: Routledge.

_____ (1997) *Gilles Deleuze's Time Machine.* Durham and London: Duke University Press.

Ross, J. (1999) 'Interview with David Lynch, BBC Online'. Online. Available at www. geocities.com/Hollywood/2093/straightstory/tssbbc.html. (20 October 2000).

Rouyer, P. (1997) 'Lost Highway. Dick Laurent est mort!', *Positif*, 431, 6–7.

Ryan, M. and D. Kellner (1988) *Camera Politica: The Politics and Ideology of Hollywood Film.* Bloomington: Indiana University Press.

Savage, J. (1992) *England's Dreaming: Anarchy, Sex Pistols, Punk Rock and Beyond.* New York: St. Martin's Press.

Sawhney, D. N. (1997) 'Palimpsest: Towards a Minor Literature in Monstrosity', in K. A. Pearson (ed.) *Deleuze and Philosophy: the difference engineer.* London and New York: Routledge, 130–48.

Schneider, S. J. (1997) 'Uncanny Realism and the Decline of the Modern Horror Film', *Paradoxa: Studies in World Literary Genres*, 3, 3–4, 417–28.

_____ (2000) 'Monsters as (Uncanny) Metaphors: Freud, Lakoff and the Representation of Monstrosity in Cinematic Horror', in A. Silver and J. Ursini (eds) *Horror Film Reader.* New York: Limelight Editions, 167–91.

_____ (2001) 'Manifestations of the Literary Double in Modern Horror Cinema', *Film and Philosophy*, Special Edition, 51–62.

Schwarz, D. (1997) *Listening Subjects: Music, Psychoanalysis, Culture.* Durham and London: Duke University Press.

Sergi, G. (1998) 'A Cry in the Dark: the role of post–classical film sound', in S. Neale and M. Smith (eds) *Contemporary Hollywood Cinema.* London: Routledge, 156–65.

Shaffer, L. (1977–8) 'Reflections on the Face in Film', *Film Quarterly*, 31, 2, 2–8.

Shatkin, E. (2000) 'Randy Thom, Sound Designer, *What Lies Beneath*', *Post Industry*, 3 August. Online. Available at www.postindustry.com/article/mainv/0,7220,112676,00.html (20 January 2001).

Shattuc, J. M. (1992) 'Postmodern Misogyny in *Blue Velvet*', *Genders*, 13, 73–89.

Shaviro, S. (1993) *The Cinematic Body.* Minneapolis and London: University of Minnesota Press.

Sheen, E. (1994) 'How Hollywood takes the waiting out of wanting' in S. Vice, T. Armstrong and M. Campbell (eds) *Beyond the Pleasure Dome: Writing and Addiction from the Romantics.* Sheffield: Sheffield Academic Press, 159–68.

Silverman, K. (1988) *The Acoustic Mirror: The Female Voice in Psychoanalysis and Cinema.* Bloomington: Indiana University Press.

Sklar, R. (1994) *Movie–Made America: A Cultural History of American Movies.* New York: Vintage.

Smalley, D. (1997) 'Spectromorphology: Explaining Sound–Shapes', *Organised Sound*, 2, 2, 107–26.

Smith, J. (1999) 'Movie Music as Moving Music: Emotion, Cognition and the Film Score', in C. Plantinga and G. M. Smith (eds) *Passionate Views: Film, Cognition and Emotion.* London: Johns Hopkins University Press, 146–67.

Smith, M. (1995) *Engaging Characters: Fiction, Emotion and the Cinema.* Oxford: Clarendon Press.

Sobchack, V. (1987) *Screening Space: The American Science Fiction Film.* New York: Ungar.

____ (1998) 'Lounge Time: Postwar Crises and the Chronotope of *Film Noir*', in N. Browne (ed.) *Refiguring American Film Genres.* Berkeley, Los Angeles and London: University of California Press, 129–71.

Spielman, Y. (1998) 'Expanding film into digital media', *Screen*, 40, 2, 143.

Sragow, M. (1999) 'David Lynch Interview', 28 October. Online. Available at www.salon.com/ ent/col/srag/1999/10/28/lynch/index.html (23 September 2000).

Stam. R. (1989) *Subversive Pleasures: Bakhtin, Cultural Criticism and Cinema.* Baltimore and London: Johns Hopkins University Press.

Stern, L. (1992) 'The Oblivious Transfer: Analyzing *Blue Velvet*', *Camera Obscura*, 30, 77–90.

Stilwell, R. (1997) '"I just put a drone under him…": Collage and subversion in the score of *Die Hard*', *Music and Letters*, 78, 551–80.

Stivale, C. (1998) *The Two–Fold Thought of Deleuze and Guattari: Intersections and Animations.* New York and London: Guilford Press.

Strauss, B. ([nd]) 'America's most enigmatic filmmaker chases his demons down a *Lost Highway*', *e–online*. Online. Available at www.geocities.com/Hollywood/2093/losthighway/ intlhonline.html (15 June 2000).

Tan, E. S. (1996) *Emotion and the Structure of Narrative Film: Film as an Emotion Machine.* Mahwah, NJ: Lawrence Erlbaum Associates.

Taussig, M. (1994) 'Physiognomic Aspects of Visual Worlds', in L. Taylor (ed.) *Visualising Theory: Selected Essays From V.A.R. 1990–1994.* London and New York: Routledge, 205–13.

Taylor, C. (2000) 'Review of *Blue Velvet*'. Online. Availaible at http://www.salon.com/ent/ movies/dvd/review/2000/06/27/blue_velvet (10 May 2002).

Thomson, R. G. (ed.) (1996) *Freakery: Cultural Spectacles of the Extraordinary Body.* New York: New York University Press.

____ (1997) *Extraordinary Bodies.* New York: Columbia University Press.

Thorne, J. and C. Miller (2001a) 'Interview with Laura Elena Harring', *Wrapped in Plastic*, 1, 55 (October), 9–11.

—— (2001b) 'Interview with Justin Theroux', *Wrapped in Plastic*, 1, 55 (October), 2–7.

—— (2001c) 'Interview with Naomi Watts', *Wrapped in Plastic*, 1, 56 (December), 2–7.

Todd, S. (1997) 'Head Trip: David Lynch'. *Black + White*, 24 April. Online. Available at www.geocities.com/Hollywood/2093/losthighway/intlhblack.html (15 June 2000).

Travers, P. (2001) '*Mulholland Drive*', *Rolling Stone*, 8 November. Also online. Available at http://www.rollingstone.com/reviews/movie/review.asp?mid=2043199 (20 April 2003).

Travers, P. (1990) 'The Wizard of Odd', *Rolling Stone*, 6 September. Also online. Available at http://www.rollingstone.com/reviews/movie/review.asp?mid=73336 (14 January 2004).

Treves, Sir F. (1923) *The Elephant Man and other Reminiscences.* London: Cassell.

Uhde, J. (2004) 'Beyond the Genre Formula: Implicit Horror in the Films of Jan Švankmajer', in S. J. Schneider and T. Williams (eds) *Horror International.* Detroit: Wayne State University Press.

Umland, R. A. and J. S. Umland (1999) 'The Lost Highways of David Lynch', *Wrapped in*

Plastic, 1, 42 (August), 2–12.

Varsava, J. A. (1995) '*Blue Velvet* and the Revisioning of the Middle-American Idyll', in T. D'haen and H. Bertens (eds) *Narrative Turns and Minor Genres in Postmodernism*. Amsterdam: Rodopi, 295–317.

Vattimo, G. (1988) 'An Apology for Nihilism', in G. Vattimo *The End of Modernity: Nihilism and Hermeneutics in Postmodern Culture*. Trans. J. Snyder. Baltimore: Johns Hopkins University Press, 19–30.

Virilio, P. (1991) *The Aesthetics of Disappearance*. New York: Semiotext(e).

____ (1994) *The Vision Machine*. London: BFI.

Wallace, D. F. (1992) 'E Unibus Pluram: Television and U.S. Fiction', in D. F. Wallace *A Supposedly Fun Thing I'll Never Do Again*. Boston: Little, Brown, 21–82.

____ (1996) 'David Lynch Keeps His Head', *US Premiere*, September. Online. Available at www.geocities.com/Hollywood/2093/papers/wallace.html (15 June 2000).

Warner, M. (1997) 'Voodoo Road', *Sight and Sound*, 7, 8, 6–10.

Williams, L. (1989) *Hard Core: Power, Pleasure and the 'Frenzy of the Visible'*. Berkeley and Los Angeles: University of California Press.

Willis, S. (1991a) '"Lynching" as Entertainment: Race and Gender in David Lynch's *Wild at Heart*', *East-West Film Journal*, 5, 2, 93–114.

____ (1991b) 'Special Effects: Sexual and Social Difference in *Wild at Heart*', *Camera Obscura*, 25–6, 275–95.

Wittenberg, J. B. and R. Gooding-Williams (1990) 'The "Strange World" of *Blue Velvet*: Conventions, Subversions and the Representation of Women', in D. Raymond (ed.) *Sexual Politics and Popular Culture*. Bowling Green, OH: Popular Culture Press, 149–57.

Wolf, B. (2001) *A Topless Cow in New York*. Online. Available at http://more.abcnews.go.com/sections/us/WolfFiles/wolffiles129.html (28 April 2001).

Wood, R. (1986) *Hollywood from Vietnam to Reagan*. New York: Columbia University Press.

Woods, P. A. (1997) *Weirdsville USA: The Obsessive Universe of David Lynch*. London: Plexus.

Woodward, R. B. (1990) 'A Dark Lens on America', *The New York Times Magazine*, 14 January. Online. Available at www.geocities.com/Hollywood/2093/intnyt.html (15 June 2000).

Wyman, B., M. Garrone and A. Klein (2001) 'Everything you were afraid to ask about *Mulholland Drive*', *Salon.Com*, 23 October. Online. Available at http://archive.salon.com/ent/movies/feature/2001/10/23/mulholland_drive_analysis/ (20 April 2003).

Zita, J. N. (1998) *Body Talk: Philosophical Reflections on Sex and Gender*. New York: Columbia University Press.

Žižek, S. (1989) *The Sublime Object of Ideology*. London: Verso.

____ (1991) 'Grimaces of the Real: Or, When the Phallus Appears', *October*, 58, 45–68.

____ (1992) *Everything You Always Wanted to Know about Lacan (But Were Afraid to Ask Hitchcock)*. London: Verso.

____ (1994) 'David Lynch, or, the Feminine Depression', in *The Metastasis of Enjoyment: Six Essays on Women and Causality*. London: Verso, 113–36.

____ (1995) 'The Lamella of David Lynch', in R. Feldstein *et al.* (eds) *Reading Seminar XI: Lacan's Four Fundamental Concepts of Psychoanalysis*. Albany: State University of New York Press, 205–20.

____ (2000a) *The Art of the Ridiculous Sublime: On David Lynch's Lost Highway* (Occasional Papers, Walter Chapin Simpson Center for the Humanities, 1). Seattle, WA: University of Washington Press.

—— (2000b) 'When Straight Means Weird and Psychosis is Normal', *Britannica.com*. Online. Available at www.britannica.com/bcom/original/article/print/0,5749,5602,00.html (17 September 2000).

Nico 63, 76
Nietzsche, Friedrich 158, 163
nihilism 91, 103, 105
nirvana 73
Nochimson, Martha P. 2–3, 16–18, 26–8, 34, 40, 46, 62–3, 81, 100, 106, 108–10, 117, 122, 129, 131, 139–40, 163, 165, 181
noise 14–15, 30–1, 53, 84, 125, 128, 130, 133–4, 138, 149
nostalgia 62, 66–7, 70, 75
nothingness 175, 178

O'Bannon, Dan 39
O'Connor, Flannery 69
Oedipus complex 48, 55, 60, 112–13
Olalquiaga, Celeste 101
On the Air 42
Orbison, Roy 53, 109, 120, 176
orifice 10, 111–12, 114
Owens, Craig 154
Ozzie and Harriet 64

Palmer, Laura 4, 14, 65, 77–90, 94, 97, 99–106, 156, 160, 163, 165
Parnet, Clare 114
parody 4, 62, 66, 70–5, 77–80, 87, 94–5, 106
pastiche 73, 79, 94–5
Penderecki, Krzysztof 129–30
Penn, Arthur 69
perceptionality 142, 148, 150
performance 3, 22, 28–9, 38, 42, 53, 72–3, 88, 90, 109, 120, 123, 126, 131, 165–6
Pfeil, Fred 117, 137–8
phallus 15, 54
phantasy 53
Pink Flag 63
Pitt, Brad 11
Place, Janey 82, 163
Plaisir 126, 133
Plastic Letters 63
Plato 116–17
Poe, Edgar Allen 13, 16
Polanski, Roman 12–13
Pollock, Jackson 108
popular culture 66, 177
pornography 116, 160
postmodernism 3–4, 36, 58, 67, 69, 72, 74, 95, 137, 138, 150
power 14, 17, 20, 25, 30, 38, 43, 53–4, 63, 66, 82, 84, 88, 90, 98–100, 106, 121–3, 130–2, 134, 139, 153, 159, 161, 166,
168–79, 181
Powermad 121–3, 132, 134
Preminger, Otto 77–80, 83, 85, 88, 91
Prendergast, Roy 83, 88, 92
Presley, Elvis 123, 131
primal fantasy 48, 51, 56, 59
production practice 124
prosthesis 153, 161
Psycho 74, 150
psychoanalysis 57, 90, 113
psychogenic fugue 41, 143
Pullman, Bill 121, 180
Pulp Fiction 80
punk 61, 63–5, 70, 73, 75
putrefaction 170–1, 173, 179–80

Quart, Leonard 66

Radio Ethiopia 63
Raising Arizona 66
Raksin, David 83, 85, 92
Rambaldi, Carlo 45
Ramones, The 63–4
Ray, Robert 63–4
Reagan, Ronald 66–70
real-impossible, the 140
realism 73, 88, 108, 140
reality 10, 34, 43, 49, 51, 57, 59, 66, 68, 70, 72, 75, 87, 105, 108, 111, 114, 116, 137, 140, 145–6, 148, 156, 160–2, 166–7, 170–2, 176, 178, 180
Rear Window 150
redemption 41, 94, 100, 106
Reed, Lou 64
Rees, A. L. 71
Reeves, Peggy 154
reification 99–100
remediation 42–3, 163
representation 17, 21–5, 27–9, 33–4, 36–8, 41, 44, 50, 55, 67, 71–2, 79, 82, 90, 94, 108, 113, 116–18, 121, 126, 133, 140–1, 145, 147–8, 153, 162, 177, 180
Repulsion 12
Return of the Jedi 40
Richard Hell and the Voidoids 63
Rockwell, Norman 107
Rodley, Chris 7–8, 16–17, 38, 40, 42, 50, 59, 65, 73, 77, 119, 124, 127, 128, 133–6, 137, 139–40, 150, 163
Rodowick, D. N. 59–60
Roeg, Nicholas 14
Rosenbaum, Jonathan 12, 17–18
Rossellini, Isabella 51, 60, 165